STUDIES IN IMPERIALISM

General editors: Andrew S. Thompson and Alan Lester
Founding editor: John M. MacKenzie

When the 'Studies in Imperialism' series was founded by Professor John M. MacKenzie more than thirty years ago, emphasis was laid upon the conviction that 'imperialism as a cultural phenomenon had as significant an effect on the dominant as on the subordinate societies'. With well over a hundred titles now published, this remains the prime concern of the series. Cross-disciplinary work has indeed appeared covering the full spectrum of cultural phenomena, as well as examining aspects of gender and sex, frontiers and law, science and the environment, language and literature, migration and patriotic societies, and much else. Moreover, the series has always wished to present comparative work on European and American imperialism, and particularly welcomes the submission of books in these areas. The fascination with imperialism, in all its aspects, shows no sign of abating, and this series will continue to lead the way in encouraging the widest possible range of studies in the field. 'Studies in Imperialism' is fully organic in its development, always seeking to be at the cutting edge, responding to the latest interests of scholars and the needs of this ever-expanding area of scholarship.

Making the British empire, 1660–1800

Manchester University Press

SELECTED TITLES AVAILABLE IN THE SERIES

WRITING IMPERIAL HISTORIES
ed. Andrew S. Thompson

GENDERED TRANSACTIONS
Indrani Sen

EXHIBITING THE EMPIRE
ed. John McAleer and John M. MacKenzie

BANISHED POTENTATES
Robert Aldrich

MISTRESS OF EVERYTHING
ed. Sarah Carter and Maria Nugent

BRITAIN AND THE FORMATION OF THE GULF STATES
Shohei Sato

CULTURES OF DECOLONISATION
ed. Ruth Craggs and Claire Wintle

HONG KONG AND BRITISH CULTURE, 1945–97
Mark Hampton

Making the British empire, 1660–1800

Edited by Jason Peacey

MANCHESTER UNIVERSITY PRESS

Copyright © Manchester University Press 2020

While copyright in the volume as a whole is vested in Manchester University Press, copyright in individual chapters belongs to their respective authors, and no chapter may be reproduced wholly or in part without the express permission in writing of both author and publisher.

Published by MANCHESTER UNIVERSITY PRESS
Oxford Road, Manchester M13 9PL
www.manchesteruniversitypress.co.uk

British Library Cataloguing-in-Publication Data
A catalogue record for this book is available from the British Library

ISBN 978 0 7190 8856 8 hardback
ISBN 978 1 5261 6700 2 paperback

First published 2020
Paperback published 2022

The publisher has no responsibility for the persistence or accuracy of URLs for any external or third-party internet websites referred to in this book, and does not guarantee that any content on such websites is, or will remain, accurate or appropriate.

Typeset by Sunrise Setting, Brixham

For Annette

CONTENTS

Notes on contributors—viii
Abbreviations and conventions—x

1 Introduction *Jason Peacey*	1
2 The pivot of empire: party politics, Spanish America and the Treaty of Utrecht (1713) *Steve Pincus*	17
3 Party politics and empire in the early eighteenth century *J. H. Elliott*	38
4 From anti-popery and anti-puritanism to orientalism *William J. Bulman*	56
5 Protestantism and the politics of overseas expansion in later Stuart England *Gabriel Glickman*	77
6 Reconciling empire: English political economy and the Spanish imperial model, 1660–90 *Leslie Theibert*	100
7 Legal geography and colonial sovereignty: the making of early English 'Bombay' *Philip J. Stern*	121
8 Compensating imperial loyalty, 1700–1800 *Julian Hoppit*	142
9 Sheffield's vision: the American Revolution and the 1783 partition of North America *Eliga H. Gould*	160
10 Legal pluralism and Burke's law of nations *Jennifer Pitts*	178

Index—198

CONTRIBUTORS

William J. Bulman is Associate Professor of History and Global Studies at Lehigh University. He is the author of *Anglican Enlightenment: Orientalism, Religion and Politics in England and its Empire, 1648–1715* (2015) and co-editor (with Robert G. Ingram) of *God in the Enlightenment* (2016). He has published articles in *Historical Journal* and *Past and Present*.

Sir John Elliott is Regius Professor emeritus of Modern History at the University of Oxford. He has published extensively on the history of Spain, Europe and the Americas in the early modern period. His books include *Imperial Spain* (1963), *Empires of the Atlantic World: Britain and Spain in America, 1492–1830* (2006) and, most recently, *Scots and Catalans: Union and Disunion* (2018).

Gabriel Glickman is Lecturer in Early Modern British History at the University of Cambridge. He is the author of *The English Catholic Community, 1688–1745* (2009) and his articles have appeared in *Historical Journal*, *Journal of Modern History*, *English Historical Review* and *Journal of British Studies*.

Eliga H. Gould is Professor of History at the University of New Hampshire. He is the author of *The Persistence of Empire: British Political Culture in the Age of the American Revolution* (2011) and *Among the Powers of the Earth: The American Revolution and the Making of a New World Empire* (2012), and he is co-editor (with Peter S. Onuf) of *Empire and Nation: The American Nation in the Atlantic World* (2015).

Julian Hoppit is the Astor Professor of British History at UCL. He is the author of *Risk and Failure in English Business, 1700–1800* (1987), *A Land of Liberty? England, 1689–1727* (2000) and *Britain's Political Economies: Parliament and Economic Life, 1660–1800* (2017).

Jason Peacey is Professor of Early Modern British History at UCL. He is the author of *Politicians and Pamphleteers: Propaganda in the English Civil Wars and Interregnum* (2004) and *Print and Public Politics in the English Revolution* (2014).

Steve Pincus is Thomas E. Donnelly Professor of British History at the University of Chicago. He is the author of *Protestantism and Patriotism: Ideologies and the Making of English Foreign Policy, 1650–1688* (1996),

CONTRIBUTORS

1688: The First Modern Revolution (2011) and *The Heart of the Declaration: The Founders' Case for Activist Government* (2016).

Jennifer Pitts is Professor of Political Science at the University of Chicago. She is the author of *A Turn to Empire: The Rise of Imperial Liberalism in Britain and France* (2005), and *Boundaries of the International: Law and Empire* (2018).

Philip J. Stern is Gilhuly Family Professor at Duke University. He is the author of *The Company State: Corporate Sovereignty and the Early Modern Foundations of the British Empire in India* (2011) and co-editor (with Carl Wennerlind) of *Mercantilism Reimagined: Political Economy in Early Modern Britain and its Empire* (2013).

Leslie Theibert completed her PhD at Yale University in 2014, and is currently preparing a book entitled *Empires of the Caribbean: Anglo-Spanish Relations and the Origins of the English Empire*.

ABBREVIATIONS AND CONVENTIONS

AHR	*American Historical Review*
BL	British Library
Bodl.	Bodleian Library, Oxford
BPP	British Parliamentary Papers
CJ	*Commons Journal*
CSPC	*Calendar of State Papers Colonial*
EcHR	*Economic History Review*
EHR	*English Historical Review*
ESTC	English Short Title Catalogue
HJ	*Historical Journal*
HLQ	*Huntington Library Quarterly*
JBS	*Journal of British Studies*
JEcH	*Journal of Economic History*
JICH	*Journal of Imperial and Commonwealth History*
JMH	*Journal of Modern History*
LPL	Lambeth Palace Library
ODNB	*Oxford Dictionary of National Biography*
OED	Oxford English Dictionary
P&P	*Past and Present*
TNA	The National Archives, Kew
TRHS	*Transactions of the Royal Historical Society*
W&MQ	*William and Mary Quarterly*

All dates before 1752 are Old Style unless otherwise indicated, but the New Year is taken to begin on 1 January rather than 25 March.

Unless otherwise stated, London is the place of publication for works printed before 1800.

CHAPTER ONE

Introduction

Jason Peacey

Historians who have reflected on the historiography relating to the British empire have often noted that this particular sub-discipline is not just prone to 'heart-searching', but is also 'quarrelsome', and it is common to find references to the tendency to engage in 'posturing' and 'ill-tempered disputes'. In commenting on what he tellingly described as the 'imperial history wars', Dane Kennedy referred to the risk that some strands within the profession might adopt a 'smugly self-righteous attitude'.[1] It is certainly true that imperial history has witnessed – probably in an exaggerated form – fairly profound shifts in intellectual fashion, in ways that are perhaps more striking than in other areas of the historical profession. In certain ways, of course, the field has witnessed changes in the fortunes of political, economic, social and cultural history that are entirely familiar across all aspects of the discipline, and that involve fairly predictable anxieties – both methodological and conceptual – as well as prejudices, some of which may indeed be politically and culturally inspired. At the same time, imperial history might be said to have become rather more acrimonious than most other sub-disciplines for two reasons. The first reflects the particular ways in which some historians have engaged with non-history disciplines in recent decades, notably post-structuralist and post-colonial thought, as well as area studies, literary studies and feminist studies, all of which are sometimes said to involve work that lacks awareness of historical methodology and of historical contexts, and that can also be somewhat impenetrable and jargon-laden. The second reason is that imperial history has been more than usually politicised, for very obvious reasons, given that the profound legacies and repercussions of our imperial past continue to be felt and debated to this day. To some, therefore, historical writing was intimately bound up with modern politics and with national identity, and there can be little doubt that this has had some kind of effect on how the British empire has been studied. However, while these divisions and disagreements can be readily understood, it might also be argued that there has at times been a risk of debates becoming over-heated, and of fault lines becoming widened unnecessarily, and it is possible to argue that there is scope to provide fresh perspectives on at least the history of what is sometimes called the 'first' British empire without the acrimony that has sometimes been present.

The aim of this volume is to provide examples of new directions in British imperial history, and of work that offers ways of bridging some of the methodological and conceptual divisions that have dogged the field in recent decades. As such, the aim of this introduction is to provide readers with an outline of the scholarly context in which the various authors are operating. This will not, and could not, involve an extremely thorough survey of the historiography, given the overwhelming volume of literature that now exists in this particularly well-populated area of scholarship. Rather, the aim here is to highlight some of the key ideas and concepts that have been developed and debated within the field, and some of the issues that have assumed greater importance within recent work, and that help to provide the context for the chapters in this volume, and are central to how the history of the British empire is currently being reconfigured.[2]

One vital issue, of course, involves inevitable questions about how much weight scholars of empire have placed, and ought to place, upon issues like 'economics' and 'politics', particularly within England or Britain, and how these issues should be handled. From Sir John Seeley and John Hobson onwards, of course, the impact of both geopolitical considerations and business interests within the metropole loomed large within what might be thought to represent the 'traditional' historiography relating to what drove imperialism, as did the perspective of policy-makers and what was sometimes called the 'official mind'. Indeed, to the extent that it is reasonable to identify 'traditional' approaches to empire, including Marxist accounts, there is certainly scope to argue that historians tended to focus upon how the empire came into being, which forces were at work and what patterns can be detected across time. This often meant tracing the ways in which control was gained over people and places, the importance of trade monopolies and the impact of rivalries between European states, either in terms of identifying the impact of mercantile interests within domestic politics, as in the work of Robert Brenner, for example, or in terms of tracing the transition from an 'adventuring' phase – based on trade, plunder and puritanism, piecemeal development and a lack of official coordination – to a later phase that more obviously involved state control and direct rule, from the takeover of the Virginia Company through the Protestant foreign

INTRODUCTION

policy of Oliver Cromwell and on to the Dominion of New England, via the evolution of the East India Company, the creation of the Royal African Company and the emergence of various boards and Councils of Trade.[3] The obvious danger with such analyses, arguments and narratives, of course, was that they were focused heavily on rather simplistic accounts of the 'interests' and visions of fairly discrete groups within the political and mercantile elite. Of course, it certainly needs to be recognised that, from John Gallagher and Ronald Robinson onwards, attention has also been paid to 'informal' as well as to 'formal' empire, and to the colonial or imperial peripheries as well as to the metropole, even if only in order to help conceptualise the shift *from* informal *towards* formal empire, and to take account of crises within colonial settings, rather than simply issues that arose at the imperial centre.[4]

More recently, of course, fresh impetus was given to an 'economic' interpretation of the British empire through the work of Peter Cain and Antony Hopkins, the importance of which lay in emphasising developments within the metropole rather than merely events on the periphery, and in stressing that economic considerations were a prime driver of imperial expansion, not least as a result of influence that was exerted on the state by financiers and financial interest groups. This intervention represented more than merely a revival of Hobson's ideas and arguments, and whatever the merits of the central claim about the role of 'gentlemanly capitalism' – either for the nineteenth century or for the earlier period from the late seventeenth century onwards – there can be no doubting its significance. This involved focusing attention upon the causes, rather than the consequences of imperial expansion; upon the relationship between metropole and periphery; and upon the complex relationship between economic interests and the state – what they referred to as 'varying influence and shifting alliances' – not least in relation to political upheaval and constitutional change in the era, as well as the aftermath, of the Glorious Revolution. What Cain and Hopkins offered, in other words, were ways of thinking about imperial expansion that focused on 'political economy', and that recognised the potential for concentrating upon the metropole without necessarily having to accept the existence of an official imperial 'mind'. For Cain and Hopkins, therefore, the 'various phases' of the empire were 'closely connected with the development of the domestic economy, the shifting balance of social and political forces ... and the varying intensity of Britain's economic and political rivalry with other powers'.[5] Indeed, these connections between economic development, imperial expansion and the rise of the fiscal state have remained central to the economic history of the early modern period.[6]

Imperial history really became controversial, of course, when challenges were laid down to the focus not just upon the metropole but also upon politics, economics and political economy. Thus, as historians took the 'cultural turn' in all sorts of different ways, and in all sorts of sub-disciplinary areas, there emerged powerful reactions against what was perceived to be the methodological conservatism of the prevailing scholarship, in terms of conceptual narrowness, disciplinary insularity and what Kennedy referred to as 'adamant empiricism'.[7] At the same time, however, such concerns and claims were clearly given piquancy by a sense that 'traditional' imperial history was also profoundly conservative in a political sense, not least in failing to probe the attitudes that underpinned imperial projects, and the impact of imperial experiments. The result, therefore, was a turn away from imperial 'policy' and towards the insights that could be offered by 'interlopers' from other disciplines, and an attempt to refocus attention on the cultural origins and consequences of empire, Orientalist attitudes towards colonised peoples and cultures, and non-western perspectives on overseas expansion, as well as the history of those from outside the elite (sometimes called 'subaltern studies'). As such, what became known as the New Imperial History focused on issues like gender, race and identity, on Foucauldian themes relating to power, knowledge and information, and on those who were on the receiving end of empire, as well as on interactions between cultures, and on perceptions and assertions of power. As Kennedy explained, the aim was to move 'from politics to cultures, from institutions to identities and from the intentions of European elites ... to the experience of colonial subjects'.[8] Ultimately, of course, the need to 'provincialise' Europe, in the words of Dipesh Chakrabarty, has also been linked to the rise to prominence of new strands within the discipline, such as transnational, global and world history.[9]

It was at this point, of course, that imperial history ran the risk of fragmenting into different and more or less incompatible sub-disciplinary strands and approaches, between which there was little common ground. It was certainly the case that cultural historians were highly critical of multi-volume projects like the *Oxford History of the British Empire*, and to the approach taken by historians such as Peter Marshall, which were seen as being too conventional and too dependent upon the ideas of Gallagher and Robinson, and which were also regarded as being insufficiently willing to address a range of cultural issues, not least gender and race. Marshall, of course, was more or less unapologetic about the value of analysing the 'official mind', and the impact of metropolitan perspectives and European competition upon developments across the British empire, not least in order to explore and explain the transition from the 'first' to the 'second' British empire. For Marshall, this was a story of a more or less decisive shift in the nature of the empire, from one that involved the projected power of a sovereign state, as a result of competition with France and Spain, and through things like plantations, to the control of both territories and people.[10] To its critics, however, such scholarship – and the Oxford History more generally – was very obviously 'reactionary', not least in its tendency to 'snipe' at cultural approaches of the kind adopted by the New Imperial History.[11]

Nevertheless, it would perhaps be too easy to overdraw the differences between different kinds of imperial history, and there is certainly scope to recognise that cultural approaches to empire are not necessarily incompatible with other methods and other ideas, and to acknowledge that at least some of its arguments and insights have had an impact on scholars who do not straightforwardly identify themselves as practitioners of New Imperial History. Indeed, it is possible to argue that recent years have witnessed a willingness to incorporate cultural dimensions into political and economic histories of the empire, just as cultural history has had an impact on social, economic and political history more broadly. It is also important to reflect on the likelihood that by looking beyond the metropole it is possible to consider the ways in which the colonies exerted influence upon Britain, and whether such influences were political rather than merely cultural. Indeed, while scholars like Marshall might be thought to be wary of such arguments, it seems clear that recent years have witnessed increasingly sophisticated and complex understandings of both the first and second British empires, which involve at least some kind of rapprochement between cultural historians of empire and those who insist on the need to address 'hard political and economic questions'.[12] This has sometimes meant critiquing, or refining, the work of Cain and Hopkins, incorporating social and cultural history into accounts that address political and economic issues, and it has also meant recognising the complex and diverse impulses and dynamics that were involved in British overseas expansion from the seventeenth century onwards. As such, there is now a degree of consensus that there were – as Marshall has said – *multiple* imperial projects.[13] Any number of examples could be cited to illustrate such trends. Mike Braddick, for example, explored links between domestic, foreign and imperial decision-making, and the influence of social, economic and indeed religious impulses, while challenging the idea that there was anything as clear as an 'imperial policy'.[14] Of course, and as Braddick recognises, the absence of a unified policy does not obviate the need to understand how decisions – including political decisions – were made. Huw Bowen, meanwhile, offered what might be thought of as an economic history of Britain's overseas empire in the century after 1688 that critiqued Cain and Hopkins, giving a more nuanced (and less metropolitan) picture of the English investors and entrepreneurs, but one that also recognised the need for an approach that blended economic, social and cultural history. This reflected a determination to complement analysis of political crises and short term change with recognition of underlying structural continuities, to acknowledge the 'less formal ... sinews or bonds which held the empire together', and to analyse the cultural ties and reciprocal influences within a transoceanic elite.[15] Another relevant example of such new thinking involves Koot's account of *Empire at the Periphery*, which analysed the emergence of an exclusive British empire in the Atlantic by taking account of government policies as well as transnational commercial developments, local economic conditions and the experiences of colonists, as well as patterns of migration, international developments and credit arrangements.[16] Indeed, it would now be possible to draw attention to any number of other historians who have recognised the need for imperial history to be 'culturally grounded', and to offer an 'integrated' approach that combines economic history with accounts of state formation and political culture, and that also explores 'shifting, uneven and often unstable inter-regional and global connections' and indeed 'entangled' histories.[17] Ultimately, of course, it is noteworthy that the *Oxford History of the British Empire* now includes a substantial series of themed volumes that incorporate issues inspired by the New Imperial History, including titles that relate to the 'black experience', gender, missions and the environment.[18]

The aim of this volume, and the contribution that its authors make, involves both acknowledging and building upon these recent trends within the historiography, in a series of precise but also challenging and conceptually rich ways. What follows in the remainder of this introduction, therefore, represents an attempt to isolate the key thematic avenues along which the authors seek to proceed, and to identify the ways in which they are helping to offer new perspectives on the early history of the British empire.

First, these chapters contribute to an ongoing attempt to re-integrate political and institutional dimensions into the history of empire. This is a key area within recent scholarship, in both domestic and imperial contexts. Attention has been paid, therefore, to transatlantic political communities, to the ideas and attitudes of leading colonists, and to rethinking the political contexts of, and impulses for, specific colonial initiatives, from the foundation of Pennsylvania to the creation of the Royal African Company.[19] Significant work has also been done on the governance of empire, in terms of the role of colonial assemblies and the influence of colonial lobbies, as well as the attitudes of colonists towards imperial oversight and the 'imperial constitution', and the ways in which attempts were made to balance local autonomy with the protection of vital interests.[20] In *Making the Empire Work*, for example,

INTRODUCTION

Alison Olson analysed the history of colonial lobbying, in ways that acknowledged the overlapping interests and connections between interest groups both in the metropole and at the periphery, and that recognised how the emergence of effective methods for influencing policymakers in London constituted a form of political representation.[21] In the work of Ken MacMillan, meanwhile, a powerful case has been made about the need to modify older arguments about the shift from a 'weak state' model of empire, based on 'salutary neglect', self-regulation and local autonomy, to a 'strong state' empire, wherein 'independence' came to an end as a result of greater centralised control in the eighteenth century. Thus, while acknowledging that colonial politics was 'negotiated', MacMillan points out that such negotiation is now recognised as being a feature of domestic politics as well, and also highlights the various ways in which governments in Whitehall and Westminster had been heavily involved in regulating colonial affairs long before the eighteenth century, and even before the Cromwellian era.[22]

Crucial to this revived and reworked politics of imperial expansion, however, has been scholarship on political economy and the New Institutional Economics, particularly in the wake of the influential scholarship of historically minded economists like Douglass North, and in terms of work on the vexed issue of 'mercantilism', and on the links between British policies in the aftermath of the Glorious Revolution. Here, of course, the work of Steve Pincus has been at the heart of recent debates, and 'The pivot of empire' forms part of a bigger project on the history of the British empire that began by challenging traditional accounts of the origins of the Navigation Act and of the ensuing Anglo-Dutch Wars after 1651. Pincus has contested the idea that there was a mercantilist consensus in early modern Britain, and has insisted that there was vigorous and partisan debate over the rationale for, and nature of, overseas expansion from the 1650s onwards.[23] Here, in other words, it is possible to observe how recognition of the complexity of imperial attitudes – arguments about the coherence of which can only be sustained by neglecting domestic politics – has been taken in new directions, not least by supplementing studies of colonial politics with studies of party politics, and indeed ideology, in the metropole. In very obvious ways, therefore, Pincus seeks to reassert the centrality of metropolitan politics for an understanding of Britain's imperial history, and as such he might be thought to be out of sympathy with key elements within the cultural history of empire.[24] Nevertheless, it is also worth noting that, for all his reservations about the contribution made by the New Imperial History, Pincus readily accepts the idea that there are complementarities, rather than merely contradictions, between his brand of political history and the ambitions of New Imperial Historians like Kathleen Wilson.[25]

This is not to say that Pincus's arguments have been, or are likely to be, accepted uncritically, as Sir John Elliott's fairly vigorous response to his chapter in this volume demonstrates, and Pincus's ideas open up three key areas for discussion and disagreement. First, debate is likely to continue about how clearly and distinctly it is possible to identify fault lines between 'Whig' and 'Tory' ideologies of empire.[26] Secondly, questions can also be raised – as they are by Elliott – about the relative importance to domestic politics within Britain of 'European' concerns on the one hand, and 'colonial' or 'imperial' visions on the other, not least in the wake of Brendan Simms' trenchant account of Britain's engagement with Europe in the eighteenth century, in *Three Victories and a Defeat*. Here, however, it is also worth noting that the views of Pincus and Simms have a great deal in common, and it might even be argued that there is more than unites them than divides them. Both, therefore, recognise the need to make connections between European and imperial politics, as well as the need to do justice to the divisions that existed between Whigs and Tories, and both insist upon the importance of 'grand strategy', and what Simms calls the 'primacy of foreign policy'.[27] Thirdly, there will very obviously be scope to recognise, as Leslie Theibert's contribution to this volume certainly does, that within colonial settings, and at the 'periphery', Whig and Tory views did not necessarily map onto English party divisions very precisely, as the views of the latter – on issues like slavery, monopolies, labour and prerogative power – were adapted on the ground.

On this last point, however, as on other issues, it is important to recognise that Pincus is not simply reviving older forms of political history. Quite apart from his insistence on the need to recognise contemporary debates and divisions, and the existence of rival modes of political economy, he has also demonstrated a lasting interest in the importance of public opinion, and in the emergence of a 'public sphere', both of which involve moving a long way from any notion that there was an official imperial 'mind'. Moreover, it also seems clear that he does not necessarily seek to privilege the metropole to the exclusion of the colonial periphery, and Pincus argues not just that domestic and foreign policy were intertwined, but also that the empire involved 'a dialectical and fruitful relationship between what was going on in the colonies and dependent states ... on the one hand, and what was going on in England on the other'.[28] Pincus's work, in other words, refocuses attention upon the metropole while also building upon the insights of previous scholarship, in order to create a novel and challenging account of the politics of empire, and to place 'policy' at the heart of the historiography once again. Indeed, this willingness to revive the political history of empire in challenging and provocative ways – by reflecting upon the impact of constitutional revolution, of parliamentary affairs, party divisions and attitudes within the colonies, as well as upon arguments regarding labour and the economy – is now increasingly evident within early modern scholarship. It is reflected, for example, in the work of Andrew Will Pettigrew on the Royal African Company, and it is also evident in the work of scholars like Abigail Swingen and Justin du Rivage.[29]

One of the things that make such work important, moreover, is the possibility of blending constitutional issues with political practice and political thought or ideology, and this might also be thought to be evident in relation to another of the themes that emerges very clearly from this volume. One of these involves the centrality of religious thought and practice to the story of the British empire. Of course, religion has scarcely been absent from histories of the empire, and scholars have certainly recognised the central importance of religious motivations for, and aspects of, colonisation, including missionary work, and they have also studied the experiences of religious diversity (and toleration) across the empire, not to mention the importance that was attached to the idea of defending and sustaining a Protestant empire.[30] Here too, however, attempts have recently been made to rethink the role of religion within the imperial context, not least by downplaying the idea of the American colonies as 'refuges' for persecuted and dissident minorities, and emphasising instead how religious pluralism served to foster loyalty, and stressing that insufficient attention has been paid to conformity, uniformity and the success of the established Anglican Church.[31] Central to this process of rethinking the role of religion in the imperial context has been the work of Gabriel Glickman, one of the contributors to this volume, whose concern has been to reflect on the role of religion within policy debates. Glickman has thus explored the ways in which religious issues fed into, and helped to polarise, contemporary debates regarding empire and colonisation.[32] Likewise, in his chapter for this volume, Glickman explores the ways in which religious controversies informed debates about overseas expansion, while also addressing how colonial issues and experiences amplified debates regarding the Church, from comprehension to toleration. In ways that complement Pincus's analysis, therefore, Glickman argues that there were different religious views about the empire, and about what a Protestant approach to foreign policy and colonisation would involve, not least in the aftermath of the English revolution, and also that the experience of empire helped to exacerbate such divisions. As such, Glickman complicates in important ways simplistic notions that the early British empire was grounded in 'Protestantism'.[33]

As Glickman has shown elsewhere, of course, it is also vital to explore the early history of the British empire by factoring in the troubled history of places like Tangier, which certainly complicate our understanding of this period of imperial expansion.[34] Central here, of course, is the need to understand contemporary perceptions of Islam, and Bill Bulman's chapter provides another example of how to acknowledge the impact of the periphery upon the metropole, and to engage with the concept of orientalism, while remaining focused upon figures from within the British elite. This means tracing the origins of orientalism back to the ways in which English churchmen and officials observed Islam through the lens of anti-puritanism and anti-Popery, and recognising that orientalist mentalities and ideologies not only had post-reformation origins but also were developed through, and in the service of, political practice, including within the empire. Bulman's chapter forms part of a much larger project which places Anglican scholars, clerics and officials at the heart of the process by which attempts were made to confront religious divisions and difference not just within Britain but across the empire, and to demonstrate the connections between political (and imperial) practice and intellectual erudition.[35]

There are, of course, other ways of recovering the intellectual history of the British empire, and here too this volume moves beyond existing approaches to the 'ideology' of empire by exploring the ideological reflections of those who were engaged in the practice of empire, and building on the work of scholars like Robert Travers and Ken MacMillan. This is certainly evident in Bulman's chapter, and it is also evident in other chapters, which use political experiences and interconnections on the ground – in both metropole and colonies – as a means of exploring issues like legitimacy and sovereignty, which have emerged as increasingly important themes within the historiography.[36] Travers, therefore, has explored modes of legitimation in eighteenth-century India, in ways that were explicitly linked to the policies and constitutional practices of men like Warren Hastings, and that revealed not just the influence of colonies upon the metropole but also the influence of 'indigenous categories'.[37] Sovereignty, and the legal basis of empire, has also been explored by MacMillan, not least as a means of moving beyond the aim of recovering the 'ideology' of empire in order to focus instead upon the constitutional and legal thinking that underpinned overseas expansion. In part this involves rethinking ideas about the transition from a 'weak' state to a 'strong' state empire. MacMillan demonstrates, therefore, that by looking at sovereignty it is possible to develop a rather different picture from the one offered by cultural historians like Alison Games, who emphasised that the cosmopolitanism, adaptability and practicality of early colonists – whereby 'cultural interaction' was 'defined by dissimulation and accommodation' – was eventually replaced by centralised authority and coercive strategies,

INTRODUCTION

such that 'accommodation' was replaced by 'brute force' from the 1650s onwards.[38] For MacMillan, in contrast, shifting the focus from cultural to intellectual issues helps suggests a different picture and a different narrative. This involves highlighting the centrality of ideas about the 'dominium' of settlers and the 'imperium' of the state, and recognising that while 'salutary neglect' of the empire was indeed replaced by a 'strong state' during the second half of the seventeenth century, and more obviously during the Hanoverian era, it is important to rethink the 'weak state' phase of empire, and to acknowledge that the English state was always 'imperially minded', and that it had placed limits on colonial autonomy from the very outset.[39]

One of the central insights of MacMillan's work is that thinking about sovereignty provides a useful means of overcoming ideas about the difference between Britain's American and Asian empires in the seventeenth and eighteenth centuries, and this has also been central to Philip Stern's work on the sovereignty of the East India Company. Stern has challenged the idea that Westphalian sovereignty predominated after 1648, by demonstrating that the company had significant jurisdictional power rather than just commercial interests, and that it was neither a public nor a private entity, in ways which highlight the existence and importance of hybrid or composite forms of sovereignty. The story of the company's power was complex, of course, in terms of the degree to which it came under the management of the state, but it nevertheless demonstrates that the evolution of the empire was intimately bound up with early modern forms of state, sovereign and political power.[40] What this also meant, as Stern explores in his contribution to this volume, is that claims to sovereignty were also made complex by geopolitical realities on the ground. Here, therefore, Stern demonstrates that the transfer of Bombay from Portugal to England in 1661 raised difficult issues for the East India Company, in terms of how far its jurisdiction reached geographically and spatially, and what authority it had over local people. In Bombay, as elsewhere, the sovereign jurisdiction of the company emerges as something that needed to be negotiated and compromised on the ground.[41]

Another way of thinking about sovereignty and the messy realities of empire involves how to deal with the perils of colonial life, the responsibilities of colonial regimes and the 'rights' of people who lived in colonial territories. This is another vital way in which it is possible to link the practical and intellectual aspects of the relations between metropole and colonies, something that MacMillan addressed by tracing the importance of the idea of 'reciprocal sovereignty', in terms of contemporary notions that allegiance was reciprocated by protection of bodies and land.[42] Within this volume, the practical issues of reciprocity that

[11]

were involved in the exercise of sovereign authority are explored by Julian Hoppit, in terms of whether and how to offer compensation for the loss (and losses) of empire. Hoppit, consciously grappling with ideas about the importance of 'credible commitment' that emerged from the New Institutional Economics, explores the ways in which colonists came to be regarded as citizens of empire, not least as a result of the kind of lobbying through which influence was exerted over the metropole, and the ways in which it became necessary to offer compensation for losses that they suffered. He demonstrates how this process was affected by ideas about the sharing of risks, and indeed about whether financial compensation was regarded as a right, or whether notions of rights were thought to undermine the loyalty that was due to the colonial regime.[43]

As Hoppit and Stern both demonstrate, the issue of sovereignty was intimately bound up with practical issues relating to relations with the inhabitants of empire, and to notions of citizenship, and this is something that also emerges from Eliga Gould's chapter, which involves a study of the effects of 'imperial partition' at the American Revolution. This is another example of the value of exploring the 'politics' of the relationship between metropole and periphery, the diversity of the imperial polity and the messy reality of empires on the ground, in terms of complex and protean patterns of loyalty in the 1770s, and the enforced changes to citizenship that resulted from the revolution. Amid such turmoil and institutional change, Gould argues, it is possible to find evidence of accommodation (as well as relocation and resistance) by those who were affected, and collaboration between Britain, the United States and other European powers, not least in new and contested borderlands. As such, Gould offers an example of the 'entangled' history of empire, which explores constitutional issues at the periphery, and which might even be thought to be influenced by post-colonial studies.[44]

A final way of exploring the intellectual history of empire, and indeed the reality of sovereignty, involves legal thought. Crucial here are issues relating to the legal systems that were employed in imperial settings, and the need to recognise the central importance of a legal pluralism that accepted the legitimacy and indeed utility and necessity of multiple legal systems. This is something that has conventionally been explored in domestic or European settings, but it is now an increasingly important dimension of work on international law, and on the history of empires. It is also another feature of Ken MacMillan's work, in terms of the way in which the British empire in America revolved around Roman law, rather than the common law, based upon the recognition that laws and legal institutions needed to be relevant

INTRODUCTION

to particular situations, and that it was important to avoid 'repugnant laws'.[45] More recently, the issue has also become central to the work of scholars like Lauren Benton, and indeed Philip Stern.[46] Here, however, legal pluralism is explored by Jennifer Pitts, in relation to the well-known trial of Warren Hastings, an episode that is used not just to explore the distinction between domestic and international law, but also to demonstrate that contemporaries were not limited to thinking about places like India in terms of categories like oriental despotism. This was true, Pitts demonstrates, of Hastings himself, at least to some degree, but it was even more true of his critics like Edmund Burke, who recognised the failings of English law in an Indian context, and that Indian laws needed to be recognised as having normative standing. Burke is thus shown to be someone who makes it possible to recognise how British law, and legal thinking, was or could be transformed through the encounter with the Indian legal system, even if such 'interpretive generosity' eventually gave way to a much more straightforward vision of law as being European in origin in the nineteenth century. Here too, therefore, it is possible to recognise the value of exploring the relationship between metropole and periphery, the theory and practice of empire, and the distinctiveness of the first British empire, as well as the timing of the most important changes that marked a shift in the nature of that empire.

Taken together, the chapters in this volume thus highlight some of the most important recent strands within scholarship on the British empire before 1800, and demonstrate ways of taking this particular subject in new directions. If they represent a response to the 'cultural turn' and to New Imperial History, then they certainly do not seek to turn back the clock to an older style of history or approach to empire, and in many ways they embrace some of the most important instincts of 'cultural' approaches to empire, albeit in somewhat different ways than were evident in studies of the 'Atlantic world'.[47] Thus, while a common thread throughout this volume involves the need to refocus attention on imperial 'policy', this does not involve a simple preoccupation with the state or the 'official mind', and it involves acknowledging that there were competing visions of, and motivations for, imperial expansion. Chapters also make connections between contemporary theories and ideologies and the practice of empire, and between political thinking, political processes and political action, in terms of religious ideas and notions of political economy, as well as in terms of the legal basis of empire and the complex nature of sovereignty and citizenship across English and British colonies, and what might be called the practice of constitutionalism. Throughout the collection, indeed, the authors work with an expanded notion of what constitutes 'intellectual' history, which incorporates thinking about empire that took place by clerics and officials, that was undertaken in concrete settings, and in that very obviously related to practical issues and problems. Beyond this, the authors certainly do not rule out, and mostly embrace, the need to explore both metropole and periphery, in terms of the complex ways in which the empire worked on the ground, was experienced and was thought about, and in terms of how colonial practice influenced metropolitan ideas. In that sense the chapters adopt a broadly 'political' approach – in terms of thinking, policy and practice – to the kinds of questions that cultural historians raised about the relationship between colonies and metropole, thereby complicating the relationship between nation and empire in ways that recognise differences and tensions, and that refuse simply to prioritise the former. Finally, in a range of different ways the chapters also help to contest established narratives, and to rethink the dynamic of imperial thought and practice. This means reflecting on the relationship between the first British empire – between 1650 and 1800 – and earlier phases of overseas expansion, as well as the later history of the British empire. (This is why this book refers to 'empire' rather than 'Empire': much of the time it deals with imperial aspirations, mentalities and thinking, rather than with formal and stable relationships.) It also means thinking about how best to detect the 'turning points' in Britain's imperial history. And it means reassessing how to situate the first British empire within broader contexts of the Reformation, the English revolution and the Enlightenment.

Notes

1. S. Howe, 'The slow death and strange rebirths of imperial history', *JICH*, 29:2 (2001), 140; S. J. Potter, *British Imperial History* (London, 2015), p. 1; D. Kennedy, 'The imperial history wars', *JBS*, 54:1 (2015), 12.
2. For relevant surveys, See A. Webster, *The Debate on the Rise of the British Empire* (Manchester, 2006); Potter, *British Imperial History*.
3. K. R. Andrews, *Trade, Plunder and Settlement: Maritime Enterprise and the Genesis of the British Empire, 1450–1630* (Cambridge, 1984); R. Brenner, *Merchants and Revolution: Commercial Change, Political Conflict and London's Overseas Traders, 1550–1653* (London, 2003); N. Canny (ed.), *The Oxford History of the British Empire, Volume 1: The Origins of Empire* (Oxford, 1998); P. Marshall (ed.), *The Oxford History of the British Empire: Volume 2: The Eighteenth Century* (Oxford, 1998).
4. J. Gallagher and R. Robinson, 'The imperialism of free trade', *EcHR*, 2nd series, 6:1 (1953), 1–15.
5. P. Cain and A. Hopkins, 'The political economy of British expansion overseas, 1750–1914', *EcHR*, 2nd series, 33 (1980), 466, 489; P. J. Cain and A. G. Hopkins, *British Imperialism: Innovation and Expansion, 1688–1914* (London, 1993).
6. P. O'Brien, 'Inseparable connections: trade, economy, fiscal state and the expansion of empire, 1688–1815', in Marshall (ed.), *Oxford History*, pp. 53–77.
7. D. Kennedy, 'Imperial history and post-colonial theory', *JICH*, 24 (1996), 345.
8. Kennedy, 'Imperial history wars', 12. See also D. Ghosh, 'Another set of imperial turns?', *AHR*, 117:3 (2012), 772–93; K. Wilson, *A New Imperial History: Culture,*

INTRODUCTION

Identity and Modernity in Britain and the Empire, 1660–1840 (Cambridge, 2006); S. Howe (ed.), *A New Imperial Histories Reader* (London, 2010).
9 D. Chakrabarty, *Provincialising Europe: Postcolonial Thought and Historical Difference* (Princeton, 2007).
10 P. Marshall, 'Britain and the world in the eighteenth century: 1. Reshaping the empire', *TRHS*, 6th series, 8 (1998), 1–18; P. Marshall, 'Britain and the world in the eighteenth century: 2. Britons and Americans', *TRHS*, 6th series, 9 (1999), 1–16; P. Marshall, 'Britain and the world in the eighteenth century: 3. Britain and India', *TRHS*, 6th series, 10 (2000), 1–16; P. Marshall, *The Making and Unmaking of Empire: Britain, India and America, c.1750–1783* (Oxford, 2005); P. Marshall, 'Introduction', in *Oxford History*, pp. 1–27.
11 A. Burton (ed.), *After the Imperial Turn* (Durham, NC, 2003), p. 4.
12 A. G. Hopkins, 'Back to the future: from national history to imperial history', *P&P*, 164 (1999), 198–243.
13 P. Marshall, 'Imperial Britain', *JICH*, 23:3 (1995), 379–94.
14 M. J. Braddick, 'The English government, war, trade and settlement, 1625–1688', in Canny (ed.), *Oxford History*, pp. 286–308.
15 H. Bowen, *Elites, Enterprise and the Making of the British Overseas Empire, 1688–1775* (Basingstoke, 1996).
16 C. Koot, *Empire at the Periphery: British Colonists, Anglo-Dutch Trade and the Development of the British Atlantic* (New York, 2011).
17 G. Rommelse, 'The role of mercantilism in Anglo-Dutch political relations, 1650–74', *EcHR*, 63:3 (2010), 591–611; T. Ballantyne, 'The changing shape of the modern British empire and its historiography', *HJ*, 53:2 (2010), 451.
18 P. D. Morgan and S. Hawkins (eds), *Black Experience and the Empire* (Oxford, 2006); P. Levine (ed.), *Gender and Empire* (Oxford, 2004); N. Etherington, *Missions and Empire* (Oxford, 2005); W. Beinart and L. Hughes (eds), *Environment and Empire* (Oxford, 2007).
19 J. Donoghue, *Fire under the Ashes* (Chicago, 2013); T. Leng, 'Shaftesbury's aristocratic empire', in J. Spurr (ed.), *Anthony Ashley Cooper, First Earl of Shaftesbury, 1621–1683* (Farnham, 2011), pp. 101–25; M. Geiter, 'The Restoration crsis and the launching of Pennsylvania, 1679–81', *EHR*, 112 (1997), 300–18; W. Pettigrew, *Freedom's Debt: the Royal African Company and the Politics of the Atlantic Slave Trade, 1672–1752* (Chapel Hill, 2013).
20 I. Steele, '"The anointed, the appointed and the elected": governance of the British empire, 1689–1784', in Marshall (ed.), *Oxford History*, pp. 105–27; J. Greene, *Peripheries and Center: Constitutional Development in the Extended Polities of the British Empire and the United States, 1607–1788* (London, 1986); O. Stanwood, *The Empire Reformed: English America in the Age of the Glorious Revolution* (Philadelphia, 2011).
21 A. Olson, *Making the Empire Work: London and American Interest Groups, 1690–1790* (London, (1992).
22 K. MacMillan, *The Atlantic Imperial Constitution: Center and Periphery in the English Atlantic World* (Basingstoke, 2011).
23 P. Stern and C. Wennerlind (eds), *Mercantilism Reimagined: Political Economy in Early Modern Britain and its Empire* (Oxford, 2013); S. Pincus, 'Rethinking mercantilism: political economy, the British empire and the Atlantic world in the seventeenth and eighteenth centuries', *W&MQ*, 69:1 (2012), 3–34; S. Pincus, *Protestantism and Patriotism: Ideologies and the Making of English Foreign Policy, 1650–1668* (Cambridge, 1996).
24 S. Pincus, 'Addison's empire: Whig conceptions of empire in the early 18th century', *Parliamentary History*, 31:1 (2012), 99–117; S. Pincus, 'Reconfiguring the British empire', *W&MQ*, 69:1 (2012), 63–70.
25 Pincus, 'Rethinking mercantilism'; Pincus, 'Addison's empire', 3; M. E. Newell, 'Putting the 'political' back in political economy', *W&MQ*, 69.1 (2012), 57–62. See also Rommelse, 'Role of mercantilism'.
26 W. Pettigrew, 'Constitutional change in England and the diffusion of regulatory initiative, 1660–1714', *History*, 99:338 (2014), 839–63. Pincus certainly accepts that Whig and Tory views became more complex over time: Pincus, 'Reconfiguring'.

27 B. Simms, *Three Victories and a Defeat: the Rise and Fall of the First British Empire, 1714–1783* (London, 2007), pp. 1–2, 15–16, 103; Pincus, 'Addison's empire'.
28 Pincus, 'Addison's empire'; Pincus, 'Reconfiguring', 63.
29 W. Pettigrew and G. van Cleve, 'Parting companies: the Glorious Revolution, company power and imperial mercantilism', *HJ*, 57:3 (2014), 617–38; Pettigrew, *Freedom's Debt*; A. Swingen, *Competing Visions of Empire: Labor, Slavery and the Origins of the British Atlantic Empire* (New Haven, 2015); J. du Rivage, *Revolution against Empire: Taxes, Politics and the Origins of American Independence* (New Haven, 2018).
30 C. Pestana, *Protestant Empire: Religion and the Making of the British Atlantic World* (Philadelphia, 2009); G. Ames, 'The role of religion in the transfer and rise of Bombay, c.1661–1687', *HJ*, 46:2 (2003), 317–40; B. Schlenther, 'Religious faith and commercial empire', in Marshall (ed.), *Oxford History*, pp. 128–50; L. Colley. *Captives: Britain, Empire and the World, 1600–1850* (London, 2002).
31 E. Haefeli, 'Toleration and empire', and J. Gregory, 'Establishment and dissent in British North America', both in S. Foster (ed.), *British North America in the Seventeenth and Eighteenth Centuries* (Oxford, 2013), 103–35, 139–69.
32 G. Glickman, 'Catholic interests and the politics of English overseas expansion 1660–1689', *JBS*, 55:4 (2016), 680–708.
33 G. Glickman, 'Protestantism, colonization and the New England Company in Restoration politics', *HJ*, 59:2 (2016), 365–91.
34 G. Glickman, 'Empire, "popery" and the fall of English Tangier, 1662–1684', *JMH*, 87:2 (2015), 247–80; T. Stein, 'Tangier in the Restoration empire', *HJ*, 54:4 (2011), 985–1011.
35 W. Bulman, *Anglican Enlightenment: Orientalism, Religion and Politics in England and its Empire, 1648–1715* (Cambridge, 2015).
36 D. Armitage, *The Ideological Origins of the British Empire* (Cambridge, 2000); A. Pagden, *Lords of all the World: Ideologies of Empire in Spain, Britain and France, c.1492–c.1830* (New Haven, 1995); A. Fitzmaurice (ed.), 'The intellectual history of early modern empire', *Renaissance Studies*, 26:4 (2012); H. V. Bowen et al (eds), *Britain's Oceanic Empire: Atlantic and Indian Ocean Worlds, c.1550–1850* (Cambridge, 2012).
37 R. Travers, *Ideology and Empire in Eighteenth Century India* (Cambridge, 2007), pp. 1–30.
38 A. Games, *The Web of Empire: English Cosmopolitans in an Age of Expansion, 1560–1660* (Oxford, 2008), pp. 12, 291.
39 K. MacMillan, *Sovereignty and Possession in the English New World: The Legal Foundations of Empire, 1576–1640* (Cambridge, 2006); K. MacMillan, 'Imperial constitutions: sovereignty and law in the British Atlantic', in Bowen et al (eds), *Britain's Oceanic Empire*, pp. 69–97; K. MacMillan, '"Bound by our regal office": empire, sovereignty and the American colonies in the seventeenth century', in Foster (ed.), *British North America*, pp. 67–102.
40 P. Stern, *The Company State: Corporate Sovereignty and the Early Modern Foundations of the British Empire in India* (Oxford, 2011); P. Stern, 'The corporation and the global seventeenth-century English empire: a tale of three cities', *Early American Studies*, 16:1 (2018), 41–63.
41 P. Stern, 'Company, state and empire: governance and regulatory frameworks in Asia', in Bowen et al (eds), *Britain's Oceanic Empire*, pp. 130–50.
42 MacMillan, 'Bound by our regal office'.
43 See also J. Hoppit, 'Compulsion, compensation and property rights in Britain, 1688–1833', *P&P*, 210 (2011), 92–128.
44 See also E. Gould, 'Entangled histories, entangled worlds: the English-speaking Atlantic as a Spanish periphery', *AHR*, 112:3 (2007), 764–86.
45 MacMillan, *Sovereignty and Possession*; MacMillan, 'Imperial constitutions'.
46 L. Benton, *A Search for Sovereignty: Law and Geography in European Empires, 1400–1900* (Cambridge, 2009); L. Benton and R. Ross (eds), *Legal Pluralism and Empires, 1500–1850* (New York, 2013).
47 D. Armitage and M. Braddick (eds), *The British Atlantic World* (Basingstoke, 2002); N. Canny and P. Morgan (eds), *The Oxford Handbook of the Atlantic World, 1450–1850* (Oxford, 2011).

CHAPTER TWO

The pivot of empire: party politics, Spanish America and the Treaty of Utrecht (1713)

Steve Pincus

British Whigs everywhere excoriated the Treaty of Utrecht, signed in April 1713, that put an end to the War of the Spanish Succession. They denounced 'the many infamous steps that have of late been taken to the dishonoring and completely ruining our country, and the Protestant interest in Europe'.[1] They bemoaned the 'infamous peace' secured with 'as much treasure as would have finished a glorious war'.[2] Above all, they felt, the peace had been an imperial betrayal. The British and their allies had fought the war for 'Spain and all her Indian treasures', but had achieved little despite the famous victories at Blenheim, Ramillies, and Malplaquet.[3] Why did the Whigs believe British imperial interests had been betrayed at the Treaty of Utrecht? Why did they think that a peace that had given the British Gibraltar, Minorca, Nova Scotia, St Kitts and the lucrative Asiento – the exclusive right to sell slaves to the Spanish empire – was an imperial disaster? What is the larger significance of this vitriolic debate for our understanding of the nature and contours of the British empire?

Unfortunately the existing scholarship makes it very difficult to answer these questions. Scholars have either insisted there was a single coherent British imperial policy over which there was little party conflict, or there was party conflict that had little to do with imperial policy.

By and large scholars who have not focused on high politics have highlighted the coherence of British imperial strategy.[4] 'Britain's empire', notes Sir John Elliott in discussing its contours post-1689, was 'to be a maritime and commercial empire'. The British, he says, aimed to create an empire that was 'the antithesis of Spain's land-based empire of conquest'.[5] England, agrees Julian Hoppit, had an 'imperial plan' – singular – that was 'economic in conception, though with important subsidiary strategic dimensions'.[6]

Political historians, by contrast, argue that the Treaty of Utrecht was a Tory but not an imperial peace. 'It is doubtful whether any other matter so continuously aggravated relations between Whig and Tory from 1708 to 1712 as the making of peace', insists Geoffrey Holmes. But the issues that divided the two parties were whether or not there should be a Bourbon on the Spanish throne and whether or not the peace ending the war should be negotiated jointly with all the members of the Grand Alliance.[7] The empire plays no role in this party political analysis.

Against these views, then, I insist that the struggle over the Peace of Utrecht was a party political struggle over the future of the British empire. The Whigs committed themselves to a notion of integrative empire. Because they rejected the notion that property was finite, they were relatively indifferent to territorial gain. For them, the War of the Spanish Succession was all about preventing Bourbon universal monarchy, and the key to preventing Bourbon hegemony was opening the markets of Spanish America to British manufactures. The best means to create a British commercial empire, they believed, was economic integration of the existing British colonial possessions in order to take advantage of free trade in South America. Tories, by contrast, committed themselves to territorial empire. Not only did they insist on territorial gains in the Treaty of Utrecht, but they also erected the South Sea Company in order to found a new British empire in South America. This party conflict over empire, conducted not only at the level of high politics, but also in popular addresses, commercial petitions, Grub Street squibs and the increasingly popular newspapers of the day, has profound implications for the ways in which we should conceptualise and narrate the history of the British empire in the long eighteenth century.

Buoyed by spectacular military victories at Blenheim (1704), Ramillies (1706), Oudenarde (1708) and Lille (1708), the Whig Junto government responded encouragingly to French feelers for peace in the spring of 1709.[8] They seized this moment to enunciate their aspirations for a peace that would put an end to the War of the Spanish Succession.

The Whigs demanded a peace that would not only prevent the possibility of French hegemony in Europe, but also entrench a Whig imperial vision. The Whigs insisted that the Bourbons cede 'the entire monarchy of Spain', that Louis XIV agree to the demolition of Dunkirk, that a barrier be erected between France and the United Provinces, and that the French agree to support the Hanoverian succession as necessary preliminaries before any further negotiation.[9] Despite all Marlborough's military victories, the Whigs had no dreams of territorial expansion.[10]

The Whigs did not, however, focus on Europe at the expense of the empire; 'economic concerns' were not 'sacrificed', as one recent scholar has suggested, in favour of strategic benefits.[11] At the same time that

Marlborough and Townshend put forth their preliminary demands for peace, the British Board of Trade, under the leadership of the Whig Earl of Sunderland advanced commercial and imperial demands. James Stanhope, at the urging of Sunderland and the Board of Trade, negotiated a commercial treaty with the Habsburg claimant to the Spanish throne Charles III that 'excluded the French from trading directly or indirectly to the Spanish West Indies; and not only lowered the Spanish duties but got us all the advantages we could desire of trading directly to the West Indies'. Had this 'treaty taken effect', opined one later Whig polemicist, 'had not we been betrayed to France, what flourishing and glorious circumstances would the nation be in'. Instead of a territorial empire, the Whigs demanded a peace that would make the Atlantic world a protected market for English manufactures.[12]

What, then, was the Whig vision for the British empire? What kind of an empire did they hope to secure in the treaty they were negotiating in 1709/1710?

The Whigs advocated an integrated commercial empire in which the key to prosperity and power was human labour. Unlike most Tories, the Whigs did not believe that the world's economic resources were finite, delimited by the amount of land in the world. Britain's economic future depended on the value that labour could add to raw materials, not on monopolising the raw materials themselves.

During the War of the Spanish Succession the Whigs gave their labour-based political economy an imperial twist. Since at least the 1680s Whig polemicists had been arguing that labour, rather than land, was the basis of property, that property was therefore infinite, and that territorial empire therefore made little sense. John Locke was typical of the later seventeenth-century Whigs in that he did not think that labour in the Americas was worth nearly as much as labour in the British Isles. In the 'waste of America', he reckoned, 'a thousand acres yield the needy and wretched in habitants as many conveniences of life, as ten acres of equally fertile land in Devonshire'.[13]

Many early eighteenth-century Whigs thought differently. In 1708, in *The British Empire in America*, the tract that more than any other detailed the Whig imperial vision instantiated in the 1709 Barrier Treaty, the Whig polemicist John Oldmixon revised Locke's assessment. While Oldmixon, like Locke, believed that labour, not land, was the basis of property, he was far more optimistic about the political economic significance of the Americas. Two decades of development had radically improved the value of Britain's colonies in America. 'A labourer in our American colonies', Oldmixon argued, is 'of more advantage to England though out of it, than any 130 of the like kind can be in it.' Oldmixon's statistical analysis revealed 'that one hand in the plantations is as good as twenty employed at home'.[14] Oldmixon, unlike Locke, prioritised colonial labour over labour in the British Isles.

Oldmixon argued, along with most Whigs, that economic growth depended on a complex interplay between production and consumption. It was not enough merely to produce goods. The British economy depended on consumers with increasingly high wages and increasingly sophisticated tastes to generate demand for its manufactures. British colonists in America had a voracious demand for British manufactures.[15]

Given his emphasis on consumption as well as on production, it was hardly surprising that Oldmixon argued for an integrated British empire, one in which the interests and activities of the colonists in the Americas were at least as important as those of the inhabitants of the British Isles. He rejected any notion of the subordination of the periphery to the metropole, so central to most scholarly accounts of the first British empire. Oldmixon shared with Edward Littleton, whom he quoted liberally and approvingly, the belief that the colonies must be treated as they had been before the Restoration of the monarchy in 1660 as 'a part of England' rather than as 'foreigners and aliens'.[16] Given this integrated imperial vision, one that would find echoes later in the eighteenth century in the works of the Whigs Thomas Pownall, Benjamin Franklin and Adam Smith, Oldmixon emphasised the economic value of all Britain's American possessions.[17]

The Whig economic world view did not rest on territorial possessions. Instead, it relied on exports of British manufactures driving the engine of British economic growth. The Whigs advocated informal empire. So, the West Indies were vital not only for what they could produce, but also because of the vital role they could play in funneling British manufactured goods into Spanish America.[18]

The Whigs wanted a manufacturing empire that stood in stark contrast to the Spanish imperial achievement. The authoritarian extractive empire of the Spanish had so weakened that kingdom that Spaniards were forced to witness a great European struggle over their own future. The Spanish had rested content with importing the fabulous riches of the Mexican and Peruvian mines rather than developing their own manufacturing sector. Despite their vast imperial riches, thought Sir Henry Sheres, the Spaniards were in a 'calamitous degree of poverty'. This was because they disdained that labour which was the ultimate key to wealth. The Spanish, according to Sheres, had 'such a contempt [of] labour of all kinds, that the poorest Spaniard will rather starve at home or transport himself than submit to any low or servile occupation'. The Spanish were thus unable to export anything to 'their vast colonies in the Indies of their own manufactures'. 'From being masters of the product of the riches of the Indies', Sheres concluded, 'they are become in effect barely the carriers thereof, and the channel as I may say to convey it (as a river) to other more wise and industrious people.'[19]

Commitment to an integrated imperial economy driven by manufacturing exports and an ever-escalating cycle of production and consumption motivated both the Whig war strategy and the Whig war aims. Whigs had no desire for territorial expansion. Britain's existing colonies, they believed, had the potential for almost infinite economic expansion. Rather the Whigs wanted to put an end to the possibility of a French universal monarchy. The Whigs wanted to prevent the French from using profits generated through exclusive trade with Spanish America to finance their war machine. 'If Spain' and Spanish America 'shall be left in the possession of the French king by a peace', warned one Whig, 'mere poverty will soon bring England and all Europe under the French dominion.'[20] We 'aim not at conquest', another Whig later explained, 'our trade giving us all the wealth we could desire'.[21]

In 1709–10, then, the Whigs were on the brink of signing a peace that would secure their imperial vision. They hoped for a world in which British manufactures, whether textiles produced in Lancashire or ships and food made in New England, would drive unprecedented and sustained economic growth. They had no interest in seizing the Spanish silver mines in South America. Rather, they negotiated a peace that would exclude the French from the Spanish American trade and would, they hoped, pave the way for the penetration of British manufactures into the vast markets of Spanish America. The Whigs had an integrated imperial strategy; one that placed as much emphasis on the Atlantic world as on Europe. After the heady victory of Malplaquet the Whigs were on the brink of implementing their imperial vision.

The French, of course, did not sign the Whig peace in 1709 or 1710. The unexpected apotheosis of a relatively obscure Oxford cleric, Henry Sacheverell, thwarted the Whig plans. Queen Anne took the opportunity provided by the widespread rioting on behalf of this high church cleric to throw over the Whig ministers who had been running the war and install a new Tory ministry, led by Robert Harley. The queen dissolved the largely Whig Parliament and the Tories secured an overwhelming electoral majority. Harley and his allies acted quickly to implement a new Tory imperial strategy.

The Tories quickly denounced the Whig peace preliminaries for granting too little to Britain. The 'advantages stipulated for Britain bear no proportion to the part she had in the war', complained Henry St John to the Earl of Orrery. The Tory ambassador to the United Provinces, Lord Raby, thought the Whig preliminaries 'pernicious'. 'We have been the dupes of the war,' he fumed, '[we] must take great care that we are not so of the peace.'[22]

The Tories pursued a two-pronged strategy as soon as they came to power in 1710. First, they sought to end the war that they believed was part of a grand Whig plot to promote social revolution in Britain. Second, they wanted to secure a massive new British empire in South America that would forever secure Britain as a leading European power and also create a permanent Tory political monopoly in Britain itself.

Many Tories were convinced that the Whigs were promoting social revolution. Whigs supported the war, they believed, in large part because its escalating costs and increasingly punishing taxes were destroying the landed interest.[23] At the time of the revolution of 1688–89, the Tory Secretary of State, Henry St John later recalled, 'the moneyed interest was not yet a rival able to cope with the landed interest, either in the nation or in Parliament'. All that had now changed, St John informed Orrery in 1709, because 'we have now been twenty years engaged in the most expensive wars that Europe ever saw'. 'The whole burden of this charge', St John was sure, was paid by 'the landed interest during the whole time.' The result was that 'a new interest has been created out of their fortunes and a sort of property which was not known twenty years ago, is now increased to be almost equal to the *Terra Firma* of our island'. According to St John, 'the landed men are become poor and dispirited'.[24] Tory 'lands' had paid for Whig wars, complained *The Examiner*.[25] 'If the war continues some years longer', warned the authors of this Tory newspaper, 'a landed man will be little better than a farmer at rack-rent to the army, and to the public funds.'[26]

Once in power the Tories, by all accounts, sought to undo this social revolution. The new Tory government, observed their former colleague Daniel Finch, earl of Nottingham, garnered popular support by using the lure of a 'present peace, and the prospect of a future plenty'. In particular they promised to lower the 'Land Tax'.[27] Tory 'Reverend Divines', complained one Whig polemicist, inveighed 'against trade, as if it were the cause of all the schisms and heresies of the world', recommending instead 'the old patriarchal ways of cow-keeping and agriculture as more innocent employments for the people'.[28]

The Tories soon discovered that they could not simply try to unmake the financial revolution. Almost immediately after the Tories took power, Robert Harley had to face a financial crisis of unprecedented proportions. British investors, who until 1710 were largely Whig investors, those who lent huge sums of money to the government to help service the debt, were well aware of Tory social proclivities. They responded to the fall of the Whig Junto ministers by shutting their wallets.

The new Tory government was faced with a terrible conundrum. They wanted to put an end to the social revolutionary pressures engendered by the War of the Spanish Succession but they detested the

Whig peace terms. In addition they faced a frightening international financial crisis that threatened to bring their new government down, and emasculate any plans to advance the Tory war aims. What were they to do?

It was at this point that Robert Harley devised a scheme that would simultaneously solve the credit crisis, save the Tory ministry and implement a Tory vision of a centralised land-based British empire. Harley came up with a plan that would pave the way for a Tory peace in which Britain would get its just rewards for its heroic efforts in the war. Harley's solution was to create a British territorial empire in South America that would be supported by a massive new financial venture, the South Sea Company. That plan was soon the talk of the town, Britain and all Europe. Newspapermen, pamphleteers, company board members, and the huge range of the middling sort who owned some portion of the national debt all contributed to the wide-ranging discussion of Harley's new company.

Harley had a long-standing interest in creating a British empire in South America. At the same time as he was building up support for his doomed National Land Bank scheme in 1696, he began gathering information about the Spanish 'gold mines near Baldivia [Valdivia]' in Chile.[29] In 1705 or 1706 Dr Moses Stringer, who himself was deeply involved in extractive mining, floated a plan for a Tory South American Company that would include 'new acquisitions' to Lord Raby, that may have also crossed Harley's desk.[30] Harley did not come up with the South Sea scheme overnight.

In May 1711, having just recovered from the assassination attempt by the deranged Frenchman, the Marquis de Guiscard, Harley ushered the South Sea Bill through the House of Commons.[31] Soon all in the City were in 'agitation' about the South Sea trade.[32]

The South Sea Company was from the first a Tory company with imperial aspirations. Prominent Whigs, men who had supported the Whig Junto's 1709 peace plans, voted against Harley's bill in the House of Commons.[33] Unsurprisingly Tories greeted the passage of the bill with outspoken enthusiasm.[34]

In fact, to ensure that the new company would be a Tory company, the queen was granted the right to name the Company's Court of Directors. The group included the Tory director of the Royal African Company and member of the Board of Trade, Arthur Moore, the Tory Hamburg merchant John Gore, whose brother was a member of the ultra-Tory October Club, the Tory merchant Francis Stratford, who had long experience of trading 'for New Spain by way of Cadiz and Sevilla', the Tory financiers Sir Richard Hoare, Sir John Lambert and Harcourt Master, and, of course the Tory Secretary of State, Henry St John.

Anne named Oxford himself governor of the South Sea Company, with the new Tory convert and East India merchant Sir James Bateman as sub-governor, and the former Land Bank commissioner and Tory East India merchant Sir Samuel Ongley as deputy governor.[35] Thirteen of the new directors of the South Sea Company were men who had unsuccessfully stood as part of Tory slates for the directorships of the Bank of England and East India Company earlier in 1711.[36] The new South Sea Company enjoyed a directorate that was not only heavily Tory but also expert in overseas and imperial trade.

Oxford designed the South Sea Company to promote the Tory imperial vision. The South Sea Company was never meant, as most scholars maintain, merely as 'a façade behind which [the Tories] could continue the business of financial manipulation'.[37] The directors, propagandists and politicians who supported the Company overwhelmingly subscribed to the Tory political economic vision. Whereas the supporters of the Whig peace of 1709, and the Whig theorists of empire like John Oldmixon, had wanted to build an integrative empire based on labour and manufacturing, the Tories wanted an authoritarian territorial empire based on extracting the mineral wealth of South America.

Tories believed the South Sea scheme provided Britain with an opportunity to reverse the imperial errors of Henry VII and Henry VIII. The early Tudors, supporters of the South Sea Company believed, had abdicated to the Spanish the opportunity to seize the fabulously rich gold and silver mines of South America. 'It was the great oversight and neglect of Henry the 7th that rejected the offers of Christopher Columbus', opined one South Sea Company advocate; had the first Tudor monarch not neglected this opportunity 'what wealth and riches [would] the mines of gold and silver [have] brought into our country'.[38]

From the first the Tory directors of the South Sea Company planned to establish a British territorial presence in South America. The credibility and viability of the South Sea Company depended on making 'a settlement on the Spanish continent of America', maintained Daniel Defoe.[39] Settlement was necessary, all of the defenders of the South Sea Company implied, in order to secure the 'real treasure ... gold and silver'.[40]

Where did the South Sea Company hope to establish its South American settlements? By the middle of the summer of 1711, the South Sea Company appears to have plumped for a southern cone strategy. First, the South Sea Company proposed to seize Buenos Aires, significantly situated on the Rio de la Plata – the silver river – from the Spanish. 'Great Britain cannot make a settlement in any place upon the face of the earth from whence reasonably it may expect to reap so many advantages as from one situated upon the River of Plate', gushed one correspondent of the earl of Oxford.[41] The Royal African Company director Thomas Pindar agreed that a British Buenos Aires would 'exceed in succeeding ages the richest colonies belonging to this kingdom'.[42] The chief reason why Buenos Aires could become so fabulously wealthy, the main aim of the Tory South Sea Company investors, was that 'any nation settled upon the River of Plate has a very commodious and certain way to the Portuguese gold mines'. The former pirate Lionel Wafer, who had recently been introduced to Oxford by the Tory duke of Leeds, thought a base on the River Plate would soon allow the British to control 'great quantities of gold and silver' that were being shipped down the river.[43]

The South Sea Company wanted a second colonial outpost at Valdivia in Chile. Valdivia, thought the active East India merchant and imperial projector Thomas Bowrey, was 'the most proper port for us to take from the Spaniards in the South Seas'. Predictably for someone long interested in piracy, Bowrey thought Valdivia would be a good vantage point from which to 'disrupt the whole Spanish trade in the South Seas'. More importantly, though, Valdivia 'produces the most gold of any place in the South Seas'.[44]

The South Sea Company hoped to establish a third port, between Buenos Aires and Valdivia, near the Straits of Magellan. Bowrey envisioned such a harbour as being necessary primarily for 'refreshment of our men, repairing of our ships after so very long and troublesome a voyage'. One of the South Sea Company's defenders had more ambitious plans. This defender of the Company wanted the Tierra del Fuego to be renamed 'Nova Britannia' because in time 'no plantation beyond the seas would be more gainful to us in furnishing this kingdom with the neighbouring gold and silver'.[45]

The South Sea Company was always designed to work hand-in-hand with the Tory Royal African Company. The long-time imperialist and naval man Sir George Byng was not alone in asking whether the South Sea directors could consider 'how to make the slave trade of Guinea useful to the Company'.[46] Thomas Pindar proposed that on the second expedition to the South Seas the Company should 'receive on board one thousand choice negroes which will be of great service in the settlements', presumably to work in the new silver and gold mines.[47] It was therefore no surprise that when the Tories did gain the Asiento contract for providing African slaves to the Spanish plantations as part of their peace negotiations in 1713, the South Sea Company agreed to work hand-in-hand with the Royal African Company to fulfil the terms of the contract.[48]

The South Sea Company hoped to create a fabulously wealthy British empire in the southern cone of South America. Unlike the Whig empire that sought to use British manufactured goods to penetrate Spanish

American markets, the Tories wanted to create their own territorial empire. They did not want to trade for Spanish bullion, they wanted to discover their own mines and conquer others from the Spanish and Portuguese. The Tories did not envisage an alternative to the Spanish Atlantic empire. They wanted to mimic it and then take it over.

Oxford designed his new company not only to create a vast territorial empire in South America, but also to solve Britain's immediate credit crisis and reverse the social revolutionary effects of the Whig financial revolution. The South Sea Company at its founding incorporated the proprietors of over £9 million of Britain's debts 'to carry on a trade to the South Seas'. At a stroke hundreds of holders of the public debt were compelled to become stockholders in the new Tory South Sea Company, with a guaranteed return of 6 per cent.[49] Oxford had designed a scheme that made hundreds of holders of the national debt, many of them Whigs, interested in the success of a Tory empire in South America. And the scheme promised to restore national and international confidence in the financial wherewithal of the British government. Once the Company, in tandem with the British government, had established its territorial empire in South America the benefit to the nation would be greater still. This South American 'commerce', predicted one of the Company's apologists, 'will open such a vein of riches, will return such wealth as in a few years will make us more than sufficient amends for the vast expenses we have been at since the Revolution'.[50] The South Sea Company and its associated territorial empire would allow Britain to pay down its debts and reverse the social revolutionary consequences of the Whig war strategy.

Oxford and the Tories always intended the South Sea Company to be a real trading and imperial concern. Oxford himself had had a long-term interest in creating a British empire in South America. He created a South Sea Company directorate filled with Tory merchants expert in long-distance trade and imperial projects. He had, it is true, used the financial crisis of 1710–11 to generate widespread support for his ingenious scheme. And he did design the Company to provide a quick fix for Britain's credit crisis. But Oxford and his friends in no way saw these two goals as incompatible. They formed a coherent ideological programme.

Immediately after creating the Company Oxford had begun plans for an expeditionary force to attack Spanish America. In September 1710 Harley was hard at work 'about the expedition to America' hoping to have it launched before October because it was not 'advisable to begin an expedition towards South America later than that'.[51] In the event that early expedition never took shape, but the following year plans began to take shape in earnest. In January 1712 the Company's Court of Directors wrote to Oxford that 'in order to make such settlements' in South America as planned, the queen needed to 'assist the Company with a sufficient sea and land force with provisions and other necessaries'. A sufficient land and sea force, they made clear, meant twenty men of war 'with 4000 land forces' and 'forty transport ships from 250 to 300 tons each'.[52] In March 1712 Queen Anne gave the final approval for a squadron sufficient 'for making settlements in America for the benefit of' the South Sea Company.[53] In the spring of 1712 the Tories launched their South American empire.

The Tories who came to power after the ministerial revolution of 1710 rejected the Whig vision of an integrated, manufacturing empire. But they were not indifferent to empire. Instead Oxford and his Tory allies launched their own imperial programme. The Tories made their new South Sea Company the lynchpin of this strategy. Oxford and his friends intended to use the South Sea Company to establish a new British empire in South America. They based their breathtaking vision on their own understanding of political economy. They believed that the key to wealth was controlling the world's finite natural resources. They did not want to provide an alternative to the Spanish empire in the Americas. They wanted to supplant it. The Tories were confident their success would allow them to halt and then reverse the corrosive social effects of the Whig-engineered financial revolution. A Tory territorial empire would once again make Britain safe for rule by landed gentlemen.

The Tories did not, in fact, create a territorial empire in the southern cone of South America. The overwhelming majority of inhabitants of Argentina and Chile still speak Spanish rather than English as their primary language. Britain's Atlantic empire in the eighteenth century remained largely north of the equator. But the Tory failure to create a territorial empire in South America was not for lack of effort. The South Sea Company was intended to be the commercial arm of Britain's new empire. That it was never able to bring back fabulous riches from the South Seas had much more to do with political developments than with the Company's initial design.

The Tory ministry's rapid success in bringing the French to the negotiating table appeared to make the British expedition against Spanish America unnecessary. The Tory government had insisted in their initial gambit for peace that the French agree to granting the British the island of St Christopher (St Kitts) in the Caribbean, the Asiento or exclusive contract for selling slaves to Spanish America for thirty years, and 'a certain extent of territory' in and around the River Plate. In addition, the British were to be given 'certain places to be named in the Treaty of Peace' that would further secure 'the British trade in the Spanish West

Indies'.[54] By November 1712, Strafford was certain that the Spanish had agreed to 'give a place on the River Plate'.[55] No wonder the Dutch were furious that the British were not merely establishing a trade with Spanish America but fully intended 'the planting of new colonies'.[56]

The Tories, of course, famously secured an exclusive contract to import African slaves to Spanish America. The Tories reasoned that the combination of the Asiento, Buenos Aires and perhaps colonies in Valdivia and on the Tierra del Fuego would secure a potent imperial base for the South Sea Company.

Just as the Tories were ostensibly securing the future of a British empire in Spanish America, so they were also securing other territorial advantages for Britain in the Treaty of Utrecht. Whereas the Whigs had sought no new territorial possessions in 1709, the Tories sought and gained them throughout the world. St John, Viscount Bolingbroke since the summer of 1712, successfully insisted that Britain retain possession of Minorca and Gibraltar despite Dutch objections. The Tories also successfully negotiated the return of Hudson's Bay and St Kitts and the acquisition of Acadia.

The Tories believed they had achieved all their goals. They had secured British territorial acquisitions in the Mediterranean, North America and the Caribbean. They had founded a British empire in South America. And they had negotiated a conclusion to a misguided war that helped their trading rivals abroad and benefitted the Whigs at home. They had, they believed, secured what the British people wanted and needed. When the news arrived in London in April 1713 that the peace had been signed at Utrecht, 'the whole British nation' seemed to express its 'approbation'. In the ensuing months well over 200 separate groups of Britons submitted addresses celebrating the peace, not a few emphasising 'the many advantages' both territorial and mercantile that Britain gained by the peace.[57]

Tory celebrations were, however, short-lived. Not only did the House of Commons reject the commercial treaty that the Tories had negotiated with France, but the new Bourbon monarchy in Spain successfully thwarted Tory plans for empire in South America.[58]

The Spanish, having granted the Asiento contract and the promise of allowing one British ship to trade with Spanish America custom free, now baulked at making the territorial concessions so central to the Tory strategy. The Spanish negotiating team, Lord Lexington complained, were refusing to honour agreements based on 'the most solemn assurances'. The Spanish, Bolingbroke understood all too well, had made sure that the peace treaty ending the war was 'signed first' so that 'the Queen would be at their mercy with respect to that of commerce'. Bolingbroke could gnash his teeth and issue threats, but Britain had demobilised. After celebrating the peace, the Tory ministers were in no position to begin a new war. When Matthew Prior pleaded with Louis XIV for help in enforcing the agreement's Britain's territories in Spanish America he was told that 'our interest in Madrid was much stronger than his own'.[59] Spanish diplomatic ingenuity put a halt to the Tory plans for territorial empire in South America.

In April 1713 Oxford and his government thought they had secured a Tory peace. Above all they had secured for Britain a territorial foothold in the southern cone of Spanish America. Buenos Aires and the other potential British bases in South America had been the fulcrum around which the Tories designed their strategy. Buenos Aires was supposed to provide the key to mineral riches as well as providing an important way station for the transportation of slaves from Africa. This was the commercial basis upon which the South Sea Company directors could promise its investors fabulous returns. That the Tories failed to secure territorial concessions in South America was an unexpected and unmitigated disaster. Forgetting the enormity of that disaster has made it impossible to understand the Tory imperial strategy of the early eighteenth century.

The British struggle over the aims and achievements of the War of the Spanish Succession needs to be understood as a party political conflict over the direction and contours of the British empire. The Whigs had sought to establish an integrative empire favourable to British manufacturing. The Whigs wanted to extend the informal tendrils of their commercial networks, but had little or no interest in seizing more territory for the British sovereign. The Tories, by contrast, had wanted to create an extractive, coercive and territorial British empire in South America. Their empire, they hoped, would soon rival and eventually displace the Spanish empire. The Tories saw nothing wrong with the Spanish imperial model. Instead, they reasoned, they should seize the imperial opportunity that Henry VII had let pass in the fifteenth century.

What then are the broader implications for this story? What have we gained by recovering the story of the failed Tory project for establishing a British empire in the southern cone? It seems to me that this story has broad implications for the ways in which we should think and write about the history of the British empire.

First, there was no single moment in which the British became authoritarian imperialists. Historians have long sought the moment in which the British turned away from liberty-loving proponents of a soft commercial empire, into the authoritarians who ruled with such a brutal hand in India and sub-Saharan Africa. Indeed historians have been so eager to uncover the moment of this remarkable epistemic shift, they have found *several* of them. In a recent and important work that theorises in innovative ways the nature of the early empire, Alison Games has discovered a 'cosmopolitan' impulse lay behind English expansion in the sixteenth and seventeenth centuries. That initial cosmopolitanism, derived from English 'weakness in the sixteenth century', Games assures us, was 'highly decentralized'. By the 1650s, however, there was 'a pronounced shift' in the nature of the empire. This shift, which 'challenged the relevance and necessity of an accommodating demeanor', involved a twofold turn toward 'centralization' and 'the use of coercion and force'.[60] The empire, in Games's view, had taken a decisive authoritarian turn by the 1650s.

Historians more focused on the tumultuous events of the 1760s and 1770s have detected an authoritarian turn in this period. Tim Breen, for example, in his exciting account of the American Revolution as bourgeois consumer revolution, has identified the period 'roughly from 1757 to 1764' as the moment when Americans began to realise that 'they were in fact colonists – perhaps nothing more than colonists – subjects of the Crown who did not quite measure up to the men and women who happened to reside in England'. Prior to this period Americans had become prosperous without 'intolerable interference by the representatives of an *ancien regime*'. This 'absence of coercion' in the period before the late 1750s allowed commerce to bring 'Americans into a closer more harmonious relationship with the mother country'. The sense of coercion, then, that began to emerge in the later 1750s was accelerated by the passage of the Sugar Act of 1764, the 1765 Stamp Act which 'instantly transformed the political landscape of Britain's Atlantic World', the Townshend duties of 1767, the Tea Act of 1773 and the Intolerable Acts of 1774. The net result was to foment a consumer revolution.[61] Breen's narrative turns on a shift in British political attitudes towards empire. In Breen's story, as in many earlier tellings, the British government turned away from a permissive commercialist attitude towards empire in the earlier period towards more coercive and authoritarian policies in the wake of the Seven Years War (1756–63).[62]

For others the period from 1780–1830 was the crucial moment in which the British empire began to 'establish overseas despotisms which mirrored in many ways the politics of neo-absolutism and the Holy Alliance of contemporary Europe'. Before that time, C. A. Bayly has maintained, the 'British empire was a ragged and conflict-ridden community of separate interests'. 'Loose control from the centre during that period had encouraged the development of an expansive settler capitalism', he maintains. Scotland, of course, was an exception, 'for Ireland and much of the rest of the western empire, centrifugal forces remained predominant'. The new British empire that emerged after 1780 was characterised 'by a form of aristocratic military government supporting a viceregal autocracy, by a well-developed imperial style which emphasised hierarchy and racial subordination, and by the patronage of indigenous landed elites'. 'Constructive authoritarian and ideological British imperialism', in Bayly's view, 'came of age in the years between 1783 and 1820.'[63]

One could go on, citing those who see an authoritarian turn in the 1680s, and others who point to the 1880s. My story of the competing Whig and Tory imperial projects of the early eighteenth century, however, suggests that the problem of a British authoritarian empire has been badly conceptualised. In a sense all these scholars are right to see an authoritarian turn in their periods. They are wrong, however, to insist on sea changes, epistemic shifts and pivotal moments of vindictive legislation. Instead, I am suggesting, the contours of the British empire were always shaped by social and political contestation. Some Britons always had an authoritarian impulse and wanted a coercive, centralised, blue-water empire. Others, who were no less imperialists, wanted a more integrative and less coercive empire.

Second, political economic conflict rather than mercantilist consensus shaped the British empire. Mercantilism was, from the publication of the influential Cambridge *History of the British Empire*, thought to be the organising principle of the so-called first British empire. After a brief interlude of intellectual doubt, the concept has returned. Recently historians of the British empire have confidently returned to the notion of a mercantilist imperial consensus. Anthony Howe insists that there was a 'mercantilist consensus on trade and power' that persisted well into the nineteenth century.[64] Nuala Zahedieh describes mercantilism as 'self-evidently a coherent system' in the seventeenth century.[65] England, Tom Devine has recently pointed out, imposed 'mercantilist regulations'.[66] David Armitage has perceived the existence of a 'mercantilist colonial system'.[67] 'From the Glorious Revolution until the defeat of Napoleonic France at Waterloo', proclaims Kenneth Morgan, 'the political economy of the British empire was underpinned by a mercantilist framework.' In his massive *After Tamerlane* John Darwin similarly finds 'mercantilist doctrines favoured in Britain' in the eighteenth century.[68]

Some scholars have doubted that there is still a belief in a mercantilist consensus. But a recent sciences citation index survey revealed over 200 uses of the term in articles published in refereed journals in the past two years alone. Recent works by eminent economic historians like Joel Mokyr and Bob Allen have insisted on the existence of such a consensus. And the new encyclopedia of economic history (2010) has an entry on mercantilism, written by a senior economic historian, that insists it was the dominant view until the 1760s.

What, then, were the organising principles of mercantilism? What were the concepts about which everyone agreed in the early modern period? The overwhelming majority of scholars agree about the fundamental underlying concept of mercantilism. Mercantilists all believed in the limits to growth. Mercantilists believed that they lived in a world of scarcity – because property and value was defined exclusively with reference to land – in which economic life was necessarily one of vicious competition. They believed, most scholars assert confidently, that trade was a zero-sum game.

Recent scholars who have reasserted the mercantilist consensus have also highlighted that a belief in the finite nature of earthly property was the touchstone of early modern political economy. 'The world's store of wealth was thought to be finite,' asserts Tom Devine, 'hence an expansion of one nation's resources could only take place at the expense of other powers.'[69] 'Mercantilists viewed overseas trade as a zero-sum game', agrees Kenneth Morgan. 'Accordingly, legitimate exchange between colonists of different nationalities was seen as a threat to the imperial strength of the nation state.'[70] 'Economics as a zero-sum game', insists Niall Ferguson in his widely circulated analysis of the British empire, is 'the essence of what came to be called mercantilism.'

These scholars, I have suggested, are not wrong to believe that many subscribed to the zero-sum views they have called mercantilism. There was, however, no mercantilist consensus. Scholars, by assuming a mercantilist consensus, have obscured the degree to which the shaping of empire was a conscious political choice. In their view, because all governments shared the same goals, the only plausible explanation for empires taking on different shapes were the constraints of environment and opportunity. I show, however, that different parties with different political economic outlooks sought to create different kinds of empires. The Tory imperialists wanted an extractive empire in South America because they were committed to the notion that there was a finite amount of wealth in the world, and that it was far better that that wealth be in British rather than Dutch or Spanish hands. The Tories did not achieve ideological hegemony. The Whigs wanted an integrative manufacturing empire devoid of more territorial possessions, because they believed that labour rather than land created value. Since they believed that property was potentially infinite, and that manufacturing was the best way to generate national wealth, the Whigs thought the Tory imperial scheme was fundamentally misguided. If I am right, then, the best way to understand the ways in which Britons shaped their empire is to pay greater attention to these fundamental political economic conflicts. Britons were divided more by differing political economic conceptions than they were by whether they lived in the metropole or in the periphery.

Finally, this contest over empire in the early eighteenth century may point to some limits of the New Imperial History. The achievements of the New Imperial History have, of course, been many and varied. We now understand a great deal more than we did before about 'issues of identity and belonging' in the British empire.[71] The 'new imperial history that is grounded on difference' has alerted us to strategies of domination not accounted for in the older histories. Nevertheless the focus on 'the ideologies and representations of difference', 'the social, cultural and epistemological networks' and the insistence on the engagement only with softer disciplines of 'literature, anthropology and history, the history of medicine and psychiatry, geography, art history and cultural studies' risks occluding the central sites of political contestation in the eighteenth century.[72] Contests over institutions were fundamental to the shaping of the eighteenth-century empire. This was true for three reasons. First, a focus on the ideologies of difference risks making illegible the Whig strategy on integrative empire, since that strategy depended so heavily on informal economic links. The New Imperial History has invariably focused on areas where the British had territorial sovereignty, not on areas of informal empire.[73] Second, by insisting on the weakness of British imperial institutions, a narrowly cultural approach to empire risks making incomprehensible the choices made to evade institutional regulation. Piracy only existed because trade regulations were frequently enforced. Third, institutions like the Board of Trade helped to structure colonial societies. It was the possibility of securing interests through institutions, as Heather Welland has recently shown, that helped to form lobbies that were so central to the eighteenth-century British imperial polity.[74]

Why, then, did the Whigs think that the Peace of Utrecht was an imperial betrayal? The answer, it should now be clear, is that the Whigs rejected the Tory view of empire. The Tories had negotiated with France in order to create the possibility of a significantly expanded British territorial empire. They succeeded in taking control of Minorca, Gibraltar, Hudson's Bay, Nova Scotia and St Kitts. They also secured the lucrative Asiento contract to supply Spanish America with slaves for thirty years. Perhaps more importantly, they had failed to secure, as they had intended from 1711, a territorial base in the southern cone for the South Sea Company. The Tory imperialists were committed to a political economic vision in which value came exclusively from the land, what could be extracted from the land, and what could be produced on the land. They believed that value was finite and that Britain, having fought heroically at great expense, deserved to increase its share of the world's scarce resources.

The Whigs rejected all of these assumptions. They believed that labour, not land, was the basis of value. Britain's future, they believed, lay not in seizing more territory, but in finding outlets for its manufactures. They thus wanted an integrated empire, in which North America, the West Indies and the British Isles all produced and manufactured what was most efficient. They thought the Tories had bungled the peace because they were fixated on territory and fears of the Dutch as Britain's greatest economic rivals. Instead of securing a substantial opening for British manufactures into Spanish America, the Tories left the majority of Spanish commercial exclusions in place. The result was that the economic basis of French power was left intact.

Whigs of all social ranks were enraged at the implementation of the Tory political economic vision. 'The merchants lie off', Oxford complained to Bolingbroke in 1713, deceived by 'the correspondence and encouragement that party [the Whigs] gives to their friends to hold out and wait for some unhappy accident to unravel all which is done'.[75] Many, observed the authors of *The Examiner*, 'censured and rejected' the terms negotiated by the Tories at Utrecht. 'Petitions', they lamented, 'swarm almost as thick as Addresses, and the [Whig] party threaten us every day to turn them into remonstrances, and to have them backed by the unrepresented multitude.'[76]

The Whigs loathed the Treaty of Utrecht because they knew it instantiated a Tory territorial empire. The Whigs, too, had fought the War of the Spanish Succession in support of empire. Their empire, however, was a manufacturing not a territorial one. The debate over the Treaty of Utrecht was a party contest over the direction of the British empire. Indeed, since the creation of the Board of Trade in 1696, England and then Britain (after 1707) had become an imperial state. British politics, in and out of doors, was necessarily imperial politics. At the same time, the contours of the British Atlantic were, throughout the eighteenth century, fundamentally shaped by British party politics.

Notes

1 *Daily Benefactor*, 2 (3 May 1715), p. 5.
2 *The Englishman*, 3 (18 July 1715), p. [2].
3 *A Letter to a Member of the October-Club* (1711), pp. 5–6.
4 I have not included the careful work of B. W. Hill in this discussion because his argument focuses more on emphasising the Earl of Oxford's central role in a peace process which he describes as fundamentally 'pragmatic': B. W. Hill, 'Oxford, Bolingbroke and the Peace of Utrecht', *HJ*, 16:2 (1973), p. 263; B. W. Hill, *Robert Harley: Speaker, Secretary of State and Prime Minister* (New Haven, 1988), pp. 159–92.
5 J. H. Eliott, *Empires of the Atlantic World* (New Haven, 2006), pp. 221–2. Elliott is not unaware of party conflict in Britain, but its only effect on colonial policy was to provide 'an opening to colonial societies and their spokesmen in London to exploit the party political divisions in England for their own purposes'. Parties did not have conflicting imperial strategies. Colonials manipulated the divisions, presumably based on non-imperial issues, to their own ends.

6   J. Hoppit, *A Land of Liberty?* (Oxford, 2000), p. 246.
7   G. Holmes, *British Politics in the Age of Anne* (London, 1967), pp. 75–81; J. Black, *Parliament and Foreign Policy in the Eighteenth Century* (Cambridge, 2004), p. 32.
8   French politicians were in fact quite desperate to end the war in 1709: TNA, PRO 31/3/196, fo. 43v.
9   BL, Additional MS 71,142, fos 29, 33.
10 *Ibid.*, fo. 37; Additional MS 38,498, fos 3–5, 7, 11.
11 B. Simms, *Three Victories and a Defeat* (London, 2007), p. 56.
12 BL, Additional MS 61,500, fo. 5; TNA, CO 391/21, pp. 99, 102; BL, Additional MS 61,500, fo. 70; *An Address to the Good People of Great Britain* (4th ed., 1715), p. 5.
13 J. Locke, *Second Treatise of Government*, ed. C. B. Macpherson (Indianapolis, 1980), ch. V, paras. 37, 40, pp. 24–5.
14 J. Oldmixon, *The British Empire in America* (2 vols, 1708), I, pp. xxii, xxvi, xxx. It should be clear here and from what follows that I disagree with David Armitage's claim that Oldmixon adopted 'the mercantilist analysis of Child and Davenant': D. Armitage, *The Ideological Origins of the British Empire* (Cambridge, 2000), p. 175. Oldmixon was writing within the Whig paradigm critical of Child and Davenant. Proper understanding of Oldmixon's political economy allows one to understand the integrative elements of his imperial strategy denied by Armitage.
15 Oldmixon, *British Empire*, I, pp. xxv, xxxii, II, p. 345. From Smith, see A. Smith, *The Wealth of Nations*, ed. E. Canaan (New York, 2000), pp. 671–5 (Bk. IV, ch. VII, Pt. III).
16 E. Littleton, *The Groans of the Plantations* (1689, 1698), p. 1.
17 Oldmixon, *British Empire*, I, pp. xxx, xxxii.
18 Oldmixon, *British Empire*, II, pp. 344–5; BL, Additional MS 70,164, unfol.
19 Oldmixon, *British Empire*, I, p. xxxv; *A Letter to a Member of the October Club* (1711), p. 19; BL, Additional MS 70,164, unfol.
20 *Letter to a Member*, p. 65.
21 *Address to the Good People*, p. 6.
22 BL, Additional MS 22,205, fo. 128v.
23 The landed interest was, of course, in large part an ideological construct: see Julian Hoppit, 'The landed interest and the national interest, 1660–1800', in *Parliaments, Nations and Identities in Britain and Ireland, 1660–1850* (Manchester, 2003), p. 84.
24 H. St John, Viscount Bolingbroke, *Letters on the Study and Use of History* (1752), Letter 8, pp. 267–8, 382–3; Bodl. MS Eng.Misc.e.180, fos 4–5. While I agree on many issues with Kramnick, I dissent from his view that Bolingbroke's thought was shaped by the credit crisis of 1710 and the later South Sea Bubble. Bolingbroke's social critique was already manifest. See I. Kramnick, *Bolingbroke and His Circle* (Cambridge, Mass., 1968), pp. 63–4. Dickinson is surely right to read this letter as expressing 'the views of the Tory squires': H. T. Dickinson, *Bolingbroke* (London, 1970), p. 69.
25 *The Examiner*, 4 (24 August 1710), p. [1].
26 *The Examiner*, 14 (26 October–2 November 1710), p. [1].
27 D. Finch, Earl of Nottingham, *Observations upon the State of the Nation in January 1712/13* (2nd ed., 1713), p. 23.
28 *Letter to Member*, p. 47.
29 BL, Additional MS 70,161, unfol.
30 BL, Additional MS 22,265, fo. 96.
31 For conflicting accounts of this development, see Hill, *Harley*, pp. 144–5; John Carswell, *The South Sea Bubble* (London, 1961), pp. 44–5.
32 BL, Additional MS 70,163, fo. 177.
33 *Ibid.*, fo. 136. While the Bank told its deputies not to petition formally against the new company, as that would create an open confrontation between the Bank and the new ministry, there was no love lost between the Whig Bank and the new South Sea Company: J. Clapham, *The Bank of England* (2 vols, Cambridge, 1945), I, pp. 80–1. I find it difficult to accept Hill's argument that the South Sea Company 'was not a rival to the Bank of England': Hill, *Harley*, p. 145.
34 E. Gregg, *Queen Anne* (New Haven, 1980), p. 338.

35 BL, Additional MS 25,494, fo. 3v; Additional MS 70,163, fo. 153; Additional MS 70,027, fo. 213. For Ongley and Bateman, See E. Cruickshanks, S. Handley, and D. W. Hayton (eds), *The House of Commons 1690–1715* (5 vols, Cambridge, 2002), V, pp. 17–8, IV, pp. 147–9. See also Carswell, *South Sea Bubble*, pp. 45–6, 244–55.
36 B. Carruthers, *City of Capital* (Princeton, 1996), pp. 153–4; J. G. Sperling, *The South Sea Company* (Cambridge, Mass., 1962), p. 7.
37 Carswell, *South Sea Bubble*, p. 46. This has been the usual interpretation of the Company: Hoppit, *Land of Liberty?*, p. 303; Carruthers, *City of Capital*, p. 79.
38 *The Considerable Advantages of a South-Sea Trade* ([1711]), p. 3. One South Sea Company advocate blamed the neglect on earlier English monarchs who had failed to capitalise on a prince of Wales's discovery of America 'long before the days of Christopher Columbus', perhaps around 1190: BL, Additional MS 70,163, fo. 249. The Tories understood the Tudor failure not as having set the British on an imperial course that would always differ substantively from the Spanish, but as a choice that could be reversed. Cf. Elliott, *Empires of the Atlantic World*, p. 411.
39 BL, Additional MS 70,291, fos 9–10; D. Defoe, *A True Account of the Design and Advantage of the South-Sea Trade* (1711), p. 10. Defoe's pamphlet was written under the close supervision of Oxford: BL, Additional MS 70,291, fos 3–v, 5, 7. For Defoe's interest, see Sperling, *South Sea Company*, p. 9; M. E. Novak, *Daniel Defoe: Master of Fictions* (Oxford, 2001), pp. 402–3.
40 Defoe, *True Account*, p. 5; *A Letter to a Member of Parliament on the Settling a Trade to the South-Sea of America* ([1711]), p. 8.
41 BL, Additional MS 70,163, fo. 233.
42 BL, Additional MS 70,164, unfol. Oxford received a similar report from one of his French spies: Additional MS 70,185, 62/78.
43 BL, Additional MS 70,163, fos 233–4; Additional MS 70,164, unfol.; BL, Additional MS 28,079, fos. 39, 40–1; Additional MS 70,164, unfol.
44 BL, Additional MS 70,163, fo. 196.
45 *Ibid.*, fo. 198; *Considerable Advantages*, p. 13.
46 BL, Additional MS 70,164, unfol. Byng, though a moderate Whig, was a long-time imperialist, having worked hand in hand with Josiah Child on James II's grand plan for an Indian empire in 1685–97.
47 *Ibid.*, unfol.
48 TNA, T 70/88, p. 401.
49 BL, Additional MS 70,163, fos 239v, 245; Defoe, *True Account*, p. 10; BL, Additional MS 25,559, fo. 2; Carruthers, *City of Capital*, p. 154.
50 BL, Additional MS 70,163, fo. 242.
51 BL, Additional MS 70,026, fo. 166.
52 BL, Additional MS 70,163, fo. 25; Additional MS 25,559, fos 8–9; Additional MS 70,163, fo. 24.
53 BL, Additional MS 25,559, fos. 7v, 9.
54 BL, Additional MS 70,342, pp. 42–4, 51.
55 BL, Additional MS 31,147, fo. 88. The British never agreed to drop these claims in exchange for the Asiento. Cf. S. J. Stein and B. H. Stein, *Silver, Trade, and War* (Baltimore, 2000), p. 136.
56 BL, Additional MS 31,136, fo. 362.
57 BL, Additional MS 78,514A, fo. 1v; *A Letter Concerning the Report from the Committee of Secrecy* (1715), p. 2; *London Gazette*, 5117 (2 May 1713).
58 The best account of the debate over the commercial treaty is now Perry Gauci, *The Politics of Trade* (Oxford, 2001), pp. 234–70.
59 BL, Additional MS 70,030, fo. 238v; Additional MS 46,543A, fo. 70; Additional MS 46,545, fos 24–5; TNA, SP 78/157, fo. 383v. I am not convinced that the Spanish Commercial Treaty 'spelled out what would become, in the long run, subordination of imperial Spain to English naval and economic hegemony': Stein and Stein, *Silver, Trade, and War*, p. 137. Instead these negotiations began the Britanno-Spanish tensions that would eventually result in the War of Jenkins' Ear.
60 A. Games, *The Web of Empire* (Oxford, 2008), pp. 289–90.

61 T. H. Breen, *The Marketplace of Revolution* (Oxford, 2004), pp. 75, 201–2, 217–18, 235, 239, 294–9.
62 For other accounts of such a shift, see E. and H. Morgan, *The Stamp Act Crisis* (Chapel Hill, NS, 1953), pp. 21–7, 54; Elliott, *Empires of the Atlantic World*, pp. 298, 301–3, 305.
63 C. A. Bayly, *Imperial Meridian* (London, 1989), pp. 8–9, 76–7, 250. With a slightly different chronology, and a different set of emphases, Jennifer Pitts has also charted 'a turn to empire' in the period 1780–1830, that is 'a sea change in opinions on empire' among liberal thinkers in favour 'of the conquest of non-European peoples and territories'. This was accompanied by 'an increasingly exclusive conception ... of national community ad political capacity': J. Pitts, *A Turn to Empire* (Princeton, 2005), p. 2.
64 A. Howe, 'Restoring free trade, 1776–1873', in D. Winch and P. O'Brien (eds), *The Political Economy of British Historical Experience, 1688–1914* (Oxford, 2002), p. 194.
65 N. Zahedieh, 'Making mercantilism work: London merchants and the Atlantic trade in the seventeenth century', *TRHS*, 6th series, 9 (1999), 158.
66 T. M. Devine, *Scotland's Empire* (Washington, 2003), p. 30.
67 Armitage, *Ideological Origins*, p. 176.
68 K. Morgan, 'Mercantilism and the British empire', in Winch and O'Brien (eds), *Political Economy*, p. 165; J. Darwin, *After Tamerlane: The Global History of Empire since 1405* (London, 2007), p. 213.
69 Devine, *Scotland's Empire*, p. 30.
70 Morgan, 'Mercantilism', p. 168.
71 C. Hall, 'Thinking the postcolonial, thinking the empire', in Hall (ed.), *Cultures of Empire* (New York. 2000), p. 2; K. Wilson, 'Histories, empires, modernities', in Wilson (ed.), *A New Imperial History* (Cambridge, 2004), p. 5.
72 Wilson, 'Histories', pp. 5, 10, 13, 19; Hall, 'Thinking', p. 24.
73 The term 'informal empire' occurs twice in Catherine Hall's introductory essay, but nowhere else in her reader. Those two mentions are about what is not discussed in her collection.
74 It should be noted that in Wilson's view at least the 'new imperial history' is supposed to supplement rather than supplant other imperial histories: Wilson, 'Histories', p. 3. One worries that not all proponents of this cultural approach will follow Wilson's wise strictures.
75 *A Report* (1715), p. 104; BL, Additional MS 70,031, fo. 19; TNA, SP 78/157, fos 418–9.
76 *The Examiner*, 4 (5–8 June 1713), p. [2].

CHAPTER THREE

Party politics and empire in the early eighteenth century

J. H. Elliott

This chapter offers a response to Steve Pincus's vigorously argued 'The Pivot of Empire', and I should like to begin by paying tribute to his prodigious achievement over the past few years. I first became aware of the extraordinary range of his research and reading when, rather belatedly, I came across his 1996 analysis of English foreign policy between 1650 and 1668, *Protestantism and Patriotism*.[1] In this wonderfully well-documented book he took up a cause that is dear to my heart by questioning the insularity of the English in the seventeenth century and demonstrating their preoccupation with the threat of universal monarchy, a threat which he presents as acquiring new characteristics as the century proceeded. In 2009, in another massively documented study, *1688*, which has rightly received widespread attention, he challenged, head-on, traditional assumptions about the moderate and peaceful nature of the Glorious Revolution, and sought to present it as neither of the above.[2] If all the forces from hell have not yet been unleashed against him, it is possible that they soon will be.

In a further challenge to accepted orthodoxies, he presents us in 'The Pivot of Empire' with the first findings of a major new enterprise. He is asking us to rethink the origins and character of English, and perhaps British, notions of empire in the seventeenth and eighteenth centuries, and the driving forces that made the eighteenth-century empire what it was. But he has complicated the task of the respondent to his piece by focusing it rather narrowly on the debates surrounding the Utrecht peace settlement of 1713–14, although he uses his analysis of those debates to raise towards the end some general questions about the recent historiography of the empire and imperial politics. The task is further complicated because this particular respondent is no specialist in British history, and one whose knowledge of the reign of Queen Anne goes little beyond the three volumes of G. M. Trevelyan, which the author generously offered as a wedding present in 1958. And if I find myself thinking about the Treaty of Utrecht, my first thought, perhaps not surprisingly, is about our shameful betrayal of the Catalans, an issue not mentioned by Steve Pincus in his chapter.

For these reasons I find myself rather inhibited in the task that has been set me, but it is nevertheless possible to raise a number of points of concern, or disagreement, arising from Pincus's analysis of the Utrecht debates, and end by following his example and making one or two summary comments on our current understanding of British attitudes to empire and imperial politics, both before and after Utrecht. What we are concerned with here is the political, economic and intellectual culture that went into the shaping of Britain's overseas empire, and led it to evolve in the way that it did. If this involves drawing contrasts with Spain and Spanish attitudes to empire, then it is to be hoped that this will help to bring the British imperial story into sharper focus.

Central to Pincus's argument about the Treaty of Utrecht is that previous historians have got it wrong – an argument not unusual when Pincus takes on a new subject. Their mistake was to claim that the issues dividing Whigs and Tories focused on whether a Bourbon should sit on the Spanish throne, and whether the peace treaty should be negotiated jointly with all the members of the Grand Alliance. This, in Pincus's view, is far too limited an interpretation of a party struggle which in reality had enormous implications for the future of Britain and its overseas possessions. Against what he sees as a restricted and partial depiction of events he insists that 'the struggle over the Peace of Utrecht was a party political struggle over the future of the British empire'.[3] 'The Whigs', he goes on, 'demanded a peace that not only would prevent the possibility of French hegemony in Europe, but also entrench a Whig imperial vision.'[4] The Tories, on the other hand, had a very different vision of empire, and their negotiation of the Utrecht settlement was seen by the Whigs as 'an imperial betrayal'.[5]

Before considering Pincus's case for seeing Utrecht as a conflict between two contrasting visions of empire, it may be worth recalling for a moment the origins of the War of the Spanish Succession. On the death of the childless Carlos II of Spain in 1700, Louis XIV decided to ignore previous international agreements and accept the terms of Carlos's final testament, which left to his grandson, Philip, Duke of Anjou, not only Spain itself but the entire Spanish Monarchy – the *monarquía española* – from Flanders to Peru. In 1702 the king's decision triggered an international conflict, described by the Admiral of Castile as 'una guerra tan universal cual no se ha visto nunca' ('such a universal war as has never been seen').[6] In June 1701 the House of Commons resolved to support the efforts of William III 'in conjunction with the Emperor and the Estates-General [the Netherlands], for the preservation of the liberties of Europe, the prosperity and peace of England, and for reducing the exorbitant power of France'.[7] In deciding to contest the succession to the Spanish throne of the Duke of Anjou and support the claims of the rival Habsburg candidate, Archduke Charles of Austria, the allies saw themselves as upholding the liberties of Europe and maintaining a balance of power which was on the point of being subverted by Louis XIV's aspirations after 'universal monarchy'.

This was a struggle, then, in the widest sense, for 'the liberties of Europe', although each individual coalition partner had vital interests of its own to sustain. At stake in England was the Protestant succession, which was called into question when in 1701 Louis came out in support of the claims of James III. But underlying everything was the fear of French universal monarchy, a fear brought appreciably closer by the prospect of French domination not only of Spain, but also of Spain's American empire, with its massive mineral resources.

From the later sixteenth century to the mid-seventeenth the overwhelming English fear had been of *Spanish* universal monarchy, and that fear was driven by the knowledge that Spain had at its command the silver reserves of Mexico and Peru. As Sir Benjamin Rudyard observed in the House of Commons in 1624, 'they are his mines in the West Indies, which minister fuel to feed his vast ambitious desire of universal monarchy'.[8] It is some indication of the continuities between seventeenth- and eighteenth-century thought that Defoe, in his *A True Account of the Design and Advantages of the Southsea Trade* of 1711, cites these very words from Rudyard's speech to the House.[9] Disruption or capture of the silver fleets, assisted by a possible acquisition of bases in the West Indies or on the American mainland from which to threaten Spain's control of the silver mines and break its American monopoly, therefore played an important part in English policy towards Spain from the time of Sir Walter Raleigh to that of Oliver Cromwell and his Western Design, and beyond. By the 1660s, however, there was a widespread perception that Spain was a declining power, and this was accompanied by growing fears that the France of Louis XIV was replacing it with designs of its own for universal monarchy. When the English and the Dutch formed their alliance at the end of the century to stop the French from gaining control of the wealth of Spanish America, they were in practice pursuing their long-sought ambition of breaking a monopoly that was seen as paving with silver the road to universal monarchy.

In his *Protestantism and Patriotism*, Steve Pincus rightly emphasised the changes in the nature of English perceptions of the character of universal monarchy over the course of the seventeenth century, although he might have placed these changes more firmly in the context of changing international ideas about the sources of national power. At the end of the sixteenth century the writings of Giovanni Botero, in particular, had brought home to his many readers across Europe the interconnection between population, productivity and national power, while also emphasising, at a time of accelerating European overseas expansion, the importance of maritime strength for the conservation of empire. The striking success of the Dutch Republic in the early seventeenth century, not only in securing its independence from Spain but also in achieving unparalleled prosperity in spite of its limited natural resources, only served to confirm the validity of Botero's arguments. The Count of Gondomar, Spain's ambassador in London, was one of those who were quick to learn the lesson. In 1619 he remarked on the changing nature of warfare: 'Today it is not a question simply of natural strength, as with bulls, nor even of battles, but of losing or gaining friends and trade.'[10]

This new perception of international realities during the opening decades of the seventeenth century was accompanied by a growing appreciation that the possession of silver was not necessarily to be equated with the possession of wealth. This was the message of the Spanish *arbitristas* (projectors) as they struggled to diagnose the sources of Spain's ills, and found them in the neglect of industry and agriculture, which they argued should be seen as the true source of a nation's wealth.[11] This internal diagnosis found confirmation in the eyes of foreign observers in the visible decline of Spain's European hegemony. By the middle of the century, bullionism in its purest form was on the defensive, and economic theorists were taking the first faltering steps towards embracing a more flexible and expansionist view of national wealth and its relation to power.

On the other hand, it is important not to underestimate the continuing importance of silver both to Britain and to Europe. The output of the American mines was regarded as crucial for offsetting Europe's unfavourable trading balance with Asia through the East India companies, and for adjusting the balance of unfavourable bilateral trading relationships. The acquisition of silver, too, remained essential for building up and maintaining the war chests of European states. Pincus draws attention to the Tory fixation on the gold and silver mines of Mexico and Peru,[12] but in the great British currency crisis of the 1690s, when silver was draining out of the country at an alarming rate, a comparable preoccupation is to be found on the other side of the party divide when John Locke reasserted the bullionist position.[13] Throughout the eighteenth century, and irrespective of party affiliation, the pursuit of American silver remained a constant in British economic thought and action. Indeed, as late as the early nineteenth century, a substantial part of the financing of the war against Napoleon was achieved by channelling the flow of Mexican silver to Britain and the Iberian peninsula, and ensuring, with the help of British naval supremacy, that it did not fall into the hands of the French.[14]

The danger was of falling into the Spanish trap, and allowing the quest for silver to predominate, at the expense of domestic productivity. Pincus cites John Oldmixon, in his *The British Empire in America* of 1708, on the error of the Spaniards in resting 'content with importing the fabulous riches of the Mexican and Peruvian mines rather than developing their own manufacturing sector'.[15] The importance of trade and of increasing national productivity, as against simply accumulating silver and spending it, seems to have been broadly accepted across the political spectrum in later seventeenth-century England.

If the English came to appreciate this importance, it was not only because of the example of the Dutch and the counter-example of Spain, but also because of their own commercial revolution during the second half of the century, which led to a dramatic increase in national wealth. As Pincus tells us in his *1688*, 'English merchant shipping more than doubled its tonnage between 1640 and 1686. Much of this growth was in foreign trade. Imports grew six fold and exports 650 per cent between 1660 and 1700', and he goes on to cite a contemporary observation that 'it is foreign trade that is the main sheet-anchor of us islanders'.[16] As the English contemplated their new-found riches, it is clear that the lesson of the Dutch had been learnt. With the learning of that lesson, as Pincus reminds us throughout his publications, an economic element came to be added to the concept of universal monarchy. This was now seen as dependent on the domination of international trade.[17] Indeed, Dutch commercial successes and their domination of the carrying trade led to implausible Tory allegations that the Dutch Republic, too, was bent on achieving universal monarchy. If the French emerged from the War of the Spanish Succession as dominating the Indies trade, and through that domination became the masters of America's mineral resources, then universal monarchy would indeed be within their grasp.

While the growing appreciation of the importance for Britain of the international and colonial trades added a new dimension to British perceptions of the sources of international power, it also broke down some of the rigidities of strict mercantilist thinking. Pincus is at pains in his chapter, as in his *1688*, to draw a distinction between Tory and Whig perceptions of wealth. For the Whigs, he tells us, 'the key to prosperity and power was human labour. Unlike most Tories, the Whigs did not believe that the world's economic resources were finite, delimited by the amount of land in the world.'[18] While it is not hard to accept that Whigs and Tories placed different emphases on commerce and land as sources of wealth, they still seem at the beginning of this period to have shared a Colbertian attitude of mind broadly accepting of finite notions of wealth and international trade.[19] As the success of the Navigation Acts made clear, protectionism was regarded as having an important part to play in economic policy, although Roger Coke, for one, came to criticise the Navigation Acts and argued for the free importation of goods into England.[20] Monopolies were much more heavily contested ground, although we find Sir Josiah Child, who appears in Pincus's *1688* as the natural ally of James II in his promotion of the monopolistic East India trade, writing in his *A New Discourse of Trade* of 1693, that 'no Company whatsoever... can be for publick good, except it may be easie for all, or any of his Majesty's subjects to be admitted into all, or any of the said Companies, at any time for a very inconsiderable Fine'.[21]

Yet if the notion of the limited nature of wealth still prevailed across the political spectrum, it is difficult not to be impressed, when reading British economic treatises of the later seventeenth century, by the way in which that notion is gradually being eroded. Joyce Appleby finds what she calls 'compelling evidence of the existence of a vision of economic growth and development' in Restoration writing on the poor.[22] This same concept of potential for growth was given further credibility by the recent history of Britain's American colonies, some of which were being transformed into striking success stories. The climate at the beginning of the Restoration period was still one of scepticism about the value of overseas colonies, which, in the days of Elizabeth, had been seen as a useful outlet for surplus population, but had now come to be looked upon as draining the mother country of useful hands – itself, surely, an indication of a growing realisation of the importance of labour to the national economy. Promoters of overseas colonisation, like Child and Locke, therefore had to develop arguments that would help them make their case for the colonies as providers of commodities that were lacking at home, and of markets for English manufactures. 'Our interest in America', wrote Charles Davenant, 'generally speaking, may bring an immense profit to this kingdom, if it is well looked after by the government here' – by which he meant avoiding the mistakes that Spain had made.[23] It was America, too, that provided the context in which Locke could develop his labour theory of value. It was becoming apparent that the mere occupation of land was an inadequate justification for holding it in the face of the prior claims of its indigenous inhabitants or, perhaps more important, of rival European powers. A far more effective argument was that it was the admixture of labour to the land that conferred rights of ownership to it.[24]

Pincus understandably places the labour theory of value at the heart of Whig economic thinking, but it is open to question whether it can be confined to a partisan ideology in this way.[25] To bring labour to the land meant to improve it, and it is hard not to be struck by the frequent use of the language of *improvement* in later seventeenth- and early eighteenth-century writing. 'Improvement' is a word that does not appear in Pincus's chapter, and it is not very noticeable in his various publications. However, the visible success of the West Indian and North American colonies gave a powerful impetus to the notion of improvement. 'Curacao', wrote Josiah Child, 'is not the tenth part so well improved as Jamaica hath been by the English within these five years; neither have the Dutch at any other time, or in other parts of the World, made any improvement by Planting.'[26] Widely used by defenders of colonisation, and by the colonists themselves, to justify the beneficial effects of overseas settlements, the word was absorbed into the national discourse, and came to be applied to trade, industry and agriculture alike.[27]

'Improvement' implies a potential for growth, and was a word that could be used equally well by the Tory squire as he brooded on means of increasing the profitability of his land, as by the industrial entrepreneur considering his potential markets or the Whig merchant poring over trade prospects in foreign parts. The new-found currency of the word 'improvement' surely helped to undermine traditional mercantilist assumptions about the finite nature of wealth. This leads me to wonder whether Whigs and Tories were really so far apart in their approach to wealth and wealth-creation as Pincus likes to present them. As John Pocock writes in *The Machiavellian Moment*, 'an anatomy of the great debate as between the "landed" and the "monied" interests, conducted by the journalists and publicists of Anne's reign, reveals that there were no pure dogmas or simple antitheses, and few assumptions that were not shared, and employed to differing purposes, by the writers on either side'.[28] Partisan politics, as we are all well aware, were extremely bitter in the reign of Queen Anne, but Pincus's interpretation suggests that he is determined, in his anxiety to promote his thesis, to widen the Whig–Tory divide further than the evidence can bear.

Take, for instance, his account of the establishment of the South Sea Company, which he describes as being 'from the first a Tory Company with imperial aspirations'.[29] It is true that the Company was Harley's device, and was looked at askance by the Whig-dominated Bank of England. It is equally true, as he tells us, that Harley's Tory supporters were heavily represented on the new company's board of directors. But he does not tell us that the directors also included some leading City Whigs and Whig merchants, or that, as Gary Stuart De Krey informs us in *A Fractured Society*, 'among those City leaders who were South Sea directors between 1711 and 1715, Whigs slightly outnumbered Tories'.

Why, then, asks De Krey, 'has the South Sea Company acquired so strong a Tory reputation in historical writing?'[30] Although Pincus goes on to widen the case for the essentially Tory character of the South Sea project, the partisan features of the project, at least where City participation is concerned, are perhaps less clear-cut than he would have us believe.

For Defoe, at least, party affiliation seems to have made little difference in matters of commerce. 'We know of no Whig or Tory in trade', he wrote in 1714.[31] But if, as seems likely, Whigs and Tories were thinking in much the same way as they contemplated the possibilities of expansion and growth, this does not, of course, preclude contrasting approaches to the means of reaching a commonly agreed goal. Pincus is keen to underline the contrasts, which are indeed crucial to the argument of his chapter as a whole. As he presents it, it is not simply a question of two opposing economic theories – land-based and labour-based – which are locked in contest, but two competing visions of empire. This begs the important question of what the word 'empire' meant to eighteenth-century Britons. It might, of course, mean territorial possessions, but it was also used of dominion, or even of dominant interests outside Britain itself. John Oldmixon's book is called *The British Empire in America*. The expression 'British Empire', without a geographical location attached, and in the sense of a single community embracing Britain and its overseas possessions, only seems to have acquired currency during the middle decades of the eighteenth century.[32]

Pincus appears to ignore these contemporary distinctions. His 'empire' is a unitary British empire, which assumes, in accordance with party affiliation, either a commercial or a territorial character. The word 'imperial', for its part, figures prominently in his chapter, and his use of it seems to be loaded. In the very first paragraph, for instance, in which he presents us with the fundamental question that he plans to answer – the reasons for the Whig denunciation of the Treaty of Utrecht – he writes that 'above all, they felt the peace had been an imperial betrayal'. Most historians would probably have phrased this as 'a commercial betrayal', and would have found nothing unexceptional about the statement when expressed in that way. But towards the end of the same paragraph he repeats the word 'imperial', and speaks of Whig ire regarding an 'imperial disaster', in his determination that his message will not be overlooked.[33]

'Why', he asks us, 'did the Whigs believe British imperial interests had been betrayed at the Treaty of Utrecht ... a peace that had given the British Gibraltar, Minorca, Nova Scotia, St Kitts, and the lucrative Asiento – the exclusive right to sell slaves to the Spanish Empire?' Dismissing the case of those – and I am classified as one of the sinners – who have asserted that there was 'a single coherent British imperial policy over which there was little party conflict, or there was party conflict that had little to do with imperial policy', he argues that the Whigs were committed to the notion of what he calls 'integrative empire'[34]; 'Because they rejected the notion that property was finite' he argues, 'they were relatively indifferent to territorial gain'. For them the war was all about preventing Bourbon universal monarchy. The Tories, on the other hand, 'committed themselves to territorial empire' and 'erected the South Sea Company in order to found a new British empire in South America'.[35] This is a striking claim. But how far can it be supported?

In his treatise, *Some Considerations on the Consequences of the Lowering of Interest*, John Locke wrote: 'In a Country not furnished with Mines there are but two ways of growing Rich, either Conquest or Commerce'. Britain had missed out on conquest, and 'Commerce, therefore, is the only way left to us.'[36] If Pincus's interpretation of Harley's ambitions and the South Sea project is correct, however, this was not enough for the Tories, who plumped for what he calls 'a southern cone strategy'. This would include the seizure of Buenos Aires and the establishment of a second colonial outpost at Valdivia, in Chile.[37] The Tory plans were in fact wild, and showed little awareness of the logistical and military problems involved, or indeed of the location of Spain's American mines, although Buenos Aires, while far from the silver mine of Potosí in the high Andes, had become a significant clandestine outlet for its silver. But it seems to me to be stretching things to suggest that the establishment of two or three English settlements in Chile and the La Plata region constituted a plan for the creation of an English 'territorial empire' in South America. The project looks more like falling squarely within the long-established tradition of securing enclaves and bases from which to attack Spanish shipping and silver fleets in time of war, and engage in clandestine trade with Spain's American possessions – trade that would deliver much-needed American silver into British pockets.

What we are witnessing once the Tories take office in 1710 is a change in the priorities that had until now dictated the conduct of the war, as the emphasis shifted from campaigning in Europe to an overseas confrontation with the French, especially in the Americas. This was later to be described as a 'blue water strategy', but it seems reasonable to share the doubts expressed by Professor Nicholas Rodger about the appropriateness of the word 'strategy', which only entered the English language a century later.[38] There were various reasons for the change in priorities: Tory antipathy to the Dutch, whose interests, both in Europe and overseas, had in their view been given precedence over British interests in the Barrier Treaty negotiated by the previous ministry in

1709; the dire situation of the state finances and the devastating burden of taxation caused by an apparently never-ending war; widespread resentment against the power and arrogance of the moneyed interest; the fact that the continental campaigns had recently been less successful than in the first years of the conflict, and would indeed come to seem increasingly pointless following the accession of Archduke Charles to the throne of the Holy Roman Empire in 1711; and the French decision to weaken the British military effort in Europe by extending the conflict to North America, and laying plans for a North American empire that would link Canada with Louisiana.[39]

The attacks made on Massachusetts by the French and their Indian allies in the course of Queen Anne's war prompted American colonists to appeal to London for help, an indication of the way in which pressures brought by the periphery to bear on the metropolis are beginning to impinge on the politics of empire. International rivalries in Europe were spilling over into the Americas, calling up responses in the American colonial societies themselves, and forcing London, Paris and Madrid to think increasingly in imperial terms.[40] If Tories like Henry St John expressed grandiose imperial ambitions, and could speak of the queen as becoming 'mistress of the whole continent of North America',[41] this was a response to the new international realities at a time when Spain gave every sign of losing control over its empire of the Indies, and the rival European powers were circling like birds of prey over the apparently prostrate corpse in the hope of carrying off the pickings. There is little obvious evidence from the later seventeenth century for Pincus's assertion that 'the Tories saw nothing wrong with the Spanish imperial model',[42] other than a very qualified observation by Davenant, who thought that Britain could usefully set up a body for the government of its overseas empire equivalent to Spain's Council of the Indies, although he admitted that it might be objected that 'the Spaniards are not very good patterns to follow in any model or scheme of government'.[43]

It is not necessary to see the Tory–Whig divide at this moment as the expression of a fundamental and lasting disagreement over the value, and the character, of overseas empire, although Doohwan Ahn in a recent article makes useful points about St John's economic and political ideas, as expressed by his mouthpiece, Davenant, in the *Mercator* – ideas that St John would still be promoting more than twenty years later in *The Patriot King*. These ideas, which made him something of a free trader, although primarily for political reasons, derived from his obsessive conviction that the Dutch and not the French were the real danger to British commercial supremacy.[44] But although St John was able to exploit the widespread anti-Dutch sentiment still prevalent in the England of Queen Anne, and manipulate public opinion to great effect in a war-weary country, it is difficult to judge how far he is putting forward theories about empire, trade and international politics that reflect, and reinforce, a lasting ideological division in the country, and how far they merely display a purely personal combination of political ambition, deep-seated prejudice and an excitable imagination.

It seems reasonable to agree with Brendan Simms, when he writes that the Tory–Whig divide of 1711–13 was not simply one between navalists and Continentalists – still less, one might add, between a Whig 'integrative' and Tory 'territorial' vision of empire, as Pincus asserts – but a conflict over 'differing conceptions of the European balance and how it should be upheld'.[45] The tension over the relative weight to be given to Europe and the world overseas was to characterise British policy-making throughout the eighteenth century, and it seems that recent work on British diplomacy and, in particular, on the effects of the Hanover connection, has begun to redraw the contours of a historiography that has tended to pay more attention to the imperial than the European dimension of eighteenth-century British policy. The British in that century looked simultaneously across the Channel to Europe and across the Atlantic to a wider world. The problem, at any given moment, was to find the point of equilibrium between the two.[46]

Why then, to return to Pincus's central question, were the Whigs made so angry by the terms of Utrecht? Here, conventional explanations are more persuasive than the one he proposes. It was not a question of competing imperial visions and Whig 'imperial ire'. The febrile party political atmosphere certainly heightened the rhetoric and sharpened the divisions. The Tories, for instance, may indeed have felt a visceral hatred for the Dutch, but they also had the embarrassing task of finding an excuse for leaving Britain's Dutch allies in the lurch. The Whigs (wrongly, as it transpired) felt that the agreement to accept a Bourbon on the Spanish throne strengthened the prospects of French universal monarchy, and that the acceptance of the terms of Utrecht, in putting the Dutch Barrier at risk, jeopardised Britain's long-term security and undermined the chances of securing and maintaining a European balance of power. In other words, the aims with which they had entered the war had been betrayed. This in itself, especially when the Tories were trumpeting their achievements from the house-tops, was surely sufficient to arouse Whig ire. On top of this, commercial elements, as Pincus makes clear, were very much at stake. The settlement may have secured the Asiento for Britain, but it failed to improve the conditions of the vital Iberian trade, which would only be salvaged, at least in part, by the new Anglo-Spanish commercial treaty negotiated by the Whigs in 1715.[47] It also – or so it was believed – left British markets wide open to French penetration, putting English cloth manufacturing at risk. Here, however, the Whigs got their revenge when the Anglo-French commercial treaty was overturned in the House of Commons three months after the signing of the peace.[48]

Pincus describes the Tories' failure to secure territorial concessions in South America as 'an unexpected but unmitigated disaster', because it deprived investors in the South Sea Company of their anticipated fabulous returns. 'Forgetting the enormity of that disaster', he writes, 'has made it impossible to understand the Tory imperial strategy of the early eighteenth century.'[49] But Harley had already given up his plan for obtaining permanent settlements in South America even before the opening of the Utrecht negotiations in January 1712, and the military expedition which everyone thought was destined for an attack on Spanish America was in fact intended for the St Lawrence. Harley, with his unrivalled skill in double-crossing, kept all this quiet when he addressed the South Sea Company directors in September 1711.[50] The disaster, if disaster it was, was not therefore exactly unexpected, at least for those in the know. Nor, given what was achieved, at least on paper, can it reasonably be described as unmitigated. In addition to the Asiento, the Utrecht settlement did permit the Company to have establishments, although not, as had been hoped, extraterritoriality, in seven ports of Spanish America, including Buenos Aires.[51] If disaster followed, it came because of Spanish obstructiveness over the Asiento once it became operative, and the Company's own incompetence.

Pincus sums up his argument by asserting that 'the British struggle over the aims and achievements of the War of the Spanish Succession needs to be understood as a party political conflict over the direction and contours of the British empire'.[52] Reasons have already been given for doubting this particular interpretation of the party conflict over the terms of Utrecht. Pincus then goes on to ask: 'What then are the broader implications for this story? What have we gained by recovering the story of the failed Tory project for establishing a British empire in the southern cone?' 'It seems to me' – he continues – 'that this story has broad implications for the ways in which we should think and write about the history of the British empire.'[53]

The first implication, as he sees it, is that 'there was no single moment in which the British became authoritarian imperialists'.[54] He points to the various claims made – notably for the 1650s, the 1750s–60s and the post-1780 period – as marking the moment of the 'authoritarian turn'. His conclusion is that, while the proponents of each of these moments of change have a good case to make, they are wrong to insist on 'sea changes, epistemic shifts, and pivotal moments of vindictive legislation'. It is unclear how many of them really are as insistent as this, but there are general grounds for agreeing with him that there is no single moment in the British imperial story when we can point to a decisive authoritarian turn, although there are good reasons to see the early nineteenth century as reinforcing the tendency in that direction, as the problem of governing India came to the fore.

Less persuasive, however, is the reason he gives for the absence of a moment in which the English became authoritarian imperialists. His argument is that 'the contours of the British empire were always shaped by political contestation. Some Britons always had an authoritarian impulse and wanted a coercive, centralised, blue-water empire. Others, who were no less imperialists, wanted a more integrative and less coercive empire.'[55] No doubt it is true that some Britons have always had an authoritarian impulse, but once again he appears to maintain that seventeenth- and eighteenth-century imperial policies, whether authoritarian or otherwise, can only be understood if they are looked at through the prism of party politics.

Pincus rightly praises Alison Games for her book, *The Web of Empire*, in which she identifies a 'cosmopolitan impulse' behind English expansion in the sixteenth and seventeenth centuries – a cosmopolitan impulse that found expression, at a time when the state was still weak, in a decentralised system of overseas expansion, including expansion through 'trading companies with loose royal oversight' and 'multiple styles of engagement with an emphasis on accommodation'.[56] But, as she says, by the 1650s, with the increase in the power of the state under Cromwell, the trend was towards centralisation and the use of coercion and force. This is surely right. But it is also possible to draw attention to Ken MacMillan's *Sovereignty and Possession in the English New World*, in which he seeks to establish the legal foundations of empire between 1576 and 1640.[57] His argument is that the Crown was acting in an imperial capacity from the beginning, asserting its right to absolute dominion over territory within its jurisdiction, and setting this assertion in a context of a Roman law which underpinned the evolving system of European international relations, and was needed by the Crown to defend its claims against its European rivals.

From a historiographical standpoint, MacMillan's argument is important because to some extent it redresses a balance in imperial history, which has in recent years tended to tilt towards Alison Games's 'cosmopolitans' – her merchants, voyagers and settlers – and away from metropolitan ideologies and policies, at least for the period before 1680. It is also important because it reaffirms the vital importance of taking international power politics and legal theories into account in explaining the origins and development of Europe's overseas empires. Every European state needed legal foundations for its empire, and, as

MacMillan explains, 'the principal legal foundations of the English New World were based on the Crown's imperial (rather than domestic) sovereign rights and responsibilities, and on the legal system that underpinned the exercise of this authority, Roman Law and its derivatives'.[58]

In practice, the Stuarts were inconsistent and erratic when it came to imposing royal control over American settlements over which they claimed imperial dominion. High-sounding assertions of royal authority, whether under Charles I or Charles II, were all too often followed by ineffective action, or by total inactivity. Only with James II's plans for the Dominion of New England was there any real consistency of action, and this was too short-lived, and perhaps came too late, to transform an 'authoritarian turn' into effective authoritarianism. Although William III refused to renew the Massachusetts charter in its original form, the war with France and the securing of the Protestant succession took priority over everything else. Only in Ireland, where the fate of the Protestant succession was at stake, did he impose a form of imperial dominion. It was surely the events of 1688–9, followed by the Anglo-Scottish Union of 1707, that set the British empire on its eighteenth-century trajectory.

Here, the comparison with Spain at the same moment is suggestive. Between 1707 and 1714 the new Bourbon dynasty transformed the composite monarchy of the Habsburgs into an authoritarian monarchy of the type to which James II had aspired – a monarchy in which the ruler at last secured the kind of sovereign power at home which he already possessed in America. Effectively Philip V's victory in the War of the Spanish Succession marked the end of the Spanish composite monarchy. By contrast, the Glorious Revolution transformed the British composite monarchy into something new, a composite parliamentary monarchy, while leaving intact the Crown's imperial power over the overseas territories, including Ireland. With the Union of 1707, an asymmetrical system came into being, with Scotland now joined to England in an incorporating union which preserved some of the characteristics of a composite monarchy, while Ireland and the American colonies were effectively consigned to a subordinate status.

The monarch's imperial claims over Ireland and America now rested not with the monarch alone, but with the king in Parliament, and would duly be asserted in the crisis of the 1760s and 1770s. In the meantime, ministerial and parliamentary politics allowed ample scope for lobbying by colonial interest groups, who succeeded in winning for themselves room for manoeuvre in the political system of the British Atlantic world. As this room for manoeuvre expanded, so the colonists began to develop their own sense of a pan-Atlantic British community – a Protestant and commercial empire of the free – and of what Jack Greene has called a British 'imperial constitution' which was essentially perceived in terms of a composite monarchy, and which rejected the notion of a subordinate status for the overseas territories.[59] The difference between this formulation of the imperial relationship and the post-1707 Westminster formulation contained within itself an obvious potential for conflict. But because of the nature of the parliamentary system itself, and because of the pressures on the metropolitan centre from the peripheral territories, there was not, it seems, much consistency in Westminster's implementation of policy towards the American colonies, at least until problems of imperial defence became paramount in the 1760s. The degree of salutary neglect may have been overemphasised, but intervention remained erratic, and lacking in consistency. It is difficult to see that this lack of consistency in imperial policy from the 1720s to the 1760s was the result, as Pincus would have it, of political contestation over the nature of empire: commercial versus territorial, coercive versus libertarian. It seems likely that a broad consensus prevailed in the British political establishment, and found wide support in the middling and lower levels of British society. This consensus was based on a belief in the supreme importance of British naval power, and in the value to Britain of its colonial trade in generating wealth for the mother country. There seems to have been no particular taste for further territorial expansion, not least because the British ruling class was well aware, from the examples of Rome and Spain, of the cyclical process of imperial rise and decline.[60] Not imperial aggrandisement but fear of, and hostility to, France remained Britain's central concern. The struggle with France inevitably meant that war spilled over into North America, but British naval supremacy was seen as essential to the defence of the British Isles and British trading interests, and not as an instrument for imperial expansion.[61] Until the costs of war rose in the 1750s to a level that made it seem reasonable to ask the American colonies to contribute their share, there is little evidence of demand from any quarter for a more coercive form of empire.

The second broad implication of Pincus's findings is, he tells us, that 'political economic conflict rather than mercantilist consensus shaped the British empire'.[62] Comments have already been offered on his interpretation of mercantilist theory and practice, and there is no reason to repeat these remarks. While he has done well to emphasise the contribution of the new political economy of the late seventeenth century to political debate, and indeed to the conduct of international power politics, it seems that late seventeenth-century and early eighteenth-century theorists and pamphleteers were still struggling to come to terms with the implications of the commercial revolution of the later seventeenth century. It is difficult to accept his stark statement that 'mercantilists all believed in the limits to growth',[63] if he means by this that the notion of a zero-sum game was a permanent fact of life under the so-called 'mercantile system', itself in many respects the retrospective invention of Adam Smith. The advent of new ideas about economic prospects and policy no doubt generated a good deal of confusion about such questions as the role of the state in the advancement of commerce, but it is unpersuasive to claim that the resulting disagreements necessarily followed party lines. As Paul Slack has pointed out, both the Tory Davenant and the Whig Defoe talked of 'natural progress' and 'growing prosperity'.[64]

Pincus's third and final assertion is that 'this contest over empire in the early eighteenth century may point to some limits of the new imperial history'.[65] Here it is possible to have considerable sympathy with him. While agreeing with him that the New Imperial History, with its emphasis on such questions as identity, representation and difference, whether of race, gender, or cultures, has 'alerted us to strategies of domination not accounted for in the older histories', it is also possible to agree that something has been lost in the process of broadening horizons. We are perhaps less interested in institutional history than historians of an earlier generation, although the eighteenth-century volume of the *Oxford History of the British Empire* hardly gives the impression that institutions have been forgotten. But there is still scope for closer study of the interaction between an institution like the Board of Trade and the variety of interest groups which tried to influence it in one way or another, although Alison Olson's *Making the Empire Work*, which finds no place in Pincus's chapter, has surely cast some bright light on murky corners.[66] Beyond this, a renovated legal history, of the kind represented by Lauren Benton in *Law and Colonial Cultures*, can do much to enhance our understanding both of imperial policy-making and of colonial responses.[67] Finally, it is very important that the history of European empires in the eighteenth century should be firmly set back into the context of international rivalries and warfare, which did so much to shape imperial and colonial developments.

All this provides an agenda for future action, and it is clear that Steve Pincus, as he moves into the study of Britain's overseas empire, has much to offer. In particular, he has brought to centre stage the vital question of the interplay between contemporary ideas about political economy and economic and political action, in a broad imperial context. If there are reasons not to be persuaded by some of his arguments, his provocative chapter has certainly provoked us into thinking again about the nature of empire and imperial policy, the role of ideology and political party in the shaping of empire, the manipulation of public opinion, and possible future directions for the writing of imperial history. We are grateful to him for his stimulating chapter, and look forward to the debate that it will certainly unleash.

Notes

1. S. Pincus, *Protestantism and Patriotism: Ideologies and the Making of English Foreign Policy, 1650–1668* (Cambridge, 1996).
2. S. Pincus, *1688: The First Modern Revolution* (New Haven, 2009).
3. See Chapter 2, p. 18.
4. *Ibid.*
5. *Ibid.*, p. 17.
6. J. A. Salvadó, *La Guerra de Sucesión de España* (Barcelona, 2010), p. 19.
7. Cited in B. Simms, *Three Victories and a Defeat: The Rise and Fall of the First British Empire* (London, 2008), p. 48.
8. L. F. Stock (ed.), *Proceedings of the British Parliaments Respecting North America* (2 vols, Washington, DC, 1924–7), II, p. 62 (19 May 1624).
9. D. Defoe, *A True Account of the Design and Advantages of the Southsea Trade* (1711), p. 10.
10. Cited in J. H. Elliott, *Spain, Europe and the Wider World, 1500–1800* (New Haven, 2009), p. 46.
11. See J. H. Elliott, *Spain and its World, 1500–1700* (New Haven, 1989), ch. 11 ('Self-Perception and Decline in Seventeenth-Century Spain').
12. See Chapter 2, p. 20.
13. J. O. Appleby, *Economic Thought and Ideology in Seventeenth-Century England* (Princeton, 1978), pp. 203 and 219–30.
14. See C. Marichal, *The Bankruptcy of Empire: Mexican Silver and the Wars Between Spain, Britain and France, 1760–1810* (Cambridge, 2007).
15. See Chapter 2, p. 20.
16. Pincus, *1688*, pp. 83–4.
17. Pincus, *Protestantism*, p. 257.
18. See Chapter 2, p. 19.
19. D. C. Coleman, 'Politics and economics in the age of Anne: The case of the Anglo-French treaty of 1713', in D. C. Coleman and A. H. John (eds), *Trade, Government and Economy in Pre-Industrial England: Essays Presented to F. J. Fisher* (London, 1976), ch. 10.
20. See, for example, R. Coke, *A Discourse of Trade* (1670) and entry for Coke in the *ODNB*.
21. Pincus, *1688*, pp. 373–5; J. Child, *A New Discourse of Trade* (1693), p. 81.
22. Appleby, *Economic Thought*, p. 136.
23. C. Whitworth (ed.), *The Political and Commercial Works of... Charles D'Avenant* (5 vols, 1771), II, Discourse 3, 'On the Plantation Trade', p. 29.
24. See B. Arneil, *John Locke in America: The Defence of English Colonialism* (Oxford, 1996), pp. 17–19.
25. See Chapter 2, p. 19.
26. Child, *A New Discourse*, p. 186.
27. See J. H. Elliott, *Empires of the Atlantic World: Britain and Spain in America, 1492–1830* (New Haven, 2006), pp. 242–3, and the references there given. On the concept of improvement in general, see P. Slack, *The Invention of Improvement: Information and Material Progress in Seventeenth-Century England* (Oxford, 2015).
28. J. G. A. Pocock, *The Machiavellian Moment: Florentine Political Thought and the Atlantic Republican Tradition* (Princeton, 1975), p. 446.
29. See Chapter 2, p. 23.
30. G. S. De Krey, *A Fractured Society: The Politics of London in the First Age of Party, 1688–1715* (Oxford, 1985), pp. 242–3.
31. Cited by P. Gauci, *The Politics of Trade: The Overseas Merchant in State and Society, 1660–1720* (Oxford, 2001), p. 264.
32. J. T. Adams, 'On the term "British Empire"', *AHR*, 27 (1922), 485–9; P. Marshall (ed.), *The Oxford History of the British Empire: Volume 2: The Eighteenth Century* (Oxford, 1998), p. 7.
33. See Chapter 2, p. 17.

34 See Chapter 2, p. 18.
35 *Ibid.*
36 P. Hyde Kelly (ed.), *Locke on Money* (2 vols, Oxford, 1991), I, pp. 222–3.
37 See Chapter 2, p. 25. Valdivia was a well fortified Pacific seaport in southern Chile. In spite of Thomas Bowrey's observation, cited by Pincus, it did not produce gold. The Dutch West India Company failed to establish a colonial outpost there in 1643, but memories of the abortive Dutch enterprise may have played a part in shaping Tory plans.
38 Marshall (ed.), *Oxford History*, p. 171.
39 See Simms, *Three Victories*, pp. 65–8.
40 Marshall (ed.), *Oxford History*, pp. 154–6.
41 Cited in Simms, *Three Victories*, p. 63.
42 See Chapter 2, p. 29.
43 Cited in Elliott, *Spain, Europe*, p. 42.
44 D. Ahn, 'The Anglo-French treaty of commerce in 1713: Tory trade politics and the question of Dutch decline', *History of European Ideas*, 36 (2010), 167–80. I. Kramnick, *Bolingbroke and his Circle: The Politics of Nostalgia in the Age of Walpole* (Cambridge, Mass., 1968), points out that St John's arguments involved no critique of mercantilism but were politically motivated. He saw an Anglo-French commercial treaty as a way of reducing the enmity between the two countries.
45 Simms, *Three Victories*, p. 65.
46 See the list of bibliographical references in note 1 of S. Conway, 'The British army, "Military Europe", and the American War of Independence', *W&MQ*, 3rd series, 67 (2010), 69–100.
47 J. O. McLachlan, *Trade and Peace with Old Spain, 1667–1750* (Cambridge, 1940), p. 69.
48 For the Anglo-French commercial treaty of 1713, see, in addition to Ahn, 'Anglo-French treaty'; De Krey, *Fractured Society*, pp. 244–5; Gauci, *Politics of Trade*, pp. 241ff.
49 See Chapter 2, p. 29.
50 B. W. Hill, *Robert Harley: Speaker, Secretary of State and Prime Minister* (New Haven, 1988), pp. 162 and 189–90; P. G. M. Dickson, *The Financial Revolution in England* (London, 1967), pp. 66–7.
51 J. Carswell, *The South Sea Bubble* (2nd edn, Stroud, 1993), p. 55.
52 See Chapter 2, p. 29.
53 *Ibid.*
54 *Ibid.*
55 *Ibid.*, p. 31.
56 *Ibid.*, p. 30, citing A. Games, *The Web of Empire: English Cosmopolitans in an Age of Expansion, 1560–1660* (Oxford, 2008), pp. 289–90.
57 K. MacMillan, *Sovereignty and Possession in the English New World: The Legal Foundations of Empire, 1576–1640* (Cambridge, 2006).
58 *Ibid.*, p. 13.
59 See D. Armitage, *The Ideological Origins of the British Empire* (Cambridge, 2000), especially pp. 180–2. For the 'British imperial constitution', see J. P. Greene, *Peripheries and Center: Constitutional Developments in the Extended Polities of the British Empire and the United States, 1607–1788* (Athens, GA, 1986), ch. 6.
60 See B. Harris, '"American Idols": empire, war and the middling ranks in mid-eighteenth-century Britain', *P&P*, 150 (1996), 111–41.
61 Marshall (ed.), *Oxford History*, p. 170.
62 See Chapter 2, p. 31.
63 *Ibid.*, p. 32.
64 P. Slack, 'Material progress and the challenge of affluence in seventeenth-century England', *EcHR*, 62 (2009), 576–603, at 576.
65 See Chapter 2, p. 33.
66 A. G. Olson, *Making the Empire Work: London and American Interest Groups, 1690–1790* (Cambridge, Mass., 1992).
67 L. Benton, *Law and Colonial Cultures: Legal Regimes in World History, 1400–1900* (Cambridge, 2002).

CHAPTER FOUR

From anti-popery and anti-puritanism to orientalism

William J. Bulman

It is well known that anti-popery and anti-puritanism were central to the political culture of post-Reformation England and the early British empire.[1] We also know that from the later eighteenth century onwards, orientalism played a crucial role in debates about the British presence in South Asia and (later) the Middle East.[2] To an extent the *via media* of English Protestantism and the construction of the Orient serve, respectively, as ideological identifiers of the so-called first and second empires, or landmarks in the shift from West to East in British imperialism. In both of these modes of analysis and critique, Britain was implicitly identified as a beacon of liberty and truth. The first, largely Atlantic empire presented itself as a defender of moderate Christianity and freedom, in supposed contrast to its imperial rivals (Spanish, French or Dutch) and its rebellious puritan subjects in North America. The second, modern British empire employed orientalist discourse to justify and organise its dominion over the supposedly despotic, priest-ridden and fanatical societies of Asia and the Middle East. No one, however, has written about the close historical relationship between these two discursive frameworks, aside from making the formal observation that both were species of 'othering' that shaped national identity.[3] Here I would like to suggest that over the course of the late seventeenth century, a change in elite understandings of popery and puritanism contributed directly to the articulation of a British form of orientalism.

This connection seems to have gone largely unnoticed as a result of both scholarly specialisation and a set of historiographical orthodoxies concerning the nature of the Enlightenment. Later eighteenth-century debates among the British elite about the supposedly corrupt polities and religions of South Asia are usually thought to have drawn upon both unchanging clichés and the theories of enlightened French philosophers. When identifying the intellectual background to these discussions, historians often single out François Bernier, Montesquieu and Nicolas Boulanger, who used pejorative accounts of Asian states to critique their own monarchy.[4] This argument about the origins of British orientalism, which is drawn not from a history of reading but from general similarities among the texts concerned, seems to be guided by three traditional but still commonly held assumptions about Enlightenment ideas: that they were French in origin, philosophical in form and ideologically determinate in content. Without denying the influence of Bernier, Montesquieu and Boulanger in Britain, this chapter asks what we might learn about British orientalism and imperialism if we proceed from a different set of assumptions about the Enlightenment in Britain in general and the Enlightenment discourse of oriental despotism in particular: that they were English in origin, historical in form and ideologically indeterminate in content.[5] These claims, which emerge from some of the most compelling recent work on late humanism, the Enlightenment and the British empire, imply that British commentaries on oriental despotism in the eighteenth century cannot be properly understood simply as revivals of an Aristotelian commonplace or as new chapters in the histories of philosophy or 'political thought'.

In his discussions of later eighteenth-century understandings of the Mughal polity, Robert Travers reminds us that '"modern" European empires had their roots in "early modern" conceptions of politics'. This chapter expands upon Travers's observation. He points out that from the deeply historical and ideologically indeterminate perspective of ancient constitutionalism, supposedly despotic forms of political and religious governance could appear utterly appropriate to the 'genius' of particular regions and peoples, and possess both their own political rationality and legal underpinning.[6] Travers gives the impression that these discussions of Asian ancient constitutions were directly inspired by the English common law tradition. But ancient constitutionalism was a much more widely employed norm in the world of late humanism. In fact, in England, it served as a guide for historical writing on the great Islamic empires from the late seventeenth century onwards. And the most important of these early works, Sir Paul Rycaut's *Present State of the Ottoman Empire* (1667), was a central source for Montesquieu himself.[7] It may be the case that early modern ancient constitutionalism was an even more direct and influential source for later orientalist discussions of Asian polities than scholars have realised.

This chapter, however, explores the early modern origins of modern imperialism from a slightly different angle, by focusing on religion. Travers and many others have noted that critiques of Asian religion were an important element of British accounts of South Asian society and its supposedly despotic political forms.[8] Yet these critiques have received far less scholarly attention than the strictly constitutional and economic aspects of British orientalist writing in the later eighteenth century. Like the global study of ancient constitutions, the historical analysis of Asian religious corruption and imposture was inherited from early modern England and the wider world of the Renaissance and Reformation. Again, though, we fail to appreciate this if we assume that such modes of writing were exclusively French in origin. Just as Montesquieu's discussion of despotic constitutions had important English precedents, the famous founding text of the anticlerical French Enlightenment, the *Traité des Trois Imposteurs*, appears to have been partly English in inspiration.[9] Similarly, from its inception and into the eighteenth century, British Enlightenment orientalism took cues from the peculiar religious polemics of post-Reformation England, which were generally characterised by competing attempts to chart a path between the Scylla and Charybdis of popery and puritanism.

In order to adumbrate the process by which anti-popery and anti-puritanism gave structure and content to British orientalism, we need to begin with the religious polemics of post-Reformation England. From Elizabeth's reign onwards, the discourses of anti-popery and anti-puritanism underwent a slow process of universalisation, in both their content and sphere of application by English Protestants. By the 1590s, the reach of anti-popery was hardly confined to Protestant attacks on Catholicism abroad and its supposed remnants in England. Conformist divines under Elizabeth I and James I consistently described the tactics and political principles of *puritans* as popish. Indeed, from their initial appearance in the 1570s, such claims became part of a positive, identifiable discourse of anti-puritanism. Sustained and mocking analyses of puritan theology, ecclesiology, ministry and piety claimed to expose the godly as hypocritical, libertine, theatrical, deluded, divisive and rebellious.[10] Critics of puritanism also began to defend numerous aspects of what other Protestants termed popery, thus subjecting anti-popery itself to political contestation. By the beginning of James's reign, purveyors of anti-popery were also offering extensive comparisons between popery and paganism. At the same time, they expanded their frame of reference for considering the more overtly political and international dimensions of Catholicism. Not only the Pope but the major Catholic princes were described as agents of popery because they were aspiring universal monarchs who threatened the sovereignty of the English empire. As anti-popery and anti-puritanism began to shape the domestic and international politics of England in new ways, they were yoked to a classical discourse of superstition and slowly uprooted from their original theological and polemical contexts.[11]

The expanding frame of reference for anti-popery and anti-puritanism in England played a small part in a much larger drama, in which scholarly developments in the late Renaissance, Reformation and Counter-Reformation led to the anthropological understanding of religion so characteristic of the Enlightenment. The education shared by all learned Christians in this period offered a set of tools for analysing religious corruption that had already been employed at length in antiquity. Early modern Catholic and Protestant historians and antiquarians put these tools to use in accounts of idolatry, superstition and many other forms of religious corruption. They observed these errors not only among other Christians, but also among the pagans of both the ancient world and the new worlds of Asia, Africa and America. Eventually, at the end of the seventeenth century, a number of European scholars eschewed a primarily theological or demonological interpretation of idolatry and religious corruption, and refashioned the ancient notion of superstition into a sociological account of religion, eventually allowing Voltaire, for instance, in his 1764 *Philosophical Dictionary*, to declare 'idolatry' a useless, pejorative term.[12]

In this process, confessional polemic, antiquarian accounts of ancient paganism and travel writing on Europe's new worlds went hand-in-hand. Guided by confessional, evangelical and imperial agendas, scholars examined religions Christian and non-Christian, ancient and modern, in each case studying similar dynamics with the tools of late humanist historical criticism.[13] The comparative possibilities offered by this fecund line of thought were so apparent in England by the early seventeenth century that in 1613 Samuel Purchas could recognise popery among Native Americans in Virginia. These men and women, he wrote, in an edited and abridged version of Thomas Hariot's famous 1588 account, believed in the immortality of the soul. On this basis they erected the popish doctrine that one's works on earth determined whether one's soul ended up in heaven or hell. They even proved the immortality of the soul itself in a popish manner. 'For the confirmation of this opinion', wrote Purchas, 'they tell tales of men dead and revived again, much like to the popish legends.'[14]

Like their Catholic counterparts, Hariot and Purchas stuck closely to a classical frame of reference in studying modern paganism. Yet Purchas could not help registering the utility of comparisons with Catholicism. By the middle of the seventeenth century, English Protestants consistently used anti-popery and anti-puritanism as tools for studying and ridiculing non-Christian religions, in a way that often rivalled the significance of the classical tradition in their accounts. This was especially true in works like Purchas's, which straddled the scholarly and middling realms of print culture and reflected, to some extent, an expansionist outlook of inevitable confrontation with corrupt religions. In these later works the discourses of popery, puritanism, enthusiasm, idolatry, superstition and priestcraft mingled constantly, to the extent that they were less separate traditions or discourses than a single, massive body of historical knowledge from which a typology of religious corruption and imposture arose. The major turning point in the creeping universalisation of anti-popery and anti-puritanism was the English Civil War. And it is therefore the immediate post-Civil War period on which this chapter focuses. In confronting the legacy of this conflict, learned commentators of all political stripes became preoccupied with studying the mechanics of religious imposture and the authoritarian and populist sources of political instability. They argued over which groups in English society were engaged in practices that all agreed could bring on another decade of devastation and extremism. Anti-popery and anti-puritanism were some of their primary analytic and polemical tools.[15]

Mark Goldie, Justin Champion and Steve Pincus have all observed in different ways how the post-revolutionary period witnessed a deeper universalisation of these essential modes of thinking about English foreign policy, empire, religion and politics. Pincus has noted how in the arena of international politics, popery and universal monarchy were to a certain extent shorn of their previous theological significance. By the Restoration period these terms were so ideologically and referentially ambiguous, and applied so widely to supposed enemies of the English state – in particular, to France and the Dutch Republic – that they no longer had any necessary relationship to the Pope, to monarchies or even to Catholics. They primarily referred to a state's pursuit of universal dominion and the activities that conduced to that end, and could be used to attack both Catholic tyrannies and Protestant republics.[16] Goldie and Champion have made a similar point about the relationship between the early Enlightenment and the religious politics of the post-Civil War period. They have noted that 'priestcraft' – a term that was apparently coined by James Harrington in 1657 and became a central slogan of both the English Enlightenment and radical Whig ideology – was, in Goldie's words, 'popery universalized'. This new term denoted the tendency of all religious leaders to act popishly, by abusing the unwarranted power they wielded over ordinary people in order to satisfy their own lust for rule and to solidify their empires, to the detriment of both true piety and sound governance.[17]

There are, however, at least three blind spots in this rather Whiggish narrative of the emergence of a universal typology of religious corruption in the later Stuart period. First of all, the use of an expansive, early Enlightenment notion of religious and political imposture and corruption was not the preserve of the Whigs and their forefathers. From the beginning of the period, these forms of analysis and critique were used just as imaginatively and persistently by their enemies: the most zealous defenders of Stuart absolutism and the persecutory Church of England. Secondly, central to this absolutist and conformist critique was a universalised version of anti-puritanism, whose sphere of application in the early modern period and beyond still awaits sustained scholarly attention. And thirdly, it is important to recognise that in both an intellectual and a physical sense, the application and development of this discourse of religious and political corruption did not end at the borders of Europe.[18] England's increasingly sophisticated and intense engagement with the great Islamic empires and the pagans, Jews, Christians and Muslims inhabiting them was integral to the development of Enlightenment notions of priestcraft and despotism. This engagement was led by servants of the Restoration empire, men who were engaged in promoting England's political, economic and religious presence in Africa and Asia. It is this fact which enables us to appreciate how in England, at least, many aspects of modern orientalism – including those most central to later eighteenth-century debates about the British empire in Asia – emerged directly from the concerns and struggles of the Renaissance and Reformation.

Servants of the trading companies, the Church of England and the Crown who wrote scholarly accounts of the Islamic empires and their inhabitants in the later seventeenth century were immersed in late Renaissance and early Enlightenment historical culture. This was above all a culture of counsel, propaganda and information management, in which historical scholarship was inherently rhetorical and ideological at the same time that it adhered to the latest methodological standards for establishing 'matters of fact'. These works were full of commentary on how both the wise management of politics and religion in these empires, and the instability, decline and excesses of the same polities, offered important lessons for English statesmen and churchmen who sought to better manage their dominions within and without the British Isles, conduct foreign policy and convert Jews, pagans and Muslims to Christianity. Working from a global understanding of the Republic of Letters, these historians also insisted on deriving useful knowledge about Asian and African history from the non-European inhabitants of these places, their literary traditions and their public records. This enterprise was driven by the late humanist dictum that the histories of all the world's peoples afforded political and religious wisdom.[19] Later eighteenth-century historical research on South Asia partly perpetuated this tradition. But these later historians were of course concerned with the governing role of the British in Asia to an extent unheard of in the political environment of the late seventeenth century, where the imperial presence of the British in both Asia and Africa was noteworthy but minuscule.

The seventeenth- and eighteenth-century orientalism with which I am concerned here is therefore drawn from a much narrower range of texts and authors than the vast discursive field famously surveyed by Edward Said from the late eighteenth century onwards. The works under consideration here were at least partly historical in nature, whether they dealt with the ancient past or the contemporary world. They featured slightly varying combinations of erudition and appeals to wider bodies of educated readers. All of them were composed as works of political counsel: they offered sustained analyses of particular Islamic empires, ostensibly in order to aid the work of state, church and colonial servants. When considering these works, at least, the dichotomy set up between scholarship and power in many of the polemics surrounding Said's *Orientalism* is beside the point. Like Said, I am well aware of, but largely uninterested in the fact that many works of orientalism were in fact texts that improved the accuracy of western views of Islamic societies, praised many of their basic characteristics, and likened some of these to the characteristics of European societies.[20] The texts under consideration here, like so many in the seventeenth and eighteenth centuries, were not wholly obsessed with either difference or critique. They contained significant commentaries on the commonalities between eastern and western states and empires, and exhibited significant appreciation for the political and religious wisdom of non-European societies.

The centrally important observation for the present discussion, however, is that works of oriental scholarship and their derivatives – whether factually accurate or inaccurate – were without exception complex political resources. The content of these works was fundamentally driven by their utility (and by implication, their legibility) for European audiences, a utility which itself demonstrated enormous variance in content and ideological orientation. Inaccuracy and accuracy, sophistication and simplicity, likeness and difference, native informants and armchair erudition could all be crucial to the political power of a particular orientalist text, depending on what forms of political activity or policy it was intended to encourage. This is why I describe the languages of popery, puritanism and priestcraft below as languages of both analysis and critique. There is obviously an important difference between orientalist commentaries on rival powers like the Ottoman empire and later studies of South Asian colonial subjects. Yet the likenesses and continuities between these two bodies of writing are equally important: orientalism in each context was both ideologically multivalent and intensely focused on the mobilisation of political activity, by means of either counsel or propaganda and polemic.[21]

ANTI-POPERY, ANTI-PURITANISM, ORIENTALISM

While historians working in the late seventeenth and eighteenth centuries can be found describing a wide variety of religions practised in the Islamic empires – including Judaism, Zoroastrianism and Christianity – as popish, puritanical, priest-ridden and conducive to tyranny, my attention here will be focused on Islam, and secondarily, Hinduism. The depiction of Islam and the Islamic empires as popish and puritanical can be found in some of the earliest learned travel literature that dealt with Asian religion. For instance, the first extensive ethnographic product of the East India Company's activities in South Asia, the chaplain Edward Terry's *A Voyage to East-India*, which was mostly written in the 1620s but published in 1655, was rife with such analysis.[22] While accounts of this sort were particularly pronounced in England, many of the most famed Protestant traveling historians from the continent also offered extensive comparisons between Islam and popish despotism when their political circumstances permitted.[23]

Yet it was only after the English revolution that anti-popery and anti-puritanism were thoroughly universalised and merged, thereby becoming a widely applicable lens for diagnosing religious corruption and its political consequences. This dynamic can be seen vividly both in the writings of men who supported the English empire in the Mediterranean and eastern Atlantic, and in the writings of those who made polemical use of incoming reports on the history of the Islamic empires. Here I will discuss the perspective of three historical writers: an armchair commentator, the freethinker Francis Osborne; a chaplain in the British colony of Tangier, Lancelot Addison; and a servant of the Levant Company and the Crown in the Ottoman empire, the aforementioned Rycaut.[24]

Osborne, Addison and Rycaut all viewed the history of Islam as an unparalleled story of both religious imposture and aspirations to universal dominion. Addison, who published a biography of Muhammad and a history of Morocco in the 1670s, believed that Muslims practised a religion that, despite all its aversion to idolatry, was in many ways popish. Like the Roman Church, Islam was a subtle mixture of truth and falsehood; any truth in it was due to its plagiaristic origins.[25] Like medieval Catholics, Muhammad had grafted his own inventions and those of priestly impostors from the past onto a pure monotheism and claimed that the entire concoction was of divine origin. The Prophet also claimed to have performed numerous miracles during his ministry, in order to prove himself to Jews and Christians, who attributed miracles to the founders of their religions.[26] Later Muslims foolishly believed, according to Addison, that seven miracles occurred at the Prophet's birth. Addison reckoned that no sober Protestant reader would be surprised to see such a tradition, such 'palpable trash'. 'It need not create our wonder', he sneered, 'that the Mahumedan doctors be thus large in the encomiums of their apostle, when as strange things are attested of St Francis, by the friars of his order; and also the Dominicans, in praise of their founder.'[27] Osborne and Rycaut expanded upon Addison's view of the Qur'an as a sacred fabrication that bolstered the authority of Muhammad and his successors by asserting that the reading and interpretation of the holy text was tightly controlled. Osborne, in his 1656 *Politicall Reflections on the Government of the Turks*, passed from Muhammad to the Ottomans in a single sentence to offer this sort of observation. 'If Muhammad exceeded the commission of discretion', Osborne wrote, 'in swelling the Qur'an to so large a volume (multiplicity of words breeding, in the same plenty, ambiguities, among divines as lawyers), yet he provided against this inconvenience, with as much caution as a by-passed error is able to admit, in prohibiting the reading of it, to any but the priests, and the interpretation to all but the mufti.'[28] Osborne believed that the Muslim strategy was even more radical than the Romanists' own restrictions on scripture reading and interpretation.

Addison also claimed that the rise of Muhammad exposed the puritanical aspects of Islam. Just as he believed that predestinarian Calvinism led to libertinism, Addison argued that Muhammad had invented a religion rooted in predestinarian theology that was perfectly equipped to indulge the carnal appetites of himself and his proselytes. 'He denied himself in no instance of lewdness, but that he entitled God to a special approbation thereof, and made it a divine testimony of the truth of his apostleship.' Like the antinomians and other sectarian proponents of radical Calvinism, Muhammad proceeded to make room in his 'conventicle' for licentiousness, in order to gain a powerful following among the people, 'to whom nothing was more acceptable, than to have the indulgence of their vile affections to be made an article of their religion, and a piece of their worship'. He marshalled their cleverly solicited support to pursue his imperial designs.[29] This style of religion was especially popular with the pagans of Arabia, whom he drew to his religion and empire by practising priestcraft better than the Arabian priests did. Priestly imposture was for Addison the engine of universal tyranny, and both were best exemplified in the life of Muhammad and the history of Islam. 'Under the pretense of religion', Addison wrote, 'he designed an empire; and he was a prophet in show, but a tyrant in project.' Indeed, Muhammad's political manipulation of religious truth was so similar to political puritanism that for Addison, the Prophet's only rival as 'the only great impostor that ever continued so long prosperous in the world' was Oliver Cromwell. Muhammad 'so well managed his ambition and injustice, under the cloak of religion, as never any have yet proved his equal', wrote Addison. 'The nearest and most exact transcript of this great impostor, was the late Usurper.'[30]

These three writers' portraits of the Islamic empires of their day were even more striking than their statements about Muhammad and Islam in general. Osborne explicitly described religion in the Ottoman empire as a system of popery that was used to solidify the empire. 'Neither is it a slight occasion of the Turkish unity', he observed, 'that their Qur'an lies patent to the exposition of none but their own Pope.'[31] In the Ottoman empire, Osborne wrote, the mufti was technically subordinate to the sultan, but his prelacy was purposely amplified to have a better effect with the people, since religion is 'esteemed by all, if not quite corrupted, yet far less pure in secular vessels, than those set wholly apart for the worship of God'. Here Osborne was presenting a version of popery appropriate to the second half of the seventeenth century, one which did not necessitate the political superiority of the pontiff. The 'Erastian' settlement in the Ottoman empire did nothing to hold back priestcraft. Here a 'circumcised Pope' was 'set up' by the sultans as 'a favorable umpire of a seeming more indifferent and sanctified allay'. The sultan had all the benefits of priestly authority, but remained in full control. 'The Turk in this is happy, that the mufti his Pope, no less than Mecca his Rome, are within the reach of his power.' Osborne made clear that he believed this was the de facto situation in Europe, since the Pope was forced to indulge every initiative of powerful Catholic princes 'for fear, like Henry the Eighth, they should do it of themselves'.[32] The mufti stood ready not to preserve the original intent of the Qur'an, but to adjust its authoritative meaning to the current needs of the empire. Rycaut, in his later, more learned work, concurred with Osborne's judgment. 'Their law', he wrote, 'was never designed to be a clog or confinement to the propagation of faith, but an advancement thereof, and therefore to be interpreted in the largest and farthest fetched sense, when the strict words will not reach the design intended.'[33] As in Catholicism, exegesis had fallen prey to evangelical and political imperatives.

In his book on Morocco, Addison focused more than Osborne and Rycaut on Muslim religious practices. Above all, he declared, the Moroccans were 'the Puritans in Mahometanism'. But he also viewed Moroccan superstition through the lens of popery. Maghribi Muslims, for instance, indulged in mindless magical beliefs. Their 'superstitiosi' attributed absurd significance to washing rituals, a belief partly rooted in scripture, since 'all the *muslimūn* of the Qur'an use washing in a mystic signification of internal purity'. Addison also saw Moroccan Islam as a carnal religion, and made this clear, for instance, in part of his description of Ramadan. Like Jews, Muslims had got fasting all wrong. 'They place a great sanctity in this fast, which yet to a scrupulist, scarce would seem to deserve that name, for the day is usually passed away in a loitering sleepiness, and the night in a junketing: the one is at best a drowsy Lent, and the other a luxurious Carnival.' Addison reserved much of his criticism for the Sufi leaders or marabouts who figured so prominently in his political history of Morocco. His description of their religious and political activities featured a mixture of anti-popery and anti-puritanism. 'There are few who are able to read, that want manuals of private devotions, which are composed by the *morabitos*, or marabouts, and are indeed rather to be termed charms, than prayers.' The marabouts, he explained, were 'a sort of Arabs which are skilled, or pretend to be, in the law of Muhammad, severe in their conversation, bearing a great ostentation of sanctity, pretending to prophesy, or predictions. They compose all sorts of charms, to which the Moor is so addicted, that he has one for every occasion: I have seen a book thereof, containing some for the child-bearing women, to facilitate their travel; some for the passenger, to guide him in the way; some for the soldier; and one for the horse, which is much in the service of the saddle: this they hang under the beast's neck, and believe that it keeps him from being blind, or dimsighted.' These Sufi-inspired superstitions covered every aspect of daily life. 'They have likewise spells to keep their cattle healthy, and make them fruitful, all composed by the marabouts or priests; the latter, of late, being given much to this sort of composures.'[34]

Rycaut similarly described Islam in the Ottoman Empire with recourse to the languages of both anti-puritanism and anti-popery. He claimed, like Osborne, that popish doctrines, ceremonies and political strategies were essential to the expansion and relative stability of the empire. In his description of Ottoman religion, he was particularly keen to describe what he called the prevalence of 'monasteries and orders of religious men' or 'friars' in the Ottoman empire, and drew on Muhammad's supposed borrowing from Christianity to explain the phenomenon. He noted that a number of religious orders in the Ottoman empire attributed miracles to the founders of their specific traditions as well. These men, he wrote, 'incline to a pretended mortification and strictness of life, to poverty, and renunciation of the world's enjoyments, according to the devotion of Christians a thousand years past'. The most well-known inhabitants of the 'Mahumetan convents', the dervishes, 'pretend to great patience, humility, modesty, charity and silence, in presence of their superior or others ... They profess poverty, chastity, and obedience, like Capuchin friars or other orders of St Francis.' Novice dervishes, he reported, usually 'exercise some kind of legerdemain, or tricks, to amuse the minds of the common people; and some really apply themselves to sorceries and conjurations by help of familiar spirits'. Many monasteries had a particular 'saint' whom they honoured.[35]

Above all, however, Rycaut was struck by the puritanical character of Ottoman Islam. Like Cromwell, Muhammad and the Ottomans had apparently built their empires on a false providentialism, attributing their military victories to the special favour of God, and claiming that anyone who died fighting an infidel was assured of salvation. Even the Ottoman religious settlement mirrored the church of the English republic. Rycaut observed that the mufti 'hath no jurisdiction over the imams, as to the good order or government of the parishes, nor is there any superiority or hierarchy as to rule amongst them; every one being independent and without control in his own parish'. This ecclesiastical regime, he noted, 'may not unaptly seem to square with the Independency in England, from which original pattern and example our sectaries and phanatick reformers appear to have drawn their copy'. These similarities also extended to theology. Considering Ottoman notions of providence and predestination, Rycaut noted that 'the doctrine of the Turks in this point seems to run exactly according to the assertion of the severest Calvinists'. Over the course of Ottoman history, such opinions had often encouraged the emergence of antinomian sects. 'To these', Rycaut wrote, 'may not improperly be compared some sectaries in England, who have vented in their pulpits that God sees no sin in his children.' In general, like puritanism, Islam in the Ottoman Empire naturally led to a proliferation of conventicles and sects that were often the fomenters of rebellion. Early on in the history of the empire, for instance, there arose 'a sort of phanatick Mahometans which at first met only in congregations under pretence of sermons and religion, appeared afterwards in troops armed against the Government of the Empire'. These revolutionaries judged a pretended reform of the ancient religion the best means to 'raise sedition'. Their leader, Rycaut claimed, 'vented doctrines properly agreeing to the humor of the people, preaching to them freedom and liberty of conscience and the mystery of revelations'. Other sects mirrored puritans in their performative characteristics. Members of the modern sect of 'Kadizadeli', Rycaut affirmed, were 'of a melancholy and Stoical temper, admitting of no music, cheerful or light discourses, but confine themselves to a set gravity ... They are exact and punctual in the observation of the rules of religion ... In short, they are highly Pharisaical in all their comportment, great admirers of themselves, and scorners of other that conform not to their tenets, scarce according them a salutation or common communication.' These Ottoman sectarians perfectly mirrored the divisive and hypocritical social practices of the godly in England.[36]

Despite their close attention to Moroccan and Ottoman religious life, Rycaut and Addison were, like Osborne, ultimately concerned with its political significance. Addison's narrative in particular serves as a vivid example of how this sort of orientalism proceeded. For him, the revolutions of sixteenth- and seventeenth-century Morocco were stunning shows of religious trickery and imposture that took forms all too familiar to students of sedition by both radical Protestants and the Catholic henchmen of aspiring universal monarchs. His overwhelming preoccupation with this theme was most evident in his account of the rise of the Sa'dī dynasty in the early sixteenth century, on the first pages of *West Barbary*. 'Near the time the Marīn family[37] approached its designed period and determination', Addison wrote, 'it fortuned that a certain *al-faqīh*, or Moorish priest, in the province of Dara, began to grow into great reputation with the people, by reason of his high pretensions to piety and fervent zeal for their law, illustrated by a stubborn rigidity of conversation and outward sanctity of life.' Addison weaved his understanding of Malikite legal expertise and Sufi religiosity into a Moroccan version of puritanism. The priest, Muhammad ibn Ahmad, knew that his 'seeming severity' would render him 'of no vulgar esteem with a generation, who from time to time have been fooled with such mountebanks in religion'.[38]

Knowing, Addison wrote, that religion was best 'fit to advance him on the estimation of the many', ibn Ahmad decided to send his three sons on pilgrimage to Mecca and Medina, to secure the basis for the long-term stability of his fledgling empire. 'Much was the reverence and reputation of holiness, which they thereby acquired among the superstitious people, who could hardly be kept from kissing their garments, and adoring them as saints.' Ibn Ahmad's sons were masters of puritan and Jesuit priestly performance. 'His admired sons failed not in their parts, but acted as much devotion, as high contemplative looks, deep sighes, tragical gestures, and other passionate interjections of holiness could express; "Allah, Allah" was their doleful note, their sustenance the people's alms.' According to Addison, ibn Ahmad then deployed his sons to hatch revolution in all the major principalities of Morocco.[39] Taking their political puritanism to another level, they offered to lead an army from Fes against the Catholic Christians who occupied numerous outposts on the northern coast of Morocco. To make the moral of this allusion to Cromwell's military campaigns even clearer, Addison included in his narrative a dissenting voice: the brother of the king of Fes, Nasr, who advised against the proposed military campaign. Nasr, he wrote, 'resisted the petition, warning the King not to arm this name of sanctity, which being once victorious, might grow insolent, and forgetful of duty in minding a kingdom. He told him likewise that war makes men aweless, and that through popularity, many became ambitious and studious of innovation.' The sons of ibn Ahmad, Addison warned through Nasr, 'took up arms, not out of love to their country and zeal for their religion, but out of a desire to rule'. Despite the advice, these young men's 'armed hypocrisy', which mirrored in detail the conduct of puritan revolutionaries, proceeded apace: 'puffed up with their successes they forgot their obedience'. Before long, they had poisoned the king of northern Morocco while on campaign, and returned to secure the kingdom of Fes from the king there, who had given them the military power they now wielded against him.[40]

The political ambitions of such 'saints' were also central to Addison's meditations on the revolutions of the seventeenth century, in the wake of the collapse of the Sa'dī dynasty. The new contenders for power in northern Morocco at this point were 'all great saints'. These figures' 'outward sanctimony equaled them in the people's affection and esteem'. One grandee 'had the learning of a *ṭālib*, and the sanctity of a marabout, by which he was esteemed as an oracle among his countrymen, who upon all emergent occasions repaired unto him for advice and instruction; which they received as infallible, and obeyed as a law'. Another headed a *zāwīya* or Sufi lodge, from which emerged the most important political actor in northwest Morocco when Addison lived there: Ghaylān. As a leader, Ghaylān was gifted with 'his plausible fortune and personage, zeal for their law, and reservation of carriage'. In this he followed a family tradition: his father had used learning to his political advantage: 'his greatest renown', Addison wrote, 'sprang from his zeal for the Mahumetan law, an artifice which seldom fails, and a knack with which whosoever is gifted, cannot want reverence among the Moors'. Ghaylān also bolstered his popularity by marrying the daughter of a Sufi saint from Tiṭwān, and positioning himself as the leader of *jihād* against the Spanish and Portuguese. 'He first showed the Moors how their Prophet, both by his example and doctrine, had taught them to exercise their revenge against all oppressors of his law; and that whoever should die in its defense or propagation, were assured of paradise.' This call to religious revenge was strikingly attractive. 'This proposal was strangely moving with people of all capacities, and the report of Ghaylān's intentions against the Christians, induced many to be his followers, who otherwise would have eschewed his company.' The continued success of his enterprises only increased his religious presence. 'It being the genius of this people', Addison explained, 'to make the prosperity of the action, and undoubted argument of its justice, and the voice of Heaven to approve it.'[41] Muhammad, like Cromwell, had brought religious zeal and selective providential interpretation to the service of military conquest and empire.

Osborne, too, explicitly linked priestcraft and the drive for universal dominion. The Ottoman sultan was, he declared, 'a universal monarch'. His wise management of religion, in consultation with the mufti, made this possible. 'But not to insist upon the equity or reason of their law', Osborne wrote, 'it gives them (as the priests manage it) a satisfactory pretense, to esteem all ways decent and consonant to religion, that are able or likely to enlarge their empire: not questioning the quarrel, no more than the future happiness of such souls, as have the fate to expire in it. And if upbraided herewith, they desire the Pope to catechize his most Catholic Son, how he came by Portugal, Naples, Milan, Sicily, etc.' The Turks were experts in popish schemes of dominion, and were even aware of how they had beaten the papists at their own game. Osborne insisted that this was a nearly universal dynamic. 'Such as look upon the Mahumetan profession', Osborne continued,

> as of the grosser allay, because so far subservient to worldly policy, that the grandees and priests, like jugglers, carry only the coal of zeal in their mouths, not being heated themselves with what they go about to inflame others ... may find other courts standing in as prophane a posture, especially that of Rome ... where churchmen like burning glasses, cast the rays of a celestial fire, into the consciences of others, carrying the mean time, themselves, a cold, chrystaline, and fragile creed, towards what they endeavor to inform the people.[42]

In 1667, Rycaut concurred in his far more influential account of the Ottomans. He recognised the threat of Europe's aspiring universal monarch, Louis XIV. Yet in *The Present State of Ottoman Empire* he faulted European governors for developing an obsession with the French potential for universal monarchy while paying little attention to the Ottomans. The Turks, he argued, were wrongly considered to be ignorant and barbarous, and partly for this reason, they had great success in encroaching upon European territories. The Habsburg emperor in particular had concluded disadvantageous terms of peace with the sultan because he was preoccupied by the French. Rycaut described the Ottoman government in the same terms he used to describe the tyranny and slavery of France, but argued that tyranny was appropriate and advantageous for a state constituted in the way the Ottoman regime was. Like the French, to a large extent the Turks accepted Justinian's notion of absolute rule. All states that aimed at universal dominion, he argued, needed this sort of regime.[43] The connection between priestcraft and universal empire was a potent one, and it knew no religious or national boundaries.

This chapter has focused attention on the Restoration-era moment in which Reformation-era anti-popery and anti-puritanism were first transformed into an element of Enlightenment orientalism. But it is clear that similar historical analyses can be found in the later writings of Britons who served the East India Company and the Church of England in South Asia during the later seventeenth and early eighteenth centuries. The accounts of the physician John Fryar, the chaplain John

Ovington and the ambassador William Norris, which were all composed or published between 1696 and 1702, followed in the footsteps of English historians of the Moroccan and Ottoman empires. They described the haunting of the Mughal dominions by particular varieties of popery, puritanism, priestcraft and despotism.[44] Fryar spent nearly a decade in the service of the East India Company in the Safavid and Mughal empires between 1672 and 1682. His *New Account of East-India and Persia* (1698) was the most striking account of the three. Fryar described Hinduism as a system of idolatry, Brahmin priestcraft and enthusiasm that featured monks, saints and canonisation processes.[45] But he paid far more detailed attention to the form of Islam practised by the Mughals. The Mughals were 'of a more puritanical sect' of Islam than the Persians, Fryer declared. Here Islam featured, for instance, the performative piety of 'conventiclers' and other hypocritical holy men, who professed strict religious observation but practised licentiousness; and a recent ban on most religious holidays by 'a religious bigot of an emperor', Aurangzeb. Mughal Islam was also popish, featuring 'guardian angels', a 'sacramental wafer' placed in the tombs of the dead, 'petitions' for the dead, rosary beads and raised and railed altars. Both in India and Persia Islam was perfectly suited for bolstering their tyrannical rule on the subcontinent, but in its most puritanical forms, it could also lead to rebellion.[46]

The connections between the languages of the Reformation and the languages of orientalism remained equally clear in early eighteenth-century accounts of the Ottoman empire and general commentaries on Islam. The poet, dramatist and projector Aaron Hill, who travelled to the Ottoman empire and lived there for four years with his relative Lord Paget, the English ambassador at Constantinople, exemplified this continuity in his *Full and Just Account of the Present State of the Ottoman Empire* (1709). This work included nearly every element of the parallels between Islam and both Catholicism and puritanism found in earlier works.[47] Even the more learned and less hostile introductory material in George Sale's famous 1734 English translation of the Qur'an expounded upon the extremity and political utility of early Islamic beliefs in 'absolute election and reprobation'. Sale also pointed out how destabilising free-will heresies were devised in reaction to such tenets.[48]

In the second half of the eighteenth century, the transition from the languages of anti-popery and anti-puritanism to the Enlightenment languages of anti-priestcraft and anti-enthusiasm was nearing completion, and explicit references to either Catholicism or radical Protestantism in works on South Asia, in particular, became less and less common. This development is what has obscured the pre-Enlightenment roots of this sort of orientalism and led historians to assume that it was theorised by French philosophers. The Constantinople ambassador Sir James Porter's much later *Observations on the Religion, Law, Government, and Manners of the Turks* (1768) featured a discussion of 'enthusiasm' and 'religious tyranny' that diagnosed Muslim forms of Pelagianism and monasticism, in a continuation of the style of analysis found in the writing of Hill and earlier writers who had spent extensive time in the empire.[49] Islam, the historian of South Asia Alexander Dow declared, was 'perfectly calculated for despotism', since Muhammad 'enslaved the mind as well as the body'. Part of this was achieved through the puritanical doctrine of 'absolute predestination', which led to absolute passivity in Muhammad's followers and the future subjects of Muslim tyrants. These antinomians, Dow claimed, trust 'the whole to Providence' and make 'God agent in [their] very crimes'.[50]

British accounts of Hinduism written early on in the period of Company rule in Bengal (when Islam became a less prominent object of inquiry) were dominated by a critique of popish priestcraft. J.Z. Holwell, a deist proponent of a 'pure' and ancient Hinduism, related the corruption of 'the simple doctrines of Bramah' by the brahmins, 'the laity thus being precluded from the knowledge of their original scriptures'. Some brahmins who were concerned about these attempts 'to inslave the laity' provoked the original schisms within Hinduism and invented the Vedas, a new set of pseudo-scriptures. 'Priestly power' prevailed everywhere, and secular rulers feared the consequences that their dependence on such men, and the 'sacerdotal slavery' reigning among the population, would have on civil order. The members of every household were turned into 'machines' by the brahmin living among them. Thus mired in superstition, Indians were led to accept 'the yoke of Mahommedan tyranny', which was a providential judgment on the corruption of their once true religion.[51] Others repeated similar observations on scriptural control, government of the mind, schism and ceremonial superstition.[52] Warren Hastings explicitly linked the 'spiritual discipline' of the brahmins to 'the religious order of Christians in the Romish Church'.[53] Hindus were also supposedly inclined to puritanical enthusiasm and fanaticism, however, and this was nowhere more evident than in their priest-inspired devotion to sati.[54] Monkery joined with puritanical enthusiasm, libertinism and performativity. Dow, for instance, reported on mendicant philosopher enthusiasts who used pilgrimages, self-flagellation and erudition to make their order 'more revered among the vulgar'.[55]

The continuities in scholarly discussions of Asian and African polities between the seventeenth and eighteenth centuries were both ideological and practical in nature. The intensely politicised, historical, philological and local nature of late eighteenth- and nineteenth-century research by the British on South Asia was in many ways a continuation of the ideals of late Renaissance humanism, and in particular, the first great era of orientalist research in Britain, which stretched from the 1630s to the 1690s.[56] It was therefore natural for the greatest orientalist of the late eighteenth century, William Jones, to place himself in dialogue with the antiquarians and philologists of the high and late Renaissance.[57] Expanding upon our sense of the Renaissance and Reformation roots of modern imperial knowledge production and debate is one of many ways in which we can appreciate the historical relationships between the Reformation and the Enlightenment, between the so-called first and second British empires and between the domestic and imperial histories of Britain.

Notes

1. Accounts of seventeenth- and eighteenth-century imperial ideology and foreign policy that examine both anti-popery and its relatively neglected counterpart, anti-puritanism, include S. Pincus, *Protestantism and Patriotism: Ideologies and the Making of English Foreign Policy, 1650–1668* (Cambridge, 1996); E. H. Shagan, *The Rule of Moderation: Violence, Religion and the Politics of Restraint in Early Modern England* (Cambridge, 2011), pp. 211–17; J. E. Bradley, *Religion, Revolution, and English Radicalism: Nonconformity in Eighteenth-Century Politics and Society* (Cambridge, 1990); J. C. D. Clark, *The Language of Liberty 1660–1832: Political Discourse and Social Dynamics in the Anglo-American World* (Cambridge, 1994); J. B. Bell, *A War of Religion: Dissenters, Anglicans, and the American Revolution* (Basingstoke, 2008); R. G. Ingram, *Religion, Reform and Modernity in the Eighteenth Century: Thomas Secker and the Church of England* (Woodbridge, 2007), pp. 226–59.
2. E. Said, *Orientalism* (New York, 1978); R. Inden, *Imagining India* (Oxford, 1990); R Travers, *Ideology and Empire in Eighteenth Century India: The British in Bengal 1757–93* (Cambridge, 2007); R. Travers, 'Ideology and British expansion in Bengal, 1757–72', *JICH*, 33:1 (2005), 7–27; R. Guha, *A Rule of Property for Bengal: An Essay on the Idea of Permanent Settlement* (Durham, NC, 1996); T. R. Metcalf, *Ideologies of the Raj* (Cambridge, 1994).
3. R. Tumbleson, *Catholicism in the English Protestant Imagination: Nationalism, Religion, and Literature 1660–1745* (Cambridge, 1998), pp. 12–13; L. Colley, *Britons: Forging the Nation, 1707–1837* (New Haven, 1992), ch. 1; L. Colley, 'Britishness and otherness: an argument', *JBS*, 31 (1992), 309–29.
4. Guha, *Rule of Property for Bengal*, pp. 16–22.
5. W. J. Bulman, *Anglican Enlightenment: Orientalism, Religion and Politics in England and its Empire, 1648–1715* (Cambridge, 2015); W. J. Bulman and R. G. Ingram (eds), *God in the Enlightenment* (New York, 2016); J. G. A. Pocock, 'Post-puritan England and the problem of the Enlightenment', in P. Zagorin (ed.), *Culture and Politics from Puritanism to the Enlightenment* (Berkeley, 1980), pp. 91–111; J. G. A. Pocock, 'The myth of John Locke and the obsession with Liberalism', in J. G. A. Pocock and R. Ashcraft (eds), *Locke* (Los Angeles, 1980), pp. 1–24; J. G. A. Pocock, 'Clergy and commerce: the conservative Enlightenment in England', in R. Ajello, E. Cortese and V.P. Mortari (eds), *L'Età dei Lumi: studi storici sul Settecento europeo in onore di Franco Venturi* (2 vols, Naples, 1985), I, pp. 523–68; J. G. A. Pocock, 'Conservative Enlightenment and democratic revolutions: the American and French cases in British perspective', *Government and Opposition*, 24 (1989), 81–105; J. G. A. Pocock, *Barbarism and Religion* (5 vols, Cambridge, 1999–2011); R. Porter, 'The

Enlightenment in England', in R. Porter and Mikulás Teich (eds), *The Enlightenment in National Context* (Cambridge, 1981), pp. 1–18; J. A. I. Champion, *The Pillars of Priestcraft Shaken: The Church of England and its Enemies, 1660–1730* (Cambridge, 1992); Travers, *Ideology and Empire*; J.-P. Rubiés, 'Oriental despotism and European orientalism: Botero to Montesquieu', *Journal of Early Modern History*, 9:1–2 (2005), 109–80.

6 Travers, *Ideology and Empire*, quotation on pp. 17–18.

7 See P. Rycaut, *The Present State of the Ottoman Empire* (1667), esp. pp. 1–3; and also among the works considered in this article, L. Addison, *West Barbary* (Oxford, 1671), pp. 73–4. On Montesquieu's sources, see M. Dodds, *Les Récits de Voyages Sources de L'Esprit des Lois de Montesquieu* (Paris, 1929), esp. pp. 41–3. On the debate over how to interpret Montesquieu's use of these sources, see Rubiés, 'Oriental Despotism', and the older works cited herein.

8 Guha, *Rule of Property for Bengal*, p. 22; Travers, *Ideology and Empire*, pp. 56–8, 62–3, 79.

9 Champion, *Pillars of Priestcraft Shaken*.

10 In this chapter I take 'anti-puritanism' to encompass not only critiques of puritans, but also critiques of those who might be more precisely identified as presbyterians and (in later periods) dissenters, independents, and sectarians. On anti-puritanism before the Civil War, See P. Lake, *Anglicans and Puritans? Presbyterianism and English Conformist Thought from Whitgift to Hooker* (London, 1988); P. Lake with M. Questier, *The Antichrist's Lewd Hat: Protestants, Papists, and Players in Post-Reformation England* (New Haven, 2002), pp. 521–78; P. Collinson, 'Ecclesiastical vitriol: religious satire in the 1590s and the invention of puritanism', in J. Guy (ed.), *The Reign of Elizabeth I: Court and Culture in the Last Decade* (Cambridge, 1995), pp. 150–70; P. Collinson, 'Ben Jonson's *Bartholomew Fair*: the theatre constructs puritanism', in D. L. Smith, R. Strier, and D. Bevington (eds), *The Theatrical City: Culture, Theatre and Politics in London, 1516–1649* (Cambridge, 1995), pp. 157–69; A. Walsham, '"A Glosse of Godlines": Philip Stubbes, Elizabethan Grub Street and the invention of puritanism', in S. Wabuda and C. Litzenberger (eds), *Belief and Practice in Reformation England* (Aldershot, 1998); Lake, 'Anti-puritanism: the structure of a prejudice', in K. Fincham and P. Lake (eds), *Religious Politics in Post-Reformation England* (Woodbridge, 2006), pp. 80–97; P. Lake, 'Puritanism (monarchical) republicanism, and monarchy: or John Whitgift, antipuritanism, and the "invention" of popularity', *Journal of Medieval and Early Modern Studies*, 40:3 (2010), 463–95.

11 The works of the conformist divine Oliver Ormerod might be the most spectacular single example of this post-Reformation analytical triangle. In 1605, Ormerod published *The Picture of a Puritane*, and attached to it a smaller treatise called *Puritano-Papismus*, which documented how the machinations of puritans matched those of the papists. Ormerod followed this in 1606 with a work called *The Picture of a Papist*, to which he attached *Pagano-Papismus, Wherein is Proved by Irrefragable Demonstrations, that Papism is Flat Paganism*. O. Ormerod, *The Picture of a Puritane* (1605), and *The Picture of a Papist* (1606). For the early intersection of these polemical resources see, e.g., A. Milton, *Catholic and Reformed: the Roman and Protestant Churches in English Protestant Thought, 1600–1640* (Cambridge, 1995); Lake, *Anglicans and Puritans*; and P. Lake, 'Anti-popery: the structure of a prejudice', in R. Cust and A. Hughes (eds), *Conflict in early Stuart England: Studies in Religion and Politics 1603–1642* (London, 1989), pp. 72–106.

12 J.-P. Rubiés, 'Theology, ethnography, and the historicization of idolatry', *Journal of the History of Ideas*, 67 (2006), 571–96; C. Eire, *War Against the Idols: The Reformation of Worship from Erasmus to Calvin* (Cambridge, 1986); P. Harrison, *'Religion' and the Religions in the English Enlightenment* (Cambridge, 1990); S. MacCormack, *Religion in the Andes: Vision and Imagination in Early Colonial Peru* (Princeton, 1991); A. Pagden, *The Fall of Natural Man: The American Indian and the Origins of Comparative Ethnology* (Cambridge, 1984); J.-P. Rubiés, *Travel and Ethnology in the Renaissance: South India Through European Eyes, 1250–1625* (Cambridge, 2000); P. Miller, *Peiresc's*

Europe: Learning and Virtue in the Seventeenth Century (New Haven:, 2000); and M. Mulsow, 'Antiquarianism and idolatry: the *Historia* of religions in the seventeenth century', in G. Pomata and N. Siraisi (eds), *Historia: Empiricism and Erudition in Early Modern Europe* (Cambridge, MA, 2005), pp. 181–210.

13 On these tools See D. Kelley, *Foundations of Modern Historical Scholarship: Language, Law, and History in the French Renaissance* (New York, 1970); A. Grafton, *What was History? The Art of History in Early Modern Europe* (Cambridge, 2007); and Markus Völkel, *'Pyrrhonismus historicus' und 'fides historica': die Entwicklung der deutschen historischen Methodologie unter dem Gesichtspunkt der historischen Skepsis* (Frankfurt am Main, 1987).

14 S. Purchas, *Purchas His Pilgrimage* (1613), pp. 948–9. Cf. T. Hariot, *Brief and True Report of the New Found Land of Virginia* (1588), p. 26. Here and elsewhere spelling, punctuation and transliteration in primary sources have usually been modernised.

15 Bulman, *Anglican Enlightenment*, chs 3–5.
16 Pincus, *Protestantism*.
17 Champion, *Pillars of Priestcraft Shaken*; M. Goldie, 'Priestcraft and the birth of Whiggism', in N. Phillipson and Q. Skinner (eds), *Political Discourse in Early Modern Britain* (Cambridge, 1993), pp. 209–31.
18 W.J. Bulman, 'Enlightenment and religious politics in Restoration England', *History Compass*, 10:10 (2012), 762–4; W.J. Bulman, 'Publicity and popery on the Restoration stage: Elkanah Settle's *The Empress of Morocco* in context', *JBS*, 51:2 (2012), 308–39; Bulman, *Anglican Enlightenment*.
19 Bulman, *Anglican Enlightenment*, ch. 3.
20 Said, *Orientalism*, p. 55. For two very different versions of the claim that early modern and modern travelers and orientalists engaged in activity that produced empirical knowledge, see Rubiés, *Travel and Ethnology*; and R. Irwin, *For Lust of Knowing: The Orientalists and Their Enemies* (New York, 2007).
21 For similar frameworks, see M.S. Dodson, *Orientalism, Empire, and National Culture: India, 1770–1880* (New York, 2007), pp. 1–17; S. Marchand, *German Orientalism in the Age of Empire* (Cambridge, 2009), pp. xvii–xxxiv.
22 E. Terry, *A Voyage to East-India* (1655), pp. 261, 271–2, 281–3, 290, 292, 309, 440. See also H. Lord, *A Display of Two Forraigne Sects in the East Indies* (1630).
23 J. D. Tracy, 'Asian Despotism? Mughal Government as seen from the Dutch East India Company factory in Surat', *Journal of Early Modern History*, 3:3 (1999): 267–78; A. Olearius, *The Voyages and Travels* (1662), pp. 341–70, 371, 373–5, 376–8. Cf. J.-B. Tavernier, *The Six Voyages of John Baptista Tavernier, Baron of Aubonne, Through Turky, into Persia and the East-Indies* (1677), Book 5.
24 L. Addison, *The First State of Mahumedism* (1678); Addison, *West Barbary*; Francis Osborne, *Politicall Reflections on the Government of the Turks* (1656); Rycaut, *The Present State of the Ottoman Empire*.
25 Addison, *First state of Mahumedism*, p. 84; Addison, *West Barbary*, pp. 143–4.
26 Addison, *First state of Mahumedism*, pp. 122–5.
27 *Ibid.*, pp. 12–15. See also Osborne, *Politicall Reflections*, p. 4.
28 Osborne, *Politicall Reflections*, pp. 13–14.
29 Addison, *First state of Mahumedism*, pp. 27–30, 184–5. See also Rycaut, *Present State*, p. 104; and Osborne, *Politicall Reflections*, p. 4.
30 Addison, *First state of Mahumedism*, Epistle Dedicatory, pp. 35, 63, 119–21.
31 Osborne, *Politicall Reflections*, pp. 13–14. See also Rycaut, *Present State*, p. 98.
32 Osborne, *Politicall Reflections*, pp. 29–32. See also Rycaut, *Present State*, p. 106.
33 Rycaut, *Present State*, pp. 106–7.
34 Addison, *West Barbary*, pp. 124, 148, 161–3, 180, 211–12.
35 Rycaut, *Present State*, pp. 97–104, 106, 126, 129, 135–9, 142–5, 149.
36 *Ibid.*, pp. 109, 115, 118, 126, 130.
37 The Marinids.
38 Addison, *West Barbary*, pp. 1–3. For Addison's awareness of the Malikī school, see Addison, *First State of Mahumedism*, pp. 55–6.
39 Addison, *West Barbary*, pp. 3–4.

40 *Ibid.*, pp. 5–6.
41 *Ibid.*, pp. 22–7, 30–7, 43.
42 Osborne, *Politicall Reflections*, pp. 21–2, 88.
43 Rycaut, *Present State*, sig. a2v. and Book I, esp. pp. 6–8; Justinian, *Institutes*, Book II, Title XVII, 8.
44 J. Ovington, *A Voyage to Suratt in the Year 1689* (1696); J. Fryer, *A New Account of East-India and Persia* (1698); S. Subrahmanyam, 'Frank submissons: the Company and the Mughals between Sir Thomas Roe and Sir William Norris', in H.V. Bowen, M. Lincoln, and N. Rigby (eds), *The Worlds of the East India Company* (Woodbridge, 2002), p. 89.
45 Fryer, *New Account of East India and Persia*, pp. 32, 44, 102.
46 *Ibid.*, pp. 92–6, 102, 107–9, 143–4, 194–6, 249, 357.
47 A. Hill, *A Full and Just Account of the Present State of the Ottoman Empire* (1733), pp. 37–42, 45, 47–9, 51, 54–6, 58–60. See also T. Shaw, *Travels, or Observations Relating to Several Parts of Barbary and the Levant* (1738).
48 G. Sale, *Koran, Commonly Called the Alcoran Of Mohammed* (1795), vol. 1, pp. 137–8.
49 J. Porter, *Observations on the Law, Government, and Manners of the Turks* (1771), pp. 12, 17, 31–2, 40–41.
50 A. Dow, *A History of Hindostan* (3 vols, 1768–1772), III, p. xvii.
51 J. Z. Holwell, 'Chapters on "The Religious Tenets of the Gentoos"', in P. J. Marshall (ed.), *The British Discovery of Hinduism in the Eighteenth Century* (Cambridge, 1970), pp. 57–60.
52 A. Dow, 'A Dissertation Concerning the Hindoos', in Marshall (ed.), *British Discovery of Hinduism*, pp. 109–10, 119; C. Wilkins, '"The Translator's Preface", from the *Bhagvat-Geeta*', in Marshall (ed.), *British Discovery of Hinduism*, pp. 192–5; R. Orme, *Historical Fragments of the Mogul Empire* (London, 1805), p. 432; R. Orme, *A History of the Military Transactions of the British Nation in Indostan* (1763), p. 3; L. Scrafton, *Reflections on the Government of Indostan* (1770), pp. 5–6.
53 W. Hastings, 'Letter to Nathaniel Smith', in Marshall (ed.), *British Discovery of Hinduism*, p. 186.
54 Holwell, 'Chapters on "The Religious Tenets of the Gentoos"', in Marshall (ed.), *British Discovery of Hinduism*, pp. 91–2; Dow, 'Dissertation Concerning the Hindoos', in Marshall (ed.), *British Discovery of Hinduism*, p. 116; N.B. Halhead, '"The Translator's Preface" to *A Code of Gentoo Laws*', in Marshall (ed.), *British Discovery of Hinduism*, pp. 149, 170; J.Z. Howell, *A View of the Original Principles, Religious and Moral, of the Ancient Bramins* (1779), 'A Dissertation on the Metempsychosis of the Bramins', p. 7.
55 Dow, 'Dissertation', pp. 117–18.
56 On which see G. Toomer, *Eastern Wisedome and Learning: The Study of Arabic in Seventeenth-Century England* (Oxford, 1996); G. Toomer, *John Selden: A Life in Scholarship* (Oxford, 2009); M. Feingold, 'Oriental Studies', in N. Tyacke (ed.), *The History of the University of Oxford: Seventeenth-Century Oxford* (Oxford, 1997), pp. 449–504.
57 See, e.g., W. Jones, 'On the Gods of Greece, Italy, and India', in Marshall (ed.), *British Discovery of Hinduism*, pp. 197, 199, 223, 224. On Jones and the advanced stage of orientalist work he helped inaugurate, see Dodson, *Orientalism, Empire, and National Culture*; O. P. Kejariwal, *The Asiatic Society of Bengal and the Discovery of India's Past, 1784–1838* (Delhi, 1988); S. N. Mukherjee, *Sir William Jones: A Study in Eighteenth-Century British Attitudes to India* (Cambridge, 1968); and J. Majeed, *Ungoverned Imaginings: James Mill's The History of British India and Orientalism* (New York, 1992).

CHAPTER FIVE

Protestantism and the politics of overseas expansion in later Stuart England

Gabriel Glickman

In 1624, a Somerset clergyman, Richard Eburne, published his vision of *A Plaine Pathway to Plantations* in the New World. Focusing on the English settlements at Newfoundland, he wrote 'for the perswading and stirring up of the people of this Land ... to effect these Attempts better then yet they doe'. Eburne insisted that 'Plantations are Actions wherein we also of the Cleargie are as farre interessed as any other'. He called upon the Crown to transpose dioceses, deaconries and parishes into the American wilderness. Above all, he appealed for the incorporation of 'Savages, Heathens, Infidels, and Idolaters', through conversion, into the colonial community. Only by 'the enlargement of *Christs Church* on Earth', he believed, could Englishmen fulfil the 'proper, and principall end of Plantations', and so attain divine favour: 'successe in wars, increase in wealth, and honour on earth'.[1] Yet Eburne's manifesto sat visibly at odds with the unfolding process of English overseas expansion. Through the seventeenth century, Newfoundland figured more consistently in English calculations not as the epicentre of a Christian mission, but as a base for control of the North Atlantic fishery.[2] Moreover, the new proprietor, and the recipient of Eburne's dedication, was Sir George Calvert: a Catholic, whose colonial initiatives in Newfoundland and Maryland served not to strengthen but dilute the confessional identity of the English overseas world. The *Plaine Pathway* inadvertently revealed a conflict between the Protestant religion and the origins of the English empire: the uneven, commercially focused methods of New World colonisation, and the strategic and patronal choices of the Crown. This tension brought unease into domestic debates over the expansion of the Stuart realm.

The birth of English Protestantism and the beginnings of the English empire were once judged to be developments not merely contemporary but coterminous. Through the seventeenth century, a genre of spiritual writing traced the providential connection between the Reformation and the discovery of America. From the Elizabethan marine conflicts to the Cromwellian Western Design, militant voices identified colonial competition as the climax of a battle with Catholic powers, to be pursued to the ends of the earth, if not the end of time.[3] Recent literature has, however, become more attentive to the frustrations and limitations implicitly captured by Eburne's treatise. Studies by David Armitage and Steve Pincus have de-emphasised the role of religion in English thought about empire, highlighting the alternative influences prised out of humanist precepts or principles of political economy.[4] The dominant trend in the historiography of the Atlantic world has been to accentuate contrasts between English and Spanish visions of dominion: between the expansionist impulses of the Counter-Reformation and the reticence of Protestants as global missionaries, between all-encompassing Councils of the Indies and more narrowly-focused Councils of Trade. Yet, as Karen Kupperman and Carla Pestana have shown, Protestant religiosity still configured the public culture and political identity of colonies across English America, however untidily it was implanted.[5] Moreover, colonisation took shape in a century when English politics was riven by confessional animosities – divisions that were not simply suspended when contemporaries eyed the New World. Absent from modern scholarship is a consideration of how colonisation affected the domestic Stuart Church, and the vision of the world entertained by Protestants in England. Hitherto, the study of England's global exchanges has focused more on the materials and commodities funnelled into domestic markets, and the stimulus given to natural philosophy, than on the spread of confessional ideas and beliefs. After the puritan dispersal of the 1630s, the plantations recede from the historiography of religion in the Stuarts' three kingdoms.

This chapter re-examines the relationship between the Protestant religion and the politics of English overseas expansion, and looks at how confessional concerns entered into debates over colonisation, between the Restoration and the death of William III. I argue that although English plantation may not have followed the coherent Protestant strategy mapped out by Richard Eburne, the debate over the dominions was inflected with spiritual, theological and ecclesiastical concerns. Confessional narratives, scriptural injunctions and missionising exhortations introduced the New World, Asia and parts of Africa to wide sections of the public domain. The challenge of enlarging insular Christianity exerted increasing influence over the restructured Restoration Church. Yet if Protestant impulses propelled private individuals across the Atlantic, the question of how to incorporate a proselytising church into the fragmented sovereign spaces of English America opened up a stream of dilemmas. Vigorous discussions were raised over how far the interest of the Crown lay in Christianising indigenous populations or reconstructing the ecclesiastical order of the domestic realm. I argue that these debates were shaped not just by local pressures, but by legal and theological contention in old England, in a confessional landscape reordered by the legacy of the Civil Wars. In the three kingdoms, as in the overseas provinces, the restored monarchy faced the question of how to bolster slender church authorities, manage the reality of religious pluralism and respond to congregations with a history of antipathy towards the Stuart crown. Colonial questions amplified fierce debates over the rival merits of comprehension, toleration or coercion in church policy. Far from extracting themselves from the politics of the three kingdoms, the leaders of American congregations sought to intervene in those exchanges, and shape them to their advantage.

The chapter argues finally that the relationship between overseas expansion and the reformed religion became problematic not because colonial policy was secularised, but because Protestants found no consensus over the sweeping moral, pastoral and political questions provoked by ventures outside Europe. English divisions undermined the possibility of a common Protestant approach towards colonisation, and gave rise to contending ideologies of empire. This disunity was compounded when shifts in world politics – the decline of Spain, the peril of French expansion in Europe – forced Englishmen to redraw the map of their spiritual and strategic obligations, casting doubt of the moral primacy of the pursuit of world dominion. I conclude that overseas expansion served not to affirm but disrupt England's Protestant identity, providing a new theatre to showcase the frailties of Restoration politics and religion. When missionaries re-engaged with America after the 1688 revolution, they were animated not by confidence in England's godly election, but by spiritual anxiety.

Through the reign of Charles II, English commentators linked the seizure of lands outside Europe to a greater salvific purpose. George Scot, promoter of settlement in East New Jersey in 1683, captured migration into America as part of the Christian 'lightning that comes out of the East unto the West', and urged settlers to rejoin the struggle against 'the bloody and cruel Spaniard ... who thirsted after the riches of that New World'.[6] Defenders of the fragile Crown colony at Tangier turned to another part of the confessional inheritance. For the surveyor general, Henry Sheres, the city's soldiers could be acclaimed as Christian knights 'who have drawn their Swords, against the Enemies of our Religion', and installed a bulwark against 'a considerable part of the Ottoman Empire'.[7] Christian exhortations gestured equally towards the commercial undergirding of English colonisation. Through traffic and navigation, God dispensed 'precious Gifts and Graces of his Spirit among his People', argued the Dissenting minister John Flavel, binding the 'Family of Christ' by common needs and mutual enticements.[8] Yet the pursuit of wealth across far-flung oceans carried spiritual dangers. For the clergyman Philip Stubbs, England had placed itself under the protection of 'the Great Sovereign of the Seas', against the 'angry elements' that had pulled down pagans, sinners and the 'proud Spaniard'. The fortunes of English mariners, who skimmed under providential guard between life and death, stood for an entire kingdom that could steer to safe harbour only by making 'suitable returns to Him of Praises and Thanksgivings'.[9] Power required a Christian foundation, these authors argued, and it was spiritual workmanship more than martial or mercantile dexterity that would take the kingdom towards *grandezza*.

Many of these writings spoke to the fragile civil and religious conditions within England in the 1660s, and identified the New World as a locale for spiritual renewal. The Oxford churchman Morgan Godwyn believed that the Church could release itself from the torments of the Civil Wars by recapturing the proselytising traditions stored within ancient British Christianity.[10] Correspondents within the Royal Society connected advances in natural philosophy to the growth of English and Christian power overseas. For the clergyman Thomas Sprat, the subjects of Charles II were attaining not merely territorial, but mental mastery, having 'describ'd, and illustrated, all parts of the Earth', as they planted, and so thrown open God's revealed book.[11] Accordingly, Sir William Petty believed, the expanding realm became a vessel for the expansion of spiritual and intellectual capability: promising to avoid the decline of the ancient empires, because its triumph would recover wisdom lost with the Fall, and enable mankind 'to advance ... towards the top of the great scale'.[12] For the clergyman John Beale, these thrilling achievements hinted that 'the greatest worke may be neere at hand'. By overcoming their popish adversaries, English adventurers had prepared the ground to move the 'thundering artillery' of a Protestant crown into the pagan wilderness, and usher in the 'Conquest of the Holy Lambe'.[13]

Yet English commentators were far from unanimous as to what Christian or 'Protestant' expansion would entail. Debates on both sides of the Atlantic opened up rival theological rulebooks for colonisation. The tradition exemplified in Richard Eburne's *Plain Pathway* called for emulation of the practices and justifications behind the Spanish missionary kingdoms in Central America. In 1584, Richard Hakluyt had contended that English monarchs, as supreme governors of the Church, possessed rights of spiritual bequest equivalent to the papal Bulls of Donation, sanctioning plantation as a means towards the advancement of the gospel. The Reformation, he suggested, had brought about a providential supersession, passing to the Crown of England the divine authority to command the conquest of the New World, for the redemption of provinces trapped under Spanish tyranny.[14] Intrinsic to this idea was the incorporation of Amerindians into the moral and religious community. For Morgan Godwyn, 'It must be piously supposed' that the conversion of heathens represented 'the only end of God's discovering those Countries to us'.[15] Calls for conversions came accompanied by reluctant admiration for Spanish missionary achievements, and dismay at the pusillanimity of Protestant settlers in matters evangelical. In 1636, the translation of the Dutch Bible into Malayan plucked further at pious consciences.[16] These arguments were matched by an appeal to reason of state. For the prosperity of the plantations, 'it were convenient', according to the MP Roger Whitley, to usher 'ye youth of ye Indians into seminaryes' alongside settler children, to be raised together as 'our own Subjectes'.[17] The clergyman Patrick Gordon bemoaned that excluding indigenous peoples disregarded not merely Christian duty, but the temporal benefits afforded by adding 'many thousands of new *English* Subjects to the *English* Empire'. For Gordon, the main obstacle to conversion – the multiplicity of native languages – obliged settlers towards a prior process of 'civilising', which would redound to the advantage of the dominions. The colonies could be transformed not merely by shared worship, but the integration of Indians into 'manufactures' and education, and finally by intermarriage, following the example of the 'Ancient Romans, whose Custom and Interest it was, to extend their own Language with their Conquests'.[18]

These ideas, however, did not command consensus. Opposing Protestant voices recoiled from appropriating the intellectual weaponry of the Counter-Reformation. By invoking missionary work to support temporal claims to empire, Protestants moved perilously close to the 'fiction' that earthly authorities might 'pretend as Vicars of Christ ... to dispose of ye kingdoms of ye world at their pleasure', protested the Scottish MP Sir John Clerk.[19] In reality, Hakluyt, and many of the Spanish authors that he followed, had caged the principle of 'dominion by grace' within a latticework of alternative claims and justifications for colonisation.[20] Yet Protestant critics were on their guard against encroachment of the doctrines of 'papists', 'tub-preachers' and barbarous empires outside Christendom. 'It is for Mahumetans to professe planting religion by the sword; it is not for Christians', pronounced Bishop Joseph Hall in 1627. The Iberian alliance of priests and conquerors transgressed, he argued, the sacred truth that Christ's kingdom was not of this world; it also flew in the face of natural law. Since 'dominion and propriety is not founded in Religion, but in a naturall, and civill right',

Hall affirmed, then 'neither doth the want of that spirituall interest debarre any man from a rightfull claime and fruition of these earthly inheritances'.[21] Colonial authors – especially those belonging to communities outside the Church of England – argued that this clash of ideas placed at stake the liberties of settlers as well as indigenous peoples. The 'popish principle' that 'kings hath a right to the lands of the heathen', put American territory into the hands of the monarch as head of the Church, warned the Boston magistrate Samuel Sewell.[22] It violated the conviction, cherished in Congregationalist and Quaker colonies, that the lands of the New World 'were not the Kings', but belonged to 'the Kings Subjects', who, according to William Penn, had 'buryed our Blood & Bones to turn it from a Desart to a pleasant Country ... upon the publick faith, of enjoying our Government as well as our Labours'.[23]

These authors reconceptualised great spaces of the New World not as the locale for a crusade, but a *vacuum domicilum* awaiting the application of human labour, and unearthed an alternative scriptural foundation for English settlement. The 'Grand Charter' of Genesis enjoined mankind to 'to increase and multiply and replenish the earth and subdue it', in the words of John Winthrop.[24] Accordingly, Englishmen could honour God as faithfully in the clearing, planting and harvesting of the wilderness as in the conquest of pagan souls. This 'agriculturalist' argument, later secularised by John Locke, carried implications for Protestant evangelism. While its tenets were not incompatible with missionary work, they de-emphasised Indian conversions as a confessional obligation, giving biblical sanction to settlers to confine their labours to 'wastes, or *asperi montes*, which the Natives make no use of', in the words of one Restoration commentator.[25] Such ideas served in practice to fortify the puritan self-image of the enclosed Elect forging protected communities in the wilderness, and gave voice to inherited Calvinist doubts over the validity of conversions through human agency. A strand of religious opinion in Massachusetts envisioned Indians instinctively as 'roaring Lyons and savage Bears', sent to scourge the sins of the faithful.[26] For one New York settler, 'the mysterious works of God', winnowing Indian numbers through Old World disease, reinforced the identity of America as a site of renewal for existing believers, rather than a place to capture new souls.[27] These notions intimated a different model of dominion. For Benjamin Worsley, secretary of the Council of Trade in 1669, the New Englanders were 'to be honoured for preserving their marriages free from mixture with Indians, soe that Their is noe Creolian seed'.[28] The Protestant imagination was ruptured in response to America. Missionising and agriculturalist arguments supplied competing intellectual frameworks for plantation, and conflicting strategies for how it should be accomplished.

For all of these inhibitions, attempts at the conversion of indigenous peoples increased after 1660, as colonial experiments, and as a feature of English Crown calculations. The new charters dispensed to Rhode Island, Carolina and Pennsylvania outlined the promulgation of Christianity as a means to 'enlarge our English Empire'.[29] Intermittently, Christian hopes encompassed unfree African labourers. The Council of Trade summoned agents for Barbados in 1661, 'to consider how the natives and slaves might be ... made capable of baptism in the Christian faith'.[30] James, Duke of York, professed a strong conviction, recalled by John Evelyn, 'that the negroes in the plantations should all be baptized, exceedingly declaiming against that impiety of their masters prohibiting it'.[31] But, faced with persistent planters' opposition, designs for conversion focused on the Indians. The most substantive experiments developed in the non-slaveholding northern colonies. Interest in Christianisation accelerated in New England in the 1660s, after tribal conflicts devastated the territorial holdings of the Massachusett Indians and flooded the Bay Colony with uprooted indigenous labourers.[32] However, the new call for conversions also pointed to a turn in confessional culture, as a second generation of preachers challenged Calvinist scruples, and posited, in Cotton Mather's words, a country 'richly bespangled with Evangelical Churches', as the mark of spiritual election.[33] Asserting the Hebraic origins of the Indians, proponents circumvented the puritan objection towards the conversion of *gentiles* as a task unachievable before the coming of the Last Days.[34] In the praying towns at Natick, Roxbury and Martha's Vineyard, John Eliot, Daniel Gookin and Thomas Mayhew constructed a template for Christianisation – with Indians offered considerable agency over the terms of their conversion – and an interim model to ease the incorporation of proselytes into colonial society.[35]

The conversion programme commanded attention across the Atlantic. A baptism service for congregants 'of riper years' entered into the 1662 prayer book, conceived for the use of 'Natives in our Plantations'.[36] In the same year, the committee of trade stamped royal approval on the praying towns, and incorporated them within the New England Company, with the natural philosopher Robert Boyle appointed as governor. Steered by a committee including eight privy councillors, the Company established a string of City investments to fund work overseas. In 1663, it organised the publication of Eliot's Algonquian New Testament, dedicated to Charles II.[37] Under its auspices, the number of praying towns rose to fourteen, and in 1674 it was proclaimed that over 12,000 Indians had received the gospel.[38] The 'holy experiment' in New England set a precedent for evangelical programmes pursued across other precincts of the English overseas world. Robert Boyle joined the board of the East India Company in 1672, lobbied for the appointment of Company chaplains with knowledge of eastern languages and raised a roll-call of City and aristocratic subscribers for the publication of Thomas Hyde's Malayan Gospel.[39] Royal Society networks mobilised funds for scriptural translations into Turkish, intended for the use of clergymen travelling with the Levant Company.[40] These designs gradually enlarged the pastoral preoccupations of the Church within the three kingdoms. The formation of the Welsh Trust in 1673 was followed eight years later by the publication of a New Testament, under Robert Boyle's sponsorship, intended for the Irish Gaels. Both enterprises espoused the twin goal of 'civilising' and Christianisation, as explored first in America.[41]

The millennial expectation around the mission mingled with moral anxiety. Lay and clerical commentaries registered old fears over the transoceanic movement of English subjects, and misgivings over the worlds they were creating beyond the walls of Christendom. 'There is nothing more dangerous to the right Religion than ... commerce with Pagans', pronounced Lord Justice Jeffreys in 1683: 'we read how the children of Israel were perverted from the true Religion by conversing with the Nations round about them'.[42] In the Mediterranean, growing English traffic heightened the number of captives lost to the Barbary corsairs: their ransom and liberation was hailed in public ceremonies of redemption, but their experiences stirred fears of an insidious penetration of Islam, through secret conversions, into domestic life.[43] America stood out equally as a zone of spiritual vulnerability, and missionaries agitated for the moral renewal of settler communities as an obligation no less urgent than the call to the unconverted. Increasingly, Restoration clergymen framed connections – developed more fully by the reformers of manners in the 1690s – between the unconverted Indians, and morally lapsed communities in old England, who were considered similarly susceptible to the heathen spirit. John Beale believed that beating down vice and luxury on both sides of the Atlantic was the precondition for successful evangelism in pagan lands.[44] Morgan Godwyn hoped that raised awareness of the New World would turn England into a 'nursery' of charitable devotion. He recommended Lenten sermons by returning missionaries before the City of London, and the endowment of parish funds from the colonies.[45] Colonial activities stimulated calls for moral reform, because missionaries pictured America as a place of divine judgement on the English nation. The Church had to be polished, dignified and positioned to extend the boundaries of Christendom, in preparation for the Last Days.[46]

Yet, in the face of these initiatives, missionary foundations remained fragile. In America, the instability of Anglo-Indian relations provided the most conspicuous obstacle to conversions. The English had not overwhelmed and absorbed Indian societies in the manner of the Spanish, and a succession of confrontations, culminating in King Philip's War in 1675, served as a reminder of the vulnerability of colonial societies. Three years after this conflict, the number of praying towns had contracted back to four, and the experience rekindled scepticism in New England, and among many Crown officials, towards the utility, and the moral importance, of conversion programmes.[47] While the project in New England was making a slow recovery by 1700, the paucity of conversions had registered on the other side of the Atlantic, provoking a barbed critique of the limits of English colonisation. 'Shame', 'sin' and 'scandal' were the watchwords with which commentators, lay and clerical, dissected the absence of converts in both the East and West Indies. In 1695, the Dean of Norwich, Humphrey Prideaux, fulminated against officers of the East India Company who had permitted temples, mosques and Catholic churches to abound throughout the English settlements, yet sponsored 'not as much as a Chappell for ye True Religion of Jesus Christ in any of them except at Fort St. George'.[48] Thirty years later, Daniel Defoe complained that English policy had been founded on the 'unaccountable mistake' that 'civilising Nations do not encrease Commerce'.[49] Plantations had not been transformed into missionary kingdoms, and the contrast with the Iberian empires was noted within and outside the Protestant fold. Wherever they ventured, jibed the Irish Catholic Hugh Reilly, the English 'took more Pains to make the Land turn Protestant than the People'.[50]

For many commentators, frustrated missionary impulses represented only one manifestation of a vacuum in ecclesiastical authority across the English territories overseas. The Church of England had not flourished on American soil, and its frailty rendered the religious lives of the settlers just as potent a cause for alarm as the absence of indigenous proselytes. 'Many of them never saw England & know not what ye nature & dignity of ye Clergy is', one resident of Virginia bemoaned to the archbishop of Canterbury.[51] In 1662, it was reported that the only religion holding together the Caribbean was 'obedience to the lawfull Power'.[52] Appointing the bishop of London in 1675 as an *ex officio* member of the committee of trade, the court of Charles II was intermittently receptive to these complaints. In the compilation of parish registers, the enforcement of correct procedure in marriages and baptism, and the development of schools, churchmen were potentially vital cognates of the civil order.[53] But the limits of transatlantic communication, and the difficulty of grappling with radically different social and cultural conditions, meant that planting the Church anew figured as a lower priority for the Restoration episcopate than the *re-establishment* of orthodox worship across the three kingdoms. Plans for 'Virginia Fellowships', proposed by ministers of the Crown in 1661 and 1685, failed to materialise at Oxford and Cambridge, and by 1677, the province supported only ten Church of England clergymen among a population of 30,000 Europeans.[54] To export the paraphernalia of worship across the Atlantic, build churches, and install legal safeguards to protect them, strained the resources of even more committed episcopal leaders.

Even in the Crown colonies, the planting of an ecclesiastical order remained dependent on the partiality of individual governors, and a whole apparatus of lay officials – magistrates, assembly members, vestrymen and colonial agents – whose support could not be guaranteed. The danger was that the Church lacked identifying features to distinguish itself from pervasive and well-staffed Protestant rivals. Before the Civil War, these inhibitions had already opened up the religious life of America to contending forms of Protestantism. Through the 1640s, the movement of rival congregations across the Atlantic further refigured the colonial world. Communities of Independents entrenched themselves in Bermuda, Surinam and the Bahamas, while Presbyterian chapels were established in Port Royal, Jamaica, and Quaker and Baptist preachers swarmed into the northern dominions. In much of New England, the confessional framework was fashioned by voluntarist association and private initiative. More robust church foundations endured in Massachusetts. But although the clergy of the Bay Colony laid claim to the inheritance of the Edwardian Reformation, they guarded their militantly Calvinist creed with a congregational model of worship incompatible with the authority of English bishops.[55]

The Crown itself sent ambiguous signals to the religious establishment. Directives from the court of Charles II obliged governors in the Leeward Islands towards 'profession of the Protestant Religion according as it is practised in England', enjoined 'due reverence & exercise' of the Church of England in Jamaica and demanded 'special encouragement' for its ministers in New Hampshire, but stopped short of granting it the legal monopoly over religious worship.[56] Reiterating that no individual was to be 'molested' or 'disquieted' as long as they owned 'the substance of Christian Religion, and entertain no tenets prejudicial to the ends of Government and Society', royal instructions upheld a principle closer to the tolerationist Declaration of Breda of 1660, than the policy of 'unity through uniformity' imposed by the Cavalier Parliament.[57] Addressing the governor of Jamaica in 1674, the Council of Trade invoked the disparity between the 'poverty and emptiness of Spain and the vast riches and number of people in the United Provinces', as evidence that toleration was the stratagem most 'agreeable with modern policy'.[58] Liberty of conscience did not, however, entail disregard for the spiritual domain. Some voices at court evinced interest in nurturing a common Protestant culture within the context of confessional plurality. The 1662 charter for Rhode Island and Providence granted exemptions from 'the liturgy, ceremonies, and articles of the Church of England', on the grounds that the inhabitants' 'serious intentions of godly edifying themselves in the holy Christian faith ... may win the Indians to the knowledge of the only true God and Saviour of mankind'.[59] Pacific strands across different congregations acknowledged that when no single church was materially equipped to gain mastery over colonial terrain, contact with pagan peoples required a philosophy that rose above Protestant divides. The Massachusetts praying towns were promoted by the New England Company in the hope of constructing a broadly-based Protestant ministry, garnering prayers and funds from the Church of England for the 'gospel work' of Boston Congregationalists.[60]

Questions over the religious life of the colonies were interwoven with debates within the British Isles, over the legitimate parameters of religious orthodoxy, and the problem of how to manage 'tender consciences' stirred in the Civil War. It was no coincidence that support for the New England Company at court came from a contingent of former puritan royalists – the earls of Anglesey and Manchester, Viscount Saye and Sele – who offered continual advocacy for a church settlement grounded on principles of 'comprehension'. For thirty years, the Company provided a vehicle for supporters of this position, marshalling the irenic instincts of supporters in and outside the Church, who wished to retain a place for the godly in the kingdoms of Charles II.[61] In parts of America nominally under the sway of the established church, the paucity of qualified clergymen made comprehension an unofficial reality. Two Swiss ministers, together with a Scotsman of Presbyterian background accounted for three-quarters of the active Anglican livings in Jamaica in 1671; ten years later, the governor of the Leeward Islands reported that 'French and Dutch Calvinists and Lutherans' staffed the parishes under his authority.[62] Underpinning the practicalities of comprehension, however, was a more far-reaching spiritual venture. The Irish MP Vincent Gookin, whose cousin Daniel supervised the praying town at Natick, had blamed internal 'bitternesses' for the shortage of conversions from the Gaels: 'the Papist sees not where to fix if he should come to us ... and ... sees not what friends or security he could partake if he should fix'.[63] The prospect of missonising in America challenged English Protestants to invigorate a rule of faith that could transcend the disputes of liturgy, theology and ecclesiology that had fractured the clergy of the Old World.

These hopes failed to come to fruition. The agenda for comprehension collapsed in 1662, and the subsequent Act of Uniformity placed antagonism between the Church and its dissenting spirits on a legal footing. Through the reign of Charles II, the suspicions sowed in recent history were reanimated, as domestic responses to the Anglo-Dutch Wars, the Popish Plot and the Exclusion Crisis laid bare the divisions within English Protestantism. The bishops had 'unchurched' the puritan tradition, and in purging Presbyterians and Congregationalists from the parishes, they hastened the decline of Calvinism in its entirety within the established church. The effect was to cut off the ideological bridges between England and Massachusetts. The Americas, a 'hiding place for some of His precious saints' in the judgement of Congregationalists, appeared in a very different shade to Anglican royalists. As the nursery of Hugh Peter, Henry Vane and Thomas Venner, and the refuge of the regicides Goffe and Whalley, New England could be perceived as simply another link in the seditious chain connecting the residue of English republicanism, the covenanting rebellions in Scotland and the Rye House Plot.[64] Edward Cranfield, appointed Crown governor in New Hampshire, appealed for the remodelling of the colony by 'loyal and orthodox ministers'.[65] By 1676, the rumour of bishops being sent across the Atlantic was reported in Massachusetts as 'a thing more dreaded than the Indian war'.[66]

The animus of the Church was vigorously returned by its opponents across the seas. For Cotton Mather, the true 'Church of England' after 1662, could be located only among ejected 'Nonconformist' consciences. Ecclesiastical authority, he argued, had been misappropriated to bolster 'none but that Faction, whose Religion lyes in Sainting their Martyr Charles I': an especially insidious brand of 'popery'.[67] Conflicts spilling out across the Atlantic amplified the local confessional tensions in English America, and presented a devastating obstacle to the project spelled out by the New England Company, for collaborative evangelism across the Protestant divide. When they were required to choose, clergymen of all stripes privileged upholding Christian orthodoxy among settlers over the propagation of the gospel among pagans. Hostility to Dissent, Richard Baxter recorded, led to the refusal of ministers of the established church to raise parish collections for the New England Company; Morgan Godwyn lamented that too many in England 'bespeak as Schismaticks and Idolaters' the sole progenitors of successful missions in English America.[68] For their part, Boston ministers prohibited Anglican worship within Massachusetts, and, even after the passing of the 1689 Toleration Act, appealed to the General Court to block the 'vile Pelagian Books, that from beyond-sea, are vended among us'.[69] For despondent Protestant critics, the consequence of England's domestic fissures was to prevent the transportation of true religion through the globe. 'Merchandizing, travaile, persecution, want of Pastors, many things hinder us from particular Church-membership', Richard Baxter insisted. Until Protestants could awaken the pastoral, inward understanding of the faith that rose above congregational difference, they would forever flounder before 'the industry of the Jesuits and Fryars'.[70]

The discontents among Protestants rendered it harder to convince secular policymakers in England to plant confessional foundations in America. The court promotion of evangelical Protestantism abated after the chartering of the New England Company. Contrary to the fears voiced in Massachusetts, Crown councils did not seek to impose the Church of England on recalcitrant settler congregations. Rather, they deployed tolerationist 'indulgences' and 'dispensations' to weaken congregational oligarchies altogether, and elevate constituencies more likely to prove loyal, regardless of their religious affiliations. The Crown blurred the confessional identity of the dominions by ushering Quakers into authority in Pennsylvania and New Jersey and allowing Catholic enclaves to develop in Tangier and the West Indies. The Stapleton family, Irish Catholics who held the governance of the Leeward Islands between 1671 and 1684, capitalised on the weakness of the Church to grant power to civil magistrates over marriage ceremonies, and devised new oaths for office-holders, free of commitments to the reformed religion.[71] Unexpectedly, the sponsorship of pluralism increased after 1675, as Charles II rolled out a plan to monitor and reorganise the dominions, challenging the legal foundations of proprietary governments. The newly convened committee of trade privileged administrative reforms and commercial statutes, rather than religious injunctions, as means to tie the colonies closer to the Crown. The Dominion of New England, constructed by James II as the culminating point in this experiment, came without any visible church policy.[72] Behind this approach lay the influence of a form of 'sceptical Toryism', briefly influential within the court of James II, which promoted toleration over coercion as the surer route towards civil peace and imperial power.[73] For the political economist Peter Pett, it was only the discovery of a 'civill interest' banishing theological 'pedantry' that would 'make us Masters' in the world.[74] Sir William Petty concurred that 'no monarch' tasked with filling up 'so great a share of the unpeopled Earth' as English America could ground his policy on 'those gibberish denominacons and uncertain phrases ... Papist, Protestant ... fanatic'.[75]

The reluctance or inability of Crown committees to develop an ecclesiastical policy for America brought waves of anxiety into the spiritual culture of the colonies. Anglicans fretted that the enlargement of the realm was creating a landscape where the scars of the Civil War split open, giving rise to 'mischiefs and growing evils for the future', as one Maryland missionary predicted.[76] In England, admonitions against the state of the overseas dominions took multiple forms. The image of New England as a fanatic's cradle represented one of the 'material objections', according to Charles Davenant, towards the maintenance of possessions overseas.[77] The more persistent claim, fixed especially on Virginia and the West Indies, was that England's outworks had become *irreligious* moral hazards, raising subjects in an alien dispensation, untutored in the gospel. John Beale appealed for the incorporation of Protestant Scots, whose 'plain and hardy breeding' would refortify the moral order against the contagion of 'pride' and 'luxury'.[78] Morgan Godwyn diagnosed the spiritual void as a factor in the confluence of crises that struck the dominions in the later 1670s, including King Philip's War and Bacon's rebellion in Virginia. Roman, Persian and Abyssinian precedents served as reminders, he contended, that it was 'more easie to build a Castle ... in the open Air, without any ground to found it upon, than to establish a Government without Religion'. If the dominion of the Spanish was damned for its cruelty and bigotry, English America had cleaved to the other extreme. Godwyn attacked the barons of the plantocracy as 'degenerated English', choosing 'trade before religion', and fattening themselves on the toil of 'pagan slaves'. By rejecting the obligation to evangelise, he believed, they had undermined the Christian spirit among their own peoples, and surrendered them to 'the Barbarity and Heathenism of the Countries they live in'.[79]

The image of the colonies as theatres of corruption, irreligion and subverted civil hierarchies spread through a wider genre of political and imaginative literature.[80] The Crown itself was not spared the invective, and by the middle of the 1670s, its critics were framing connections between the debility of the Protestant religion in the overseas territories and the apparent growth of 'popish' tendencies within the court of Charles II. In 1679, the Exclusionist Parliament at Westminster turned its fire upon the embattled royal colony at Tangier, pinpointing the degeneration of the city into 'a nursery for popish soldiers', and 'a seminary for priests', under a succession of governors, who, according to one former mayor, had 'made it their business to ruine the Protestant Interest'.[81] Repeatedly, Whig MPs refused to supply the city with funding against its Moroccan combatants without the prior removal of the Catholic Duke of York from line of succession. In the absence of this concession, the collapse and evacuation of Tangier in 1684 vindicated, according to one critic, the ancient verity that no province 'ever prosper'd since the beginning of the World that slighted the Religion of its Countrie'.[82]

PROTESTANTISM AND OVERSEAS EXPANSION

Many of the critiques of royal policy were inflected with awareness of an international context beyond America. For earlier generations of commentators, it had not been difficult to spell out the connection between conquests in the New World and the international Protestant interest. The vision of empire brought to a head in the Western Design was steeped in a world view defined by the power of Spain, and an understanding of America as a witness to the peril of the Counter-Reformation. Even without bibles, missionaries and well-staffed colonial parishes, voyages across the Atlantic could be praised as doing the work of God, by cutting off the inflow of Central American bullion that made Spanish ambitions possible in Europe. After 1660, however, the tectonic plates of power in European were shifting. Spain, seen through English eyes, was a force in decline, its economic strains compounded by the revolt and secession of key continental territories. Peace with Madrid was established in 1667, and extended to the Americas three years later. In the southern and island colonies, English governors schemed not to bring down the Iberian Babylon, but to tame it through favourable commercial relations.[83] Under Charles II, English colonial wars were more likely to be fought out against Protestant Dutchmen: the competitors for commerce in the East and West Indies. Yet while Spanish power contracted, new candidates were emerging as contenders for the universal monarchy in Europe. By the middle of the 1670s, the court of Madrid had been unseated by Louis XIV as the principal threat to the international Protestant interest.[84] More consequentially – and despite its military build-up in Canada – France was identified less as a colonial usurper than a force for expansion in Europe: a peril to Huguenots within its domain, and Vaudois, Dutch and Palatinate Protestants beyond its borders.

Viewed against these changing horizons, the preoccupation of the Crown with conquest and plantation outside Europe could be indicted as a corrupting diversion from England's inherited moral and religious bonds. To lavish resources on distant colonies while Louis XIV pillaged the strongholds of the faithful was to act, as one Whig MP put in 1680, 'like Nero, when Rome was on fire, to fiddle'.[85] The diplomat Sir William Temple concurred that in neglecting 'the deplorable state of the Protestants abroad ... we have not made ourselves fit for what God has appointed us'.[86] In surveying all parts of the world, English commentators, Whig and Tory, tempered confessional exhortations with a competing appeal to 'reason of state' and the 'national interest'. Yet the colonialist preoccupations of the court of Charles II risked severing those two foundations of policy altogether. 'The undoubted Interest of England is Trade' averred the duke of Buckingham in defence of the third Anglo-Dutch War; 'it is that only which can make us either Rich or Safe'.[87] The French alliance, sealed at the Treaty of Dover in 1669, was conceived by Lord Treasurer Thomas Clifford as a way to tempt Louis XIV towards seeking continental hegemony at the Dutch expense, leaving England a free hand across 'all the places and countries in America'.[88] By contrast the Whig call to arms in defence of European coreligionists brought temporal and confessional interests back into conjunction. England could build 'gold and silver palaces' overseas, the Earl of Shaftesbury affirmed in Parliament in 1678. But palaces would crumble if the 'walls and defences' provided by 'foreign Protestants' in Europe fell before the popish deluge.[89]

These complaints spoke to older abrasions in the relationship between Protestantism and the idea of territorial empire. English confessional literature looked naturally outwards. The consciousness of Milton's 'slaughtered saints' overseas flowed within the bloodstream of domestic Protestant congregations.[90] But Protestant internationalism was universal not imperial: if its concerns overlapped with the interests of the expanding English monarchy, they were not confined to the same borders. Even after the Elizabethan Spanish wars, the conception of England as a uniquely elective actor in sacred history was more contested among Protestants than many historians have credited.[91] The shifting of the Catholic threat from Habsburg to Bourbon reactivated an alternative lineage of godly polemic that had long questioned the merit of sinking Protestant blood and treasure into 'these windswept conquests of ours', as Sir Philip Sidney had put it.[92] Attacks on specific colonial projects released wider anxieties in works that drew attention to the association between 'empire', 'popery' and universal monarchy. 'Let us for bear to vaunt, as we have done, of Conquests', or 'overween as if we thought none were our Equals', appealed the poet George Wither in 1665.[93] In a 1678 Commons sermon, Edward Stillingfleet proclaimed that the Christian path diverged from 'the ways of rapine and oppression', by which 'mighty Empires have been raised and maintained'.[94] Puritans, Dissenters and a considerable strand of opinion with the Restoration Church submerged the 'chosen' status of the English people within a wider ocean of ideas and allegiances, and judged the godliness of the nation by its capacity to protect spiritual brethren beyond its borders.[95] When English colonies had fallen seemingly into 'popery' and 'barbarity', it was harder to make the case for their providential value.

Through the decade that followed the 1688 revolution, lay and clerical networks in England and America crafted a campaign to remoralise the overseas dominions, and reclaim them for a nation vigorously asserting its Protestant identity. Missionary interests were reawakened in the disputed territories north and west of New York, provoked by reports of French Jesuits moving through the Great Lakes, to 'allure' the Indian Five Nations into allegiance to Louis XIV, 'with their beads and crucifixes and little painted Images'.[96] In 1701, the Church of England announced its venture into the missionary arena with the creation of the Society for the Propagation of the Gospel (SPG), on a tripartite mandate covering Indians, African slaves and English settlers.[97] Pitching printed literature at planters, merchants and mariners, the society preserved the distinction between 'apostolical conquests' and 'dominion by grace', but identified evangelical work as moral legitimation for power overseas. Even if Englishmen had settled on 'derelict' wastelands untouched by Indian habitation, argued the clergyman White Kennett, they held their lands under a 'feudal tenure' from God that hinged on their capacity to propagate the gospel.[98] The revolution had, however, left an ambiguous dual legacy in America. The fall of James II had strengthened the Church overseas, principally at the expense of Catholics, with the assumption of ecclesiastical authority in Maryland, and the reconfiguration of laws across the provinces to strengthen the Anglican position.[99] Yet the 1689 Toleration Act weakened the episcopacy at home, and delivered a precedent to support opponents of church establishments within the New World. The Crown and the Board of Trade promoted the Church within the context of appeals for closer collaboration between Protestants, putting governors on high alert against clerical divisions likely to 'divide the people'.[100] Thomas Bray, the founding president of the SPG, held out an olive branch to New England, insisting that his purpose was 'not to intermeddle, where Christianity under any Form has obtained Possession'.[101] While English governments supported church-building, book transmission and the creation of Anglican schools, they blocked repeated appeals for the consecration of bishops in America.

Calls for Protestant reunion heightened after war with France broke across transatlantic frontiers in 1689, and when Bourbon claims over the Spanish Succession threatened to re-establish a Catholic powerbase within the New World. These pressures revived the idea of an Atlantic community with common Protestant interests, spanning kingdoms, colonies and congregations. Defending the Scottish expedition to Darien, the Presbyterian Robert Ferguson urged English readers to 'be thankful to God, that the *Reformed Religion* is like to obtain some footing where it never had any', even if it was to flower under 'a Form of Ecclesiastical Government and Discipline ... different from those of the *Church* of *England*'.[102] By speaking of the New World as a locale to unite the reformed churches, clergymen of different stripes wrenched English America back into the cultural universe of European Protestantism. 'Though Jerusalem is yet in Ruines; the French Churches are dissipated, the Hungarian Churches are desolated', lamented the

Congregationalist Cotton Mather, the restoration of Protestant virtue in England would create 'glorious' outposts of true religion in the New World.[103] The SPG aspired to 'communicate their good designs to other Protestant Nations', sent representatives to the reformed churches of Grisons, Geneva and St Gallen, and dispatched the call for subscriptions through Bohemia and northern Germany.[104] The committee threw its weight behind projects for resettling Protestant refugees, and prepared the ground for Huguenot, Palatinate and Vaudois incomers to fill up vacant colonial parishes. Colonial evangelism may have been intended to 'retrieve in some measure the Genius of the English Nation', as the future SPG secretary John Chamberlayne informed the governor of Jamaica in 1697, but the mission was not represented as the exclusive property of English sovereign power.[105] The task of making the colonies Christian was obliging the Church of England, paradoxically, to become more European.

It proved, however, harder to transfer this vision from the realm of language and communication into political reality. The ecumenical enthusiasm stimulated in the 1690s was challenged as newly arriving missionaries encountered the reality of the multi-credal environment. For the Anglican clergyman John Talbot in East Jersey, the 'heathens' to be confronted in East Jersey were not Indians but Quakers and Independents; the governor Lewis Morris concurred that most Dissenters 'cannot with truth be called Christians'.[106] The SPG diverged from its domestic partner, the Society for the Propagation of Christian Knowledge, in resisting collaboration with Protestants outside the Church. Quaker, Congregationalist and Scottish Presbyterian ministers worked equally assiduously to seal off their own operations among the Amerindians.[107] Programmes of refugee settlement created equally thorny tests of moral and spiritual scruples for the upholders of church establishments, both Anglican and Congregationalist. In Boston, Samuel Sewall fretted over the celebration of 'the Holy-Days' and 'Christmas-day as they abusively call it' by French Huguenots at their chapel in School Street. While English bishops added Huguenots in America to the domestic charity briefs, SPG supporters in South Carolina lobbied for the Church Act of 1704, legislating for an Anglican establishment, and requiring French settlers to maintain it through the public purse.[108] Clergymen may have adhered to the pieties of Protestant reunion, but they struggled to settle the terms on which it would proceed.

By the middle of the eighteenth century, colonial conquests were being retailed and received in domestic politics as tokens of providential virtue.[109] The 1707 Act of Union, in preserving the Presbyterian Church of Scotland, formalised a broad, cross-confessional conception of the Protestant religion as the spiritual foundation of the British state. But if religion provided rhetorical legitimation for empire, it was not straightforwardly imported into the practice of colonisation. Paradoxically, as Protestant triumphalism increased, the dominions were spilling out beyond the clutches of the reformed religion, gathering Catholic subjects in Gibraltar, Minorca and Acadia in 1713 and incorporating non-Christians in Asia and among the soaring numbers of African slaves. Governors and clergymen had failed to bring an Anglican empire into being; increasingly the claims of the Protestant religion in general were rivalled in provinces, garrisons and trading enclaves by a de facto pluralism that elevated civic bonds over confessional unities. 'In my dominions are a great many religions but no disputes as to the civil affairs ... every man must do as I command', boasted the Baptist Joseph Collet, governor for the East India Company in Madras in 1718.[110]

The enlargement of the English realm had kindled new dilemmas for believers – questions over the eschatological meaning of the New World, and whether Christian duty lay in missionary emulation of the Catholic Church or the careful cultivation of Elect virtue in a derelict wilderness. More dangerously, overseas expansion reawakened older forms of discord buried at the heart of the English Reformation. The New World challenged Anglicans to define the soul and the substance of their religion in a landscape devoid of the historic and institutional buttresses that supported the clergy at home. The frictions in Restoration politics tested the willingness of all churches to open up their provincial lockholds, and establish America as the shared possession of the Protestant world. Spiritual uncertainties shaded into political questions, in which the interests of secular authorities and Protestant ministers overlapped, but did not totally conform. When clerical conflicts threatened stability not merely in fragile colonial societies but within the three kingdoms, the Crown retreated from the role of 'nursing father' in the wilderness and repositioned itself as the – occasionally reluctant – sponsor of confessional pluralism. The result was that by 1700, the reformed religion was a visible presence in the English overseas world, but it was also a frustrated one.

Notes

1 R. Eburne, *A Plaine Pathway to Plantations* (1624), preface, pp. 4–5.
2 P. E. Pope, *Fish into Wine: The Newfoundland Plantation in the Seventeenth Century* (Chapel Hill, 2004), pp. 65–78.
3 A. H. Williamson, 'An empire to end empire: the dynamic of early modern British expansion', *HLQ*, 68 (2005), 227–56.
4 D. Armitage, *The Ideological Origins of the British Empire* (Cambridge, 2000), pp. 61–98; S. Pincus, 'From holy cause to economic interest: the study of population and the invention of the state', in S. Pincus and A. Houston (eds,) *A Nation Transformed: England after the Restoration* (Cambridge, 2001), pp. 272–98.

5   K. Kupperman, 'Errand to the Indies: puritan colonization from Providence Island through the Western Design', W&MQ, 3rd series, 45 (1988), 70–99; C. G. Pestana, *Protestant Empire: Religion and the Making of the British Atlantic World* (Philadelphia, 2009).
6   G. Scot, *Model of the Government of East New Jersey* (1682), pp. 32–3.
7   H. Sheres, *A Discourse touching Tanger* (1680), p. 33.
8   J. Flavel, *Navigation Spiritualiz'd: Or, A New Compass for Seamen* (1664), pp. 37–9.
9   P. Stubbs, *God's Dominion over the Seas, and the Seaman's Duty Consider'd* (1701), pp. 23–5.
10 M. Godwyn, *The Negro's & Indians Advocate* (1680), pp. 94–6.
11 T. Sprat, *Observations on Monsieur de Sorbier's Voyage into England* (1665), pp. 46, 49–50.
12 Marquis of Lansdowne (ed.), *The Petty–Southwell Correspondence, 1676–1687* (London, 1928), p. 46; S. Irving, *Natural Science and the Origins of the British Empire* (London, 2008).
13 M. Hunter, A. Clericuzio and L. M. Principe (eds), *The Correspondence of Robert Boyle 1636–1691* (6 vols, London, 2004), V, p. 241.
14 R. Hakluyt, *A Particular Discourse Concerning the Great Necessity and Manifold Commodities that Are Like to Grow to This Realm of England by the Western Discoveries Lately Attempted* (1584), p. 1; D. Boruchoff, 'Piety, patriotism, and empire: lessons for England, Spain, and the New World in the works of Richard Hakluyt', *Renaissance Quarterly*, 62 (2009), 809–58.
15 Godwyn, *Negro's & Indians Advocate*, p. 172.
16 I. Mather, *A Brief History of the War with the Indians in New-England* (1676), pp. 1–3; Hunter, Clericuzio and Principe (eds), *Boyle Correspondence*, V, p. 246.
17 Bodl. MS Eng.Hist.e.309, c712, fo. 608.
18 P. Gordon, *Geography Anatomiz'd* (1699), pp. 400–2, original emphasis.
19 National Archives of Scotland, GD/28/5177/36, fo. 3.
20 A. Pagden, *Lords of All the World: Ideologies of Empire in Spain, Britain and France 1492–1830* (New Haven, 1998), pp. 32, 46–7, 51.
21 J. Hall, *Resolutions and Decisions of Divers Practical Cases of Conscience* (1623, republished 1659), pp. 234–5, 247–8.
22 S. Sewall and E. Rawson, *The Revolution in New England Justify'd* (1691), pp. 13–15.
23 M. M. Dunn and R. S. Dunn (eds), *Papers of William Penn* (5 vols, Philadelphia, 1981–6), II, p. 633.
24 J. Winthrop, 'Reasons to be considered for justifying the undertakers of the intended Plantation in New England', 1628; Armitage, *Ideological Origins*, pp. 96–7.
25 C. Molloy, *De Jure Maritimo et Navali: or, A Treatise of Affaires Maritime, and of Commerce* (1676), pp. 421–2; J. Tully, 'Rediscovering America: the *Two Treatises* and Aboriginal Rights', in *An Approach to Political Philosophy: Locke in Contexts* (Cambridge, 1993), pp. 137–76.
26 *The Soveraignty & Goodness of God ... Being a Narrative of the Captivity and Restauration of Mrs Mary Rowlandson* (1682), p. 64.
27 D. Denton, *A Brief Description of New York* (1670), pp. 6–7.
28 Mapperton House, Dorset, Earl of Sandwich's journal, x, 404.
29 M. E. E. Parker (ed.), *North Carolina Charters and Constitutions* (Raleigh, NC, 1963), p. 76; Dunn and Dunn (eds), *Penn Papers*, II, p. 64.
30 *CSPC 1661–8*, item 3.
31 W. Bray (ed.), *The Diary of John Evelyn* (4 vols, London, 1930), II, p. 234.
32 J. H. Pulsipher, *Subjects unto the Same King* (Philadelphia, 2005), pp. 74–9.
33 C. Mather, *The Wonders of the Invisible World* (1693), preface.
34 Bodl. MS Rawlinson A175, 382.
35 R.W. Cogley, *John Eliot's Mission to the Indians before King Philip's War* (Cambridge, MA, 1999); D. J. Silverman, *Faith and Boundaries* (Cambridge, 2005), pp. 1–48.

36 J. Gregory, 'The later Stuart Church and America', in G. Tapsell (ed.), *The Later Stuart Church 1660–1714* (Manchester, 2012), p. 152.
37 M. Sylvester (ed.), *Reliquiae Baxteriana* (1696), bk I, part II, p. 290; Hunter, Clericuzio and Principe (eds), *Boyle Correspondence*, II, pp. 44–5; W. Kellaway, *The New England Company 1649–1776* (London, 1961).
38 M. Goldie et al (eds), *The Entring Book of Roger Morrice* (6 vols, Woodbridge, 2007), IV, p. 10.
39 Bodl. MS Tanner 36, fo. 67; Hunter, Clericuzio and Principe (eds), *Boyle Correspondence*, IV, p. 427.
40 Royal Society Archives, RB1/4/18; Nabil Matar, *Islam in Britain, 1558–1685* (Cambridge, 1998), pp. 125, 142.
41 N. Tyacke, 'From Laudians to Latitudinarians: a shifting balance of theological forces', in Tapsell (ed.), *Later Stuart Church*, pp. 51–2; F. A. MacDonald, *Missions to the Gaels: Reformation and Counter-Reformation in Ulster and the Highlands and Islands of Scotland, 1560–1760* (Edinburgh, 2006), pp. 209–10.
42 G. Jeffreys, *The Argument of the Lord Chief Justice of the Court of King's Bench Concerning the Great Case of Monopolies* (1683), p. 24.
43 Matar, *Islam in Britain*, pp. 50–71; L. Colley, *Captives: Britain, Empire and the World* (London, 2002), chapters 2–4.
44 Hunter, Clericuzio and Principe (eds), *Boyle Correspondence*, V, pp. 309, 311–12.
45 M. Godwyn, *A Supplement to the Negro's [and] Indian's Advocate* (1681), p. 8.
46 J. A. De Jong, *As the Waters Cover the Sea: Millennial Expectations in the Rise of Anglo-American Missions 1640–1810* (London, 1970).
47 BL, Egerton MS, 2,395, fos 433–5; L. A. Breen, 'Praying with the enemy: Daniel Gookin, King Philip's War and the dangers of intercultural mediatorship', in M. J. Daunton and R. Halpern (eds), *Empire and Others: British Encounters with Indigenous Peoples, 1600–1850* (London, 1999), pp. 101–22; J. Drake, *King Philip's War: Civil War in New England 1675–6* (Boston, 1999).
48 LPL, MS 933, 2.
49 D. Defoe, *A Plan of the English Commerce* (1728), pp. 338–9.
50 H. Reilly, *The Impartial History of Ireland* (1749), p. v.
51 Bodl. MS Tanner 29, fo. 126.
52 R. Sanford, *Surinam Justice* (1662), p. 44.
53 Longleat, Coventry MS 76, fo. 63; *CSPC 1677–80*, item 339.
54 P. S. Haffenden, 'The Anglican church in Restoration policy', in J. M. Smith (ed.), *Seventeenth-Century America: Essays in Colonial History* (Chapel Hill, NC, 1959), pp. 179–81; J. B. Bell, *The Imperial Origins of the King's Church in Early America 1607–1783* (Basingstoke, 2004), pp. 13–19.
55 C. G. Pestana, *The English Atlantic in an Age of Revolution, 1640–1661* (Cambridge, Mass., 2004), pp. 3–11, 185–93, 210–17.
56 BL, Additional MS 12,430, fo. 22; TNA, CO 153/1/11; *CSPC 1677–1680*, item 1058.
57 *CSPC 1661–8*, item 512; *CSPC 1669–74*, item 1423.
58 *CSPC 1669–74*, item 1425.
59 *CSPC 1661–8*, item 512.
60 N. H. Keeble and G. F. Nuttall (eds), *Calendar of the Correspondence of Richard Baxter* (2 vols, Oxford, 1991), II, p. 65; D. Pulsifer (ed.), *Acts of the Commissioners of the United Colonies* (2 vols, Boston, 1859), II, pp. 255–60.
61 Sylvester (ed.), *Reliquiae Baxteriana*, II, pp. 265, 279; J. Spurr, *The Restoration Church of England* (New Haven, 1991), pp. 31–42.
62 BL, Additional MS 11,410, fol. 199; *CSPC 1681–5*, item 188.
63 V. Gookin, *Great Case of Transplantation in Ireland Discussed* (1659), p. 3.
64 National Library of Scotland, Wodrow Quarto CV, fol. 111.
65 *CSPC 1681–5*, item 1129.
66 *CSPC 1675–6*, item 953; R. N. Toppan and A. T. Goodrick (eds), *Edward Randolph: Including His Letters and Official Papers* (7 vols, Boston, 1898–1909), IV, p. 272.
67 C. Mather, *A Letter of Advice to the Churches of the Non-conformists in the English Nation* (1700), pp. 3–4, 28.

68 Keeble and Nuttall, *Calendar*, II, pp. 40–1; M. Godwyn, *Trade Preferr'd before Religion and Christ* (1685), pp. 24–5.
69 *Diary of Cotton Mather* (2 vols, New York, 1957), I, p. 429; Rhodes House Library, Oxford, USPG MS A1, fol. 49.
70 Sylvester (ed.), *Reliquiae*, II, pp. 295–6.
71 G. Glickman, 'Catholic interests and the politics of English overseas expansion 1660–1689', *JBS*, 55:4 (2016), 680–708.
72 O. Stanwood, 'The Protestant moment: antipopery, the Revolution of 1688–1689, and the making of an Anglo-American empire', *JBS*, 26 (2007), 481–508.
73 M. Goldie, 'Sir Peter Pett, sceptical Toryism and the science of toleration in the 1680s', in W. J. Sheils (ed.), *Persecution and Toleration* (Studies in Church History, 21, Oxford, 1984), pp. 247–73.
74 P. Pett, *The Happy Future State of England* (1688), pp. 184, 200.
75 Marquis of Lansdowne (ed.), *The Petty Papers* (2 vols, London, 1927), I, pp. 256–7.
76 LPL, Fulham papers, ii, fols 98–9.
77 C. Davenant, *Discourses on the Publick Revenues, and on the Trade of England* (1698), p. 195.
78 Hunter, Clericuzio and Principe (eds), *Boyle Correspondence*, V, pp. 309, 311–12.
79 Godwyn, *Negro's & Indians Advocate*, epistle dedicatory, pp. 132, 172.
80 B. Orr, *Empire on the English Stage, 1660–1714* (Oxford, 2001).
81 BL, Sloane MS 3,512, fol. 283.
82 *The Present interest of Tangiers* (1679), 2; G. Glickman, 'Empire, popery and the fall of English Tangier', *JMH*, 87:2 (2015), 247–80.
83 BL, Additional MS 11,410, fol. 180; Leslie Theibert, 'The making of an English Caribbean' (Yale University PhD dissertation, 2013).
84 S. Pincus, 'From butterboxes to wooden shoes: the shift in English popular sentiment from anti-Dutch to anti-French in the 1670s', *HJ*, 38 (1996), 333–61.
85 A. Grey, *Debates of the House of Commons, from the year 1667 to the year 1694* (10 vols, 1763), VIII, p. 11.
86 *Ibid.*, p. 19.
87 Duke of Buckingham, *A Letter to Sir Thomas Osborn* (1672), pp. 10–11.
88 BL, Additional MS 65,138, fols 77–80.
89 W. Cobbett (ed.), *The Parliamentary History of England* (36 vols., London, 1820), IV, pp. 1116–7.
90 Tony Claydon, *Europe and the Making of England* (Cambridge, 2007), pp. 44–65.
91 J. C. D. Clark, 'Protestantism, nationalism and national identity, 1660–1832', *HJ*, 43 (2000), 249–76.
92 Williamson, 'Empire to end empire', 240–1.
93 G. Wither, *Sigh for the Pitchers* (1666), p. 13.
94 E. Stillingfleet, *A Sermon Preached on the Fast-day, November 13, 1678* (1678), pp. 46–7.
95 T. Claydon and I. McBride (eds), *Protestantism and National Identity: Britain and Ireland c. 1650–1850* (Cambridge, 2007), pp. 1–29.
96 Toppan and Goodrick (eds), *Edward Randolph*, IV, pp. 276, 281.
97 LPL, SPG papers, VII, fols 4–7; Brent S. Sirota, *The Christian Monitors: the Church of England and the Age of Benevolence 1680–1730* (New Haven, 2014), pp. 223–47.
98 R. Strong, 'A vision of an Anglican imperialism: the annual sermons of the Society for the Propagation of the Gospel in Foreign Parts 1701–1714', *Journal of Religious History*, 30:2 (2006), 184–5.
99 E. Haefeli, 'Toleration and empire', in S. Foster (ed.), *British North America in the Seventeenth and Eighteenth Centuries* (Oxford, 2013), pp. 128–30.
100 *CSPC 1698*, item 593.
101 T. Bray, *A Memorial Representing the Present State of Religion, on the Continent of North-America* (1700), p. 9.
102 R. Ferguson, *A Just and Modest Vindication of the Scots Design for having Established a Colony at Darien* (1699), p. 203, original emphasis.
103 *Diary of Cotton Mather*, I, pp. 206–7, 214.

104 *Account of the Society for Propagating the Gospel in Foreign Parts* (1706), pp. 69, 72; Rhodes House Library, Oxford, USPG MS A1, 13, fo. 41.
105 Cambridge University Library, Wanley MSS, SPCK E/1/1.
106 Rhodes House Library, Oxford, USPG MS A1, 119, fo. 45.
107 Kellaway, *New England Company*, p. 192; J. A. Grigg, '"How This Shall be Brought About": the development of the SPCK's American policy', *Itinerario*, 32:3 (2008), 43–60.
108 Gregory, 'Later Stuart church', p. 238.
109 L. Colley, *Britons: Forging the Nation* (London, 1992), pp. 11–71; K. Wilson, *The Sense of the People: Politics, Culture and Imperialism in England 1715–1775* (Cambridge, 1995).
110 P. Stern, *The Company-State: Corporate Sovereignty and the Early Modern Foundations of the British Empire in India* (Oxford, 2011), p. 104.

CHAPTER SIX

Reconciling empire: English political economy and the Spanish imperial model, 1660–90

Leslie Theibert

Spain, 'though Lord of all the treasure of the West-Indies', was in unmistakable decline by the 1670s.[1] From Europe's dominant power in the sixteenth and early seventeenth centuries, when Hapsburg threats of universal monarchy had frightened all of Protestant Europe, Spain had become 'weak and feeble', particularly in the face of the rising menace from Louis XIV's France.[2] Across the continent, political and economic commentators recognised that years of warfare and economic mismanagement, combined with weak leadership under King Carlos II, had resulted in a series of embarrassing defeats to the French and Portuguese and the loss of Spain's European supremacy.[3] To Whig political economist Roger Coke, this decline appeared paradoxical, as Spain possessed 'greater dominions than any kingdom of the western or perhaps of the eastern world'.[4] Yet the conquest of territory and influx of treasure from around the globe had not made the country powerful.

Coke and other seventeenth-century political economists argued that possession of this overseas empire had rendered the Hapsburg monarchy obsolete, as it sapped the country of its most valuable resource: its people. When discussing the benefits or dangers of empire, Coke and his allies used 'the example of Spain, which they say is almost ruined by the depopulation which the West-Indies hath occasioned'.[5] The loss of domestic population to the American colonies, they believed, had proved devastating for the economic health of the nation. With this cautionary tale before them Coke and others warned of the dangers to England if it followed in the path of Spain, as 'his Majesty's plantations abroad, have very much prejudiced this kingdom by draining us of our people'.[6] For these political economists, imperial expansion, and the population loss that it engendered, were ultimately against the interests of the nation.

Yet Coke's warnings fell on deaf ears, as the English empire expanded rapidly through the 1660s and 1670s. While the calls to emulate the

Spanish that had permeated early English colonial projects faded from English imperial discourse, the Stuart monarchs of the Restoration took firm steps to bring the governance of empire under greater metropolitan control and regulate the economy of that empire through monopoly companies.[7] In so doing, they sought to create an empire like that of their Spanish counterparts – conquering territory, acquiring a subservient labouring population and organising colonial trade through the metropole in favour of the Crown. For all their critique of the Spanish empire and England's ostensible differences from it, the English empire came to resemble the Spanish far more over the course of the second half of the seventeenth century, and Spain remained the dominant, if no longer hegemonic, power in the Americas.[8]

Across the English Atlantic empire, conflicting understandings of the prosperity and failures of the Spanish empire reflected wider divisions about imperial political economy that emerged through the Restoration. Historians disagree on the exact nature of the ideology and practice of this political economy, variously calling the later seventeenth-century programmes 'mercantilist' and 'land-based'. According to imperial historians of the early and mid-twentieth century, mercantilists believed there was a finite amount of land, trade and bullion in the world, and whatever was not owned by one nation would be controlled by another. Mercantilism, the shared political economic ideology of all European states, considered trade to be a zero-sum game in which land, labourers, plantations, mines and the power that accompanied these economic resources could be transferred from one European power to another.[9] Recent historiography has complicated this picture, demonstrating that a mercantilist political economy was far from universal and consisted of multiple strands of belief about the production and value of land, labour and trade.[10] According to Steve Pincus, mercantilist ideas held by the emerging Tory party stemmed from the belief that wealth was based in land and therefore finite, while the emerging Whigs believed in the prospect of infinite wealth produced through labour.[11] Other historians argue that these programmes were both less monolithic and less ideologically motivated than Pincus suggests, as members of both parties held a wide range of political economic positions and actions often resulted from immediate circumstance rather than firm ideology.[12]

Divergent ideas about the source of wealth and rival programmes for how to increase this wealth did emerge in the second half of the seventeenth century and map onto Whig and Tory party platforms.[13] Furthermore, these conflicting beliefs led to distinctive ideas about the value of and programmes for the development of an imperial political economy. Yet these agendas were neither monolithic nor based solely in differing ideas about land and labour: both groups understood that economic expansion depended to an extent on an increase in production through labour, and deep divisions ran through these parties as to how best to increase England's prosperity.

The Stuart and then Tory mercantilists believed that wealth was potentially finite, and therefore they advocated for an empire like that of Spain based on the capture of limited resources like territory, bullion and trade from rival empires. They sought to protect and regulate this trade through the creation of monopolies like the Royal African Company (RAC). Yet they also recognised the central role of labour in the production of goods and advocated for the import of labour from both Europe and Africa in an effort to reproduce the labour supply Spain had discovered in the New World. Domestic production, they argued, would not suffer so long as the goods produced in the colonies returned to be manufactured at home.

Emerging Whigs, meanwhile, believed in the potential for infinite growth. They advocated for an increase in English domestic labour and production and sought to free overseas trade from stifling regulations like monopolies. For these Whigs, Spain served as a warning of what could occur when a country became depopulated. Yet at the same time, differing ideas about whether colonists constituted English labourers led to conflicting perceptions of the value of overseas colonies to English economic development. On the frontiers of empire, colonists put these programmes into action and adapted their ideas about political economy to circumstances on the ground. While they largely aligned with English domestic politics, promoting the seizure of resources from overseas rivals or peaceful circumstances in which to expand trade, imperial regulations like those of the RAC that held support at home met with a variety of resistance in a local colonial setting. Formulated in England and tested on the frontiers of empire, transatlantic ideologies of imperial political economy emerged throughout the Restoration.

We can see these diverging ideas about the political economy of empire and the extent to which political economic thinkers hoped to build a Spanish-style empire in attitudes towards the RAC. In many ways, this company resembled the trading monopolies of the Spanish state-controlled but privately owned *casa de la contratación* (house of trade), but was designed to penetrate Spanish American markets and usurp trade from their rivals, most particularly the Dutch. While Whigs and Tories in England debated the value and structure of the Company, their colonial counterparts developed linked, though by no means identical, ideas about what a monopoly slave-trading company meant for the progress of empire. Ultimately, the question of slavery, the slave trade and the RAC would prove central to English debates about the potential for empire. For Tories in both London and the Caribbean, the import of slaves would allow them to Hispanise the Caribbean, creating a subservient labour force like that of the Spanish empire, while both infiltrating markets controlled by their imperial rivals and regulating the trade in favour of the state through a monopoly company.[14] For the Whigs, slavery and the slave trade provided a solution to the problem of population loss from the mother country, expanding the total productive capacity of Britain across the Atlantic world.[15] Though a topic of serious controversy through the later seventeenth century, the RAC helped to reconcile competing ideas about imperial economic development and create a British plantation economy in the Caribbean to rival that of Spain.

Tory political economy
Metropolitan goals and the RAC

Though they did not directly compare themselves with the Spanish empire, through the Restoration Charles II and James II pursued a series of economic programmes designed to create a British empire in the Spanish image and challenge their most powerful rival in the Caribbean. They disagreed with Whigs like Coke about the causes of Spanish imperial decline, and believed that control of colonial land, labour and 'the excess and predominancy [sic] of foreign trade' regulated by the state was necessary for England's increasing overseas wealth and power.[16] As a result, they sought to expand the land mass of their empire across the world, import a labour supply and increase trade at the expense of their rivals through state regulation and monopoly companies like the RAC. By the 1680s, these ideas about the political economy of the empire would become identified with a wider Tory programme that included alliance with the French against the Dutch, primacy of the monarchy and use of the royal prerogative.

One of the goals of the emerging Tories was the expansion of imperial territory, which they did through marriage, warfare and proprietary grants. The Stuart kings gained Tangier and Bombay with the Portuguese match, supported new proprietary colonies in coveted areas like Carolina, New Jersey and the Bahamas, and promoted attacks on the Dutch and Spanish in New York and across the Caribbean. In so doing, they took land either claimed or occupied by their European rivals in the Americas. They hoped to expand further, suggesting the plantation of colonies in the valuable land near the Spanish empire where, 'if they have been at first planted … they would be this time have run down as far as the silver mines'.[17]

This territory would need to be held by a settler population and worked by labourers coming from Europe, the Americas or Africa. Stuart imperial promoters and Tory political economists like Carew Reynell and president of the East India Company Josiah Child recognised 'lands (though excellent) without hands proportionable will not enrich any kingdom'.[18] In this they resembled their Spanish counterparts, who argued for the centrality of settlement to the success of the early empire.[19] Yet while they accepted that labour was essential to imperial production, they did not believe that empire had depopulated Spain, and therefore were not concerned that it would prove a danger to England's domestic population or economic capabilities. Instead, Tory political economists argued that it was Spain's intolerant religious policies, such as the use of the Inquisition and expulsion of the *moriscos*, that had led to population decline. More importantly, poor monetary policy, interest rate management and a decline in manufactures resulting from a flood of cheap foreign imports were ultimately responsible for a large portion of Spain's economic trouble. The profits of empire accrued to other European countries because Spain imported rather than producing goods for colonial consumption, a problem that England could easily avoid in its own empire by promoting domestic manufacturing.[20] The colonies would provide raw materials to fuel manufacturing in England, and as it was 'customary in most of our islands in America, upon every plantation, to employ eight or ten blacks for one white servant', the total number of labourers producing goods to be refined in England would expand exponentially.[21]

An increase in colonial goods to be refined at home would allow England to produce new commodities and usurp the trade of their rivals, particularly the Dutch. Yet in order to ensure that population movement to the colonies was not a drain on the kingdom and that these goods returned to provide employment at home, England had to require that 'trade be restrained to their mother kingdom'.[22] In addition, further regulations were needed to ensure that the benefits of trade accrued to the state, rather than just individual merchants. According to Child, 'trading merchants' were not necessarily 'the best judges of trade, as it relates to the profit or power of a kingdom', because of their focus on individual profit rather than 'what is most advantageous to the kingdom in general'.[23] Thus, as with the Spanish *casa de la contratación*, the state needed monopoly companies to regulate that trade for the financial benefit of the nation. The Stuarts granted certain joint-stock and regulated companies the exclusive right to trade, particularly in areas that demanded infrastructure and fortification like the western coast of Africa.[24]

One of the most important realms of regulation was in the trade of people themselves through the RAC. As the RAC would bring more labourers to the Americas and ensure that the profits from that trade found their way to state coffers, the RAC became a model of Stuart political economic policy. Re-chartered by Charles II in 1672 under the governorship of his brother James, Duke of York, the joint-stock company received exclusive monopoly trading rights to the west coast of Africa and 'such powers and privileges as shall be most convenient for the advancement and carrying on' of a 'sole trade'.[25] The Company argued that this monopoly was necessary to both protect the trade and render it economically viable – bringing labourers to the colonies and profit to merchants and the state. Because it limited the trade to a few English merchants, excluding all those outside of the Company structure, the RAC could negotiate for slaves at lower prices and sell their limited supply of slaves at higher prices in the Caribbean, providing revenues which could then be used to maintain the fortified factories along the African coast that protected the English from Dutch, French and local African attack.[26] One petition from the RAC argued that 'we have struggled under great difficulties to support the great expense of maintaining our forts and factories abroad, whereby we have kept the African trade from falling wholly into the hands of the Dutch'.[27]

As Stuart political economists believed that trade was a zero-sum game, the acquisition of trade from rival European states was a central goal of their policies. Monopoly companies like the RAC would aid them in the capture of this trade through both the defense of their bases on the western coast of Africa and the infiltration of the Spanish monopoly of trade to the West Indies, challenging the Dutch for the right to the *asiento de negros* in order to prevent them 'from monopolising all the wealth of the Indies'.[28] Spain was entitled only to colonies in the western hemisphere under the 1494 treaty of Tordesillas, and therefore contracted foreign merchants to bring slaves from the African coast to the Spanish ports of the Caribbean through the Asiento. While the Genoese merchant Domingo Grillo held the Asiento in the 1660s and sub-contracted out to the Dutch West India Company, by the 1670s governor of Jamaica John, Lord Vaughn, suggested that there was 'a good opportunity for our Royal Company to endeavor the making of a contract with them, which would exceedingly contribute to the interest of England and of this island'.[29] Within six years Vaughn's programme succeeded, as Spanish American governors began to send to Jamaica for slaves provided by the RAC.

Monopoly companies not only advanced a particular vision of political economy, however, but also the relative power of the monarchy in relation to Parliament through the privileging of the royal prerogative. This 'special right or privilege exercised by a monarch over all other persons', included the powers of 'making treaties, making war and concluding peace', choosing ministers, regulating the succession and calling

Parliament.[30] Through the 1670s, Charles II sought to extend these prerogative rights, and his increasingly Whig opponents argued that the charters given by the king were invalid because the right to regulate trade and commerce belonged to Parliament.[31] In the 1685 case of *Sandy's vs. the East India Company*, Tory Lord Chief Justice George Jeffreys confirmed that, as the king had the right to make war and peace, and as commercial treaties and alliances depended on the control of trade, the king possessed and could continue his 'prerogative, of restraining, disposing, and ordering matters of commerce and foreign trade, by royal licenses, charters, and dispensations'.[32] This extension of the prerogative represented only one strand of a much broader attempt by the later Stuart monarchs to extend their control over both the nation and the empire, by, for example, revoking colonial charters and appointing royal governors who answered directly to the king, just as their Spanish counterparts did.[33] Thus, the legality of the monopoly upon which the early slave trade depended was inextricably linked to Stuart and increasingly Tory ideas about the role of the monarch and the political future of the nation.

By the 1680s, a strain of political economic thought that promoted an increase in wealth through the seizure of economic assets from rival empires and control through monopoly companies dominated the Stuart imperial economic agenda. For the emerging Tories of the 1680s the Spanish empire was not an example to be avoided, but one to be both seized and emulated through imperial expansion, growth of labour and company regulation. Moreover, these ideas had become linked to the emerging Tory party within England under Charles II and James II. An imperial programme that challenged Dutch control of trade, combined with a belief in the value of the royal prerogative which underpinned these companies and the support of many Tory leaders, most notably James himself, made this a political programme as well as an economic one.

Tory political economy in practice: the case of Jamaica

These debates about the political economy of empire and the example of Spain extended to the colonies through the Restoration period. As in England, multiple perspectives on the value of imperial expansion, economic regulation and the RAC divided those making economic choices on the fringes of empire, where colonists adapted debates to local circumstances. These fissures are particularly evident in the Caribbean, where colonies depended on the slave trade for economic growth and Spain was not a theoretical empire to be discussed but a potent imperial rival that required regular engagement. On the island of Jamaica, rival factions endorsed conflicting economic programmes, and these factions came to identify with Tory and Whig ideas of empire and political economy by the 1680s. The Company was widely unpopular across all sections of the island, but competing factions offered different kinds of opposition to the RAC, and those who sympathised with the Tories directed their antagonism not towards the monopoly, but the RAC's choice to prioritise the slave trade to Spanish America at the expense of increased plantation labour.

One group within the island endorsed what would be a Tory vision of imperial economy by the 1680s, and advocated a programme in which Jamaica should seize the assets of the Spanish empire and build powerful plantations through the import of a native labour force.[34] Dominated by governors Sir Thomas Modyford and Sir Henry Morgan with the support of more 'mercantilist' imperial agents like the duke of Albemarle, this faction promoted Stuart programmes of imperial expansion and bullion extraction through privateering and treasure hunting.[35] They actively pursued the acquisition of new colonies, taking the islands of Providence from the Spanish in 1665, Saba and St Eustasia from the Dutch in the same year, and sending an expedition to expel the Carib Indians from St Lucia in 1667. Into the 1670s they continued to assure supporters in England that, if given the opportunity, they could continue their expansion at the expense of rival empires.[36]

In Jamaica, privateering offered one potential way to seize land, bullion and trade from Spanish enemies, and the English hoped that this 'forced trade' would encourage the Spanish to open their ports.[37] Port Royal became a privateering centre through the 1660s, as Governor Modyford offered letters of marque for legal raids and the city provided a safe haven in which admiralty courts condemned goods.[38] Under the leadership of Henry Morgan, the buccaneers sacked towns across the Spanish Main through the 1660s and despite initial attempts to suppress privateering through the 1670s, Governor Vaughn complained that Sir Henry continued in his support of the privateers despite direct orders to the contrary.[39] As defence of privateering became politically untenable in the 1680s, this faction pursued other forms of bullion acquisition, primarily through the fishing of wrecked Spanish treasure ships under Morgan and the second duke of Albemarle, appointed governor in 1687.[40] Albemarle's 1686 expedition to Hispaniola under William Phips found the *Concepción* and brought back £300,000 in gold and silver.[41]

This faction sought to put the Stuart programmes of imperial political economy into practice, seizing the economic assets of rival empires, and by the 1680s this faction declared their affiliation with the Tories at home, naming themselves the 'Loyal Club' and leaving their political opponents to opine that Morgan 'hoped to be thought head of the Tories' rendering their opponents 'of the Whigs'.[42] Again as in England, they linked their economic programmes with support for the royal prerogative through support for the royal governor in the Jamaican Constitution Crisis and James, Duke of York, in the Exclusion Crisis.[43] Yet despite this link between economic and other political programmes under a party banner, the self-identified Tory faction opposed one major tenant of Tory political economy in England – the RAC and the Asiento trade to Spanish America.

Jamaican Tories' dislike of the Asiento was not a result of opposition to slavery itself, or even a challenge to the RAC's monopoly.[44] Rather, they resented that their political allies in England suppressed Jamaican Tory programmes designed to capture assets from their imperial rivals in favour of peace and trade with Spain, which the Tories deemed a low priority.[45] They complained that the Asiento took much-needed slaves from the island's planters, whose burgeoning sugar plantations could not be productive without a labour supply, damaging the production of colonial goods advocated by Child and others. In response to the RAC's pro-Spanish policies, the Jamaican Tories sought to tax any slaves exported to Spanish colonies, 'occasioned by the merchants supplying the Spaniard with great numbers of negroes rather than the planters, whose necessities pressed them much for a good supply'.[46] Their opposition also manifested itself in outright attacks on both the Company factors and attempts to 'seize the Spaniards' who came to the island to trade.[47]

For the Jamaican Tories, wealth came from the acquisition of new territory, labourers and bullion. The sacrifice of programmes in which these men not only believed but also participated for trade with the Spanish meant that the economic goals of the RAC did not translate on the imperial periphery. Instead, the Company threatened colonial efforts to build an empire like that of Spain in the Caribbean through the capture of resources from their rivals.

Whig political economy
Empire, labour and the emergence of Whig political economies

Despite the power of Tory imperial political economy and the monopoly companies it protected, many people across the empire disagreed with its vision, fearing the dangers of imperial expansion and gesturing to the Spanish as a model of how empire could destroy a national economy. Far from a monolithic mercantilist ideology, questions about the sources of wealth and the value of empire were hotly debated. Political economists who would become identified with the Whig party argued that trade was not a zero-sum game in which any gains had to be made at the expense of an imperial rival. Rather, the potential for trade was infinite and depended on labour to produce new manufactured goods, labour they could ill afford to lose to the growing colonies.[48] Advocates of this policy agreed that foreign trade and manufacturing would bring wealth to the kingdom, but as they did not see it as finite, they opposed any restrictions, like monopoly companies, that might limit the potential for growth. In so doing, they argued that Spain was not an imperial model to be emulated but one to be avoided, either because empire had caused domestic decline, or because that empire was incorrectly managed.

These Whig political economists argued that labour, industry and trade lay at the heart of economic prosperity. 'Trade must be the principle interest of England', and was 'the only means to enrich this kingdom'.[49] Unlike the mercantilists, however, they argued that wealth was not taken directly from rivals, but created through the production of new goods, which could then be traded both within England and overseas. For successful economic growth through manufacture and trade, these political economists believed that the nation needed a strong domestic labour supply and a flourishing population. They asserted that the 'multitude and concourse of people advance trade', and promoted policies like easy immigration and naturalisation that would lead to population growth.[50]

Yet if the strength and wealth of the nation depended on the labour of its people, England faced a crisis because of its declining population.[51] Early seventeenth century colonial promoters had drawn on concerns that England was overpopulated to promote emigration to the empire, arguing that colonies were valuable as an outlet for a poor population grown too numerous to be sustained on English soil.[52] With the reversal of this demographic trend, many labour-centred political economists argued that the empire weakened England by drawing off its much-needed labour supply. According to Roger Coke in his 1671 *A Discourse of Trade*, the 'trade of *England*, and the fishing trade, are so much diminished, by how much they might have been supplied, by those men who are diverted in our *American* plantations'.[53] William Petty, author of the seminal *Political Arithmetick*, agreed that colonies could be 'a source of competition or a drain on population'.[54] Whig author Slingsby Bethel argued that empire was not in the true interest of the nation, writing that 'the experience of all former times showeth us, that foreign acquisitions, have ever been chargeable, and prejudicial to the people of England'.[55] These political economists opposed continued imperial expansion, arguing that projects like the 1660 Carolina colony 'so much more enfeeble this nation, and reduce the trade thereof to so much a less proportion by how many men shall be withdrawn from it'.[56]

These authors looked directly to Spain as an example of the damage that empire could do to a country. All agreed that Spain had been 'brought at this time low, and into a languishing condition', with a decline in agricultural output and manufacturing that translated into weakness on the international stage.[57] Authors like Coke argued that the Spanish decline had come from a loss of population, particularly from the 'the transporting so many Spaniards into the West-Indies' and the lack of immigration due to 'the Inquisition which bars out any future supply'.[58] These political economists feared that England was following this path, suggesting that 'Ireland and our plantations do in proportion to England more exhaust it of men than the West-Indies do Spain; and if no provision be made will in less time than since the West-Indies came to be subject to the Crown of Spain leave it less peopled.'[59] Furthermore, as the colonies failed to attract large enough populations to protect themselves against foreign encroachment, 'all the smaller Kingdoms and Dominions, instead of being additions, are really diminutions'.[60] For these political economists, who would become increasingly Whig through the 1670s, empire weakened the economic base of the nation and hindered, rather than expanded, the manufacturing and trade upon which national wealth depended. They argued against the increase in imperial territory, particularly that taken from European rivals, as a drain on England's population.

Despite concerns about a decline in labour, however, many other Whig political economists who accepted value in labour and trade instead saw the colonies as a source of ever-expanding wealth, recognising that empire had brought new products and trade to the Spanish throughout the sixteenth and seventeenth centuries. If goods grown or manufactured in the colonies could be considered the produce of 'greater England', then the emigration of men and women to the New World did not mean a net loss of labour. The plantations, they argued, did not deplete the nation's productive labour supply, but turned the poor and prisoners into productive servants and planters who could produce new 'English' products as they had done in the early seventeenth century. These political economists did not see the colonies as separate from England, but an extension of England's land mass; those labourers leaving the mother country would still be used to produce products and consume goods within a widened domestic market. One commentator, Andrew Orgill, argued that in the colonies 'as their number of inhabitants increase so will the commodities increase, and so much the more of the manufactures of this place will be taken off from the merchant for ready pay, to the great augmentation of the trade in general'.[61] The colonies provided opportunities for previously under-utilised labour to work in the production of new commodities.

For these political economists, the colonies provided new opportunities for import substitution and an increase in general trade. Like their

Tory counterparts, they argued that goods that could not be produced in England could be grown in the Americas and provide new sources of trade and manufacturing at home. A 1671 account argued that the Caribbean colonies 'produce all such commodities as are fit for our market, and cannot be produced here, which if encouraged will prove of infinite advantage to the trade and navigation of this kingdom'.[62] The instructions for the 1672 Council of Trade written by future Whigs Shaftesbury and Locke argued that the plantations benefitted the nation by growing produce not available in England, and they gave explicit orders for the planters to attempt to grow East Indian produce in the Americas.[63]

However, these Whig political economists differed from the Tories in the ways in which they believed this trade should be regulated. They argued that plantation production led to an increase in manufacturing, which in turn led to an increase in trade. As trade was potentially unlimited, regulations like the Navigation Acts and monopolies like the RAC damaged national wealth by restricting the growth of trade. Roger Coke asserted that 'the trade of *England*, and the fishing trade are so much hindered, by how many men, and so much money and stock as are excluded by corporations ... For any business will be so much hindered, by how much the means of improving it are excluded.'[64]

Because they considered the colonies to be part of a greater England, these Whigs recognised the potential of these colonists as new consumers of English products. As an increase in colonial wealth led to a growth in consumption, the state export monopoly dictated by the Navigation Acts hurt domestic production by restricting the growth of plantation wealth and therefore consumption. The plantations, they argued, provided a profitable market for English manufactures, as the colonists 'must be supplied with clothes and all kind of our manufactories from hence, because their countries are not capable of producing them'.[65] This need for manufactures in the colonies, it was argued 'will beget great employment for his Majesty's subjects' in England, as well as work for 'our merchants ships to export our commodities to them, and import theirs to us'.[66] The number and diversity of manufactures exported to the colonies grew exponentially over the Restoration period, and by 1686 the London merchants exported over £200,000 a year in manufactured goods to the American and West Indian colonies.[67]

These Whig political economists supported the slave trade, recognising that imported African slaves increased the total number of labourers producing and consuming in the English market, but argued that monopoly companies like the RAC had the same limiting effect as the Navigation Acts. According to one colonial estimate, by the 1670s the slave trade brought in 20,000 new labourers to produce colonial commodities like sugar, indigo, tobacco, cotton and cacao.[68] Many of these political economists hoped that the expanded trade in slaves would open access to the Asiento and provide a new and legal path to trade in Spanish America that would avoid the costly route through Seville.[69] The slave trade also served to reconcile those Whigs most concerned about a decline in the domestic labour supply. In notoriously unhealthy Caribbean colonies like Jamaica where thousands of new immigrants died each year, replacing English immigrants and indentured labourers with African slaves relieved the burden on the English population, and the changing sources of labour in vast swaths of the English American empire helped to allay fears of fleeing labour by the end of the century.[70] Yet Whig political economists vehemently opposed the organisation of this trade through the RAC and argued against the use of monopolies.[71] By the early 1690s, merchants across the Atlantic world were clamouring for an end to the monopoly of the joint-stock company and their exclusion from the African trade.[72] If one believed that growth from trade was limited, then the creation of monopoly companies that could establish and defend factories from trade rivals made sense, especially if the person in question had access to that monopoly. If trade was unlimited, however, the restriction of that trade to a small group of people curtailed the possibilities for growth. This was particularly important in the slave trade, as these slaves could provide additional plantation labour, allowing Englishmen to remain in England.

Just as the emerging Tories saw the connection between the promotion of monopolies and the expanded power of the royal prerogative, the Whigs recognised that royal monopolies advanced the authority of the monarch at the expense of Parliament.[73] They further opposed all attempts to extend royal power through the crises of the 1670s and 1680s, seeing in these monarchical efforts the potential transformation of both the nation and empire into an absolutist state like that of their southern rivals, where 'tyrannous princes and their wicked ministers' governed a weakened Spain.[74] According to Bethel, Spain had over-expanded, enfeebled the nation domestically, and rendered the American colonies vulnerable by 'disdaining all dominion not founded in arbitrary and absolute will'.[75] A push to alter the balance of power between the monarch and Parliament endangered English freedoms in both England and the empire, freedoms that underpinned the economic health of the nation. It was 'justice, good laws, and liberty', rather than any natural advantages that led to an increase in people and industry and made the nation economically, and therefore politically, powerful.[76] Thus, these political economists linked their economic programmes to political concerns.

For the Whig political economists, the Spanish empire represented a positive danger to be avoided, rather than one to be emulated. Many of them feared continued colonial expansion and the drain on domestic labour that it produced. Even those who saw the advantages of empire opposed the Spanish-style trading monopolies advanced by their Tory rivals, arguing that, if wealth and trade were infinite, then there was no need to challenge the Spanish for imperial dominance or limit that trade to companies that promoted monarchical power over that of Parliament. By the 1680s, rival political economies of empire had emerged that mapped onto Whig and Tory party positions, as fears of the royal prerogative, which protected monopolies and a Tory idea of imperial political economy, joined with rising concerns about an absolutist and Catholic monarch into a Whig ideology.[77]

Whig political economy in Jamaica

Like their English counterparts, many planters and merchants in Jamaica strongly supported programmes of plantation growth and inter-imperial trade underpinned by a belief in infinite wealth. While no one in the colonies doubted the value of the empire in which they participated, many agreed with the programmes of men like Shaftesbury and Locke that promoted plantation production and sugar manufacturing on the island and searched for a legal means to access the trade to Spanish America as sources of ever-expanding economic growth. Like the Whigs in England, this group connected a desire for infinite economic wealth to a fear of attempts to regulate the imperial government and wealth production, and strongly opposed the RAC and its monopoly, arguing that it excluded merchants and limited supply. In both their promotion of plantations and trade and in their support for the island's assembly in the Jamaican Constitutional Crisis, this faction became 'Whiggish'.[78]

This faction, led by Thomas Lynch, included a variety of planters and merchants on the island such as William Beeston, Peter Beckford and Samuel Long. These colonists argued that rival programmes of imperial expansion and privateering threatened their efforts at economic expansion. Like many political economists in England, they opposed the acquisition of new islands, asserting that further conquest would damage the current plantations, causing war and 'an end to the improvement begun and designed at Jamaica'.[79] They argued that the privateers drew away needed labour in the form of white indentured servants in the 1660s, angered the Spanish government and caused the inhabitants of coastal communities to flee from a newly arrived ship, fearing that it was a buccaneer come to sack the town rather than a peaceful trader.[80] As lieutenant governor in the 1670s and 1680s, Lynch effectively ended the island's reputation as a bastion of privateering.

Lynch and his faction argued the direct capture of land and bullion was not in the best interest of the island. Instead they asserted that trade with the Spanish Indies would allow the island to thrive economically.[81] Like their patrons in England, their arguments for this trade prioritised English access to new goods in exchange for English manufactures, rather than on depriving their imperial rivals. By the 1680s, a prominent smuggling trade between Jamaica and Spanish America had emerged in the smaller ports around the Caribbean, as merchants sent a variety of manufactured goods, particularly cloth, to the Spanish colonies, in exchange for 'much money and great quantities of hides, cocoa etc. imported by our trading sloops'.[82] For trade with the major Spanish American outposts, the English needed a legal means, which they found in the *asiento de negros*. While the English had been trying to send slaves to Spanish America since the revivification of the RAC, the 1682 reports that the Asiento in Spain is 'broke' provided an opening for the English in Jamaica to trade directly with the Spanish, as governors from Havana to Panama, desperate for slaves to work the newly discovered gold mines, received permission to buy slaves in other parts of the Caribbean.[83] The location and supply of slaves to Jamaica meant that Spanish governors sent their factors to trade on the island, and the English soon convoyed slaves to major ports like Cartagena, taking the slaves into Spanish territory and returning with Spanish bullion and merchandise.[84]

Lynch and his merchant allies, particularly Hender Molesworth and Charles Penhallow, his fellow RAC factors, actively promoted this trade with the Spaniards, which was extremely profitable.[85] Yet the island's commerce was limited by the RAC's willingness and capability to send slaves to Jamaica, and even RAC factors like Lynch and Molesworth complained that a dearth of slaves prevented them from filling the demands of either the planters or the *asientistas*: Molesworth wrote home, 'what precious opportunities' in the Spanish slave trade 'are lost for want of negroes'.[86] A limited supply of slaves jeopardised both the desire for an expanding population of labourers in the colonies and an expansion of the trade to Spanish America. Lynch and his Jamaican allies prioritised supply over the RAC's desire to preserve its monopoly and suppress interlopers. Lynch allowed interloping merchants to land slaves on the island when necessary.[87] While about 27,730 slaves arrived on the island of Jamaica in the 1680s, more than 7,000 more than in the previous decade, the RAC's deliveries account for only 17,449 slaves between 1680 and 1689.[88] Lynch wrote home in 1683 that, despite a new agreement with the Company to provide 3,000 slaves a year, 'these little hopes of a supply for such a trade, while the planters themselves want so exceedingly' were 'like to be lost' due to the RAC's failures to supply the market.[89]

Lynch and the Company's factors offered tacit support for the Company, but many members of this faction openly opposed the

Company's monopoly because it excluded them from legal participation in the Spanish slave trade. Through the 1670s merchants participated in an active smuggling trade importing slaves to Jamaica and the Spanish colonies against the monopolies of both the RAC and the Asiento, despite the Company's efforts to suppress the interloping merchants.[90] Moreover, like the Whigs in England, this faction began to connect their opposition to the monopoly of the RAC to wider concerns over attempts to use the royal prerogative to secure greater direct metropolitan control over the island's government. In 1680, the middle of Jamaica's Constitutional Crisis, several Jamaican proto-Whigs arrived to England with a petition from Jamaica's planters and merchants that the Duke of York 'interpose with the Royal African Company to furnish this island annually with a plentiful supply of negroes at moderate rates'.[91] Jamaica's merchants further requested that the RAC be forced to open up the African trade and restructure the company as a regulated rather than a joint-stock company, available to 'any of his Majesty's subjects' who 'may at any time be admitted to trade'.[92] According to the Jamaican merchants, the new company would bring in much-needed labour and replace the joint-stock company, which, they asserted, had not 'added any thing to the increase, support, and maintenance of any of his Majesty's dominions'.[93] The Lords of Trade offered a compromise over the RAC to the island's planters, suggesting that the company be required to provide the island with 3,000 slaves at £18 a head, yet through the 1680s merchants and planters repeatedly complained that the 'Royal Africa Company have not in any reasonably measure complied' with the post-Crisis agreement.[94]

Divergent views of political economy that mirrored those of their metropolitan counterparts divided Jamaica's planters and colonists. While one faction endorsed a mercantilist Stuart imperial programme based on the capture of land, bullion and trade from imperial rivals and sought to Hispanise the English Caribbean, the other promoted ideas of infinite economic growth through plantation produce and trade in slaves and manufactured goods with foreign empires, hoping to trade with rather than replicate their Spanish neighbours. Their increasing dependence on slave labour and the Spanish American slave trade led both of these factions to oppose the RAC, as those who called themselves 'Tories' protested against the prioritisation of the Spanish trade, while those who embraced infinite wealth complained of the limits the monopoly placed on the island's economic growth. Yet despite this dislike of the RAC, the island remained dependent upon the continued import of slaves, made possible by the Company's infrastructure, financing and English political support. As in England, one of the most divisive imperial programmes also proved vital to the political and economic success of the empire.

In the second half of the seventeenth century, divergent ideas about the future economic development of England and its empire emerged across the Atlantic world and became identified with Whig and Tory party platforms. For the Tories, who identified wealth with production from the land, the capture of territory, bullion and foreign trade became an economic priority. In so doing, they sought to emulate the Spanish by both replicating and seizing the assets of their imperial rivals. For the Whigs, the potential for production through increased manufacturing depended on the growth of labour, an increase in production and the freeing of trade from state regulations. For many Whigs, the Spanish provided a cautionary tale of the dangers of depopulation through imperial over-extension. Yet for others, imperial expansion, if done correctly, could increase the total number of labourers within the English empire, provide new products and markets and expand the trade of the country. In the Caribbean, colonists held similar diverging ideas about imperial political economy, promoting confrontation or trade with their Spanish rivals. Yet imperial regulations like the RAC proved a source of tension, driving political allies apart as they battled for control of labour in the region.

For all the controversy it generated, the RAC proved vital to the success of the early English empire. By the late 1690s, political change and the rise of the Whigs and merchants to power allowed them to alter the nature of the company itself, opening to merchants as the regulated company so desired by the Jamaican interlopers. Yet one of the fundamental goals and sources of division, the Spanish trade and the Asiento, would soon be taken again by a monopoly in the form of the South Sea Company. While Whigs and Tories disagreed about the importance of labour in the production of imperial wealth, the RAC and the slave trade it made possible to reconcile those who wished to Hispanise the Caribbean with those who feared a loss of domestic labour and those who wished to trade with the Spanish in the Caribbean.

Notes

1 R. Coke, *A Discourse of Trade in Two Parts* (1670), p. 11.
2 *Ibid*. The English criticised not only Spain's overseas programme, but also their monarchical form of government and religious intolerance. J. Elliott, 'Learning from the enemy: early modern Britain and Spain', in *Spain, Europe, and the Wider World* (New Haven, 2009), pp. 41–3.
3 For traditional views of Spanish economic and political decline in the seventeenth century see R. Trevor Davies, *Spain in Decline, 1621–1700* (London, 1957); J. Elliott, 'The decline of Spain', *P&P*, 20 (1961), 217–40; J. Elliott, 'Self-perception and decline in early seventeenth century Spain', *P&P*, 74 (1977), 41–61; J. Israel, 'The decline of Spain: a historical myth?', *P&P*, 91 (1981), 170–85; J. Lynch, *The Hispanic World in Crisis and Change* (Oxford, 1992). For claims that Spain remained powerful and that this decline was relative rather than absolute See H. Kamen, 'The decline of Spain:

a historical myth?, P&P, 81 (1978), 24–50; C. Storrs, *The Resilience of the Spanish Monarchy, 1665–1700* (Oxford, 2006). For a historiographical account of the decline of Spain see R. L. Kagan, 'Prescott's paradigm: American historical scholarship and the decline of Spain', *AHR*, 101:2 (1996), 423–46.
4 Coke, *Discourse of Trade*, p. 11.
5 J. Child, *A New Discourse of Trade* (1668), pp. 164–5. This idea originally came from Giovanni Botero, *The Reason of State*, trans. P. J. and D. P. Waley (London, 1956), pp. 143–6, 11–12, cited in Elliott, 'Learning from the enemy', p. 40.
6 Coke, *Discourse of Trade*, p. 12; Child, *A New Discourse*, pp. 164–5.
7 On early emulation, see J. Hart, *Representing the New World: English and French Uses of the Example of Spain* (New York, 2001); A. L. Hatfield, 'Spanish colonization literature, Powhatan geographies, and English perceptions of Tsenacommacah/Virginia', *The Journal of Southern History*, 69:2 (2003), 245–82; E. S. Morgan, *American Slavery, American Freedom* (New York, 1975, 2003), pp. 77, 99; L. Roper, *The English Empire in America, 1602–1658: Beyond Jamestown* (New York, 2009); E. Griffin, 'The specter of Spain in John Smith's colonial writing', in R. Applebaum and J. Sweet (eds), *Envisioning an English Empire: Jamestown and the Making of a North Atlantic World* (Philadelphia, 2005), pp. 111–34; J. Canizares-Esguerra, *Puritan Conquistadors: Iberianizing the Atlantic, 1550–1700* (Stanford, 2006).
8 This contradicts the prevailing narrative that the British empire became 'Protestant, commercial, maritime, and free', advocated by David Armitage and Linda Colley. It demonstrates instead how multiple ideas about English/British imperial development competed for political primacy through the second-half of the seventeenth century. See D. Armitage, *The Ideological Origins of the British Empire* (Cambridge, 2000), p. 173; L. Colley, *Britons: Forging the Nation, 1707–1837* (New Haven, 1992), pp. 5, 368.
9 G. L. Beer, *The Old Colonial System* (2 vols, New York, 1912), I, pp. vii, 38; Eli F. Heckscher, *Mercantilism*, trans. M. Shapiro (2 vols, New York, 1955), I, p. 27; C. M. Andrews, *The Colonial Period of American History* (4 vols, New Haven, 1934–1938), IV, pp. 7–9.
10 P. J. Stern and C. Wennerlind (eds), *Mercantilism Reimagined: Political Economy in Early Modern Britain and Its Empire* (Oxford, 2013); 'Forum: Rethinking Mercantilism', W&MQ, 69:1 (2012), 3–70.
11 S. Pincus, *1688: The First Modern Revolution* (New Haven, 2009), pp. 372–81.
12 'Forum: Rethinking Mercantilism', 3–70.
13 These positions were, broadly, that the Tories supported Anglican conformity, the power of the monarch against Parliament, and an alliance with the French, while the Whigs supported nonconformist religious views, an increase in the power of Parliament vis-à-vis the Crown, and an alliance with the Dutch against the French. See R. Hutton, *Charles the Second, King of England, Scotland, and Ireland* (Oxford, 1989); M. Knights, *Politics and Opinion in Crisis, 1678–81* (Cambridge, 1994); J. R. Jones, *Court and Country: England 1658–1714* (Cambridge, Mass., 1978); Pincus, *1688*; J. Spurr, *England in the 1670s: This Masquerading Age* (Oxford, 2000).
14 Edmund Morgan argues that the English, who early sought to replicate the Spanish empire in Virginia, had, by the early eighteenth century, 'Hispanised' Virginia by creating a labour force similar to the one found by the Spanish: E. Morgan, 'The labor problem at Jamestown, 1607–1618', *AHR*, 76:3 (1971), 611.
15 A. Swingen, *Competing Visions of Empire: Labor, Slavery, and the Origins of the British Atlantic Empire* (New Haven, 2015), pp. 1–2, 31, 143–51.
16 J. Child, *A Treatise Wherein is Demonstrated ...* (1681), p. 3.
17 C. Reynell, *The True English Interest* (1674), p. 91.
18 Child, *A New Discourse*, p. 165.
19 J. Elliott, *Empires of the Atlantic World: Britain and Spain in America, 1492–1830* (New Haven, 2006), p. 20; R. Konezke, 'Hernan Cortes como poblador de Nueva Espana', *Estudios Coresianos* (Madrid, 1948), pp. 341–81. Additionally, English colonisation was theoretically based on the concept that land had to be planted and improved to be owned, justifying their colonisation of territory claimed by the

Spanish by right of discovery: E. Botella-Ordinas, 'Debating empires, inventing empires: British territorial claims against the Spaniards in America, 1670–1714', *Journal for Early Modern Cultural Studies*, 10:1 (2010), 142–68.
20 Child, *A New Discourse*, pp. 176–7.
21 *Ibid.*
22 *Ibid.*, p. 184.
23 Child, *Treatise Wherein is Demonstrated*, p. 1.
24 These could be used to invest in colonial projects, like the joint-stock Virginia or Providence Island Companies, or for trade to a particular region, like the joint-stock East India Company or the regulated Levant Company.
25 C. T. Carr (ed.), *Select Charters of Trading Companies* (London, 1913), pp. 186–92. For a history of the Company see K.G. Davies, *The Royal African Company* (London, 1957, 1999); D. Galenson, *Traders, Planters and Slaves: Market Behaviour in Early America* (Cambridge, 1986), pp. 13–28. The new company included in its membership a large number of courtiers, merchants and colonials administrators with interests in English imperial expansion. These included courtiers responsible for handling colonial affairs like the duke of York, Prince Rupert, and Sir Anthony Ashley Cooper, later Earl of Shaftesbury, imperial administrators like Thomas Povey and Shaftesbury's secretary, John Locke, colonial governors such as Ferdinando Gorges, Peter Colleton, Charles Modyford, and Sir Charles Lyttleton, and a variety of merchants trading to Spain, Africa, the East Indies, and the Americas.
26 *Certain Considerations relating to the Royal African Company* (1680), p. 8.
27 TNA, CO 324/4, pp. 120–2.
28 Child, *Treatise Wherein is Demonstrated*, p. 3; A.P. Thornton, *West India Policy under the Restoration* (Oxford, 1956), pp. 67–123.
29 TNA, SP 94/58, fo. 74; K. G. Davies, *The Royal African Company*, pp. 327–35; BL, Egerton MS 2,395, fo. 523.
30 'Prerogative', *OED*.
31 W. Pettigrew, *Freedoms Debt: The Royal African Company and the Politics of the Atlantic Slave Trade, 1672–1752* (Chapel Hill, NC, 2013), pp. 23–5; 27–9, 88–9.
32 T. B. Howell (ed.), *A Complete Collection of State Trials* (34 vols, London, 1816), X, pp. 532–5.
33 L. Theibert, 'Making an English Caribbean, 1650–1688' (Yale University PhD dissertation, 2013), pp. 431–68.
34 This challenges the planter vs privateer dichotomy argued by Richard Dunn. See R. Dunn, *Sugar and Slaves: The Rise of the English Planter Class in the English West Indies, 1624–1713* (Chapel Hill, NC, 2000), pp. 156–62; Theibert, 'Making an English Caribbean', p. 277.
35 Modyford was governor from 1664–70; Morgan served as admiral of the Buccaneers under Modyford and then as lieutenant-governor from 1675–81; Albemarle was Modyford's cousin and secured him the position on the island: S. S. Webb, *The Governors-General: The English Army and the Definition of the Empire, 1569–1681* (Chapel Hill, NC, 1979, 1987), pp. 225–7.
36 TNA, CO 1/20, No. 24; CO 1/21, No. 170; BL, Additional MS 11,410, fos 6–7; TNA, CO 1/18, No. 65; Westminster Abbey Muniments, 11912.
37 TNA, HCA 49/59; C. Pestana, 'Early English America without pirates', *W&MQ*, 71:3 (2014), 321–60.
38 TNA, CO 138/1 p. 22; CO 1/19, No. 109; CO 140/1 p. 143–7.
39 Vaughan to Sec. Williamson, 2 May 1676, TNA: CO 1/36, No. 58. On Morgan's exploits see A. O. Exquemelin, *The History of the Buccaneers of America* (3 vols, 1684), II, pp. 60–149, III, pp. 1–76.
40 P. Earle, *The Pirate Wars* (London, 2003), pp. 133–56; BL, Sloane MS 2,724, fo. 30.
41 National Maritime Museum, John Narborough Letterbook 1; P. Earle, *Wreck of the Almiranta, The Treasure of the Concepcion* (New York, 1980).
42 TNA, CO 1/53, No. 32.
43 They also adopted Tory programmes like support for the French and opposition to religious dissenters. See TNA, CO 1/53, No. 32. In the Jamaican Constitutional

Crisis, the Lords of Trade and Plantations sought to place new restrictions on the appointment of governors, approval of laws, and Assembly voting on local taxation: Agnes Whitson, *The Constitutional Development of Jamaica, 1660–1729* (Manchester, 1929), pp. 70–109.
44 Swingen, *Competing Visions*, pp. 136–8.
45 This challenges Nuala Zahedieh's argument that it was merely control over the Asiento that this group opposed: N. Zahedieh, 'Regulation, rent-seeking, and the Glorious Revolution in the English Atlantic economy', *EcHR*, 63:4 (2010), 878–80.
46 TNA, CO 1/46, No. 145.
47 TNA, CO 1/54, No. 93; CO 1/54 No. 97; CO 1/54, No. 132.
48 Pincus, *1688*, pp. 369–72, 383–93.
49 S. Bethel, *The Interest of Princes and States* (1680), p. 3; Coke, *Discourse of Trade*, p. 5.
50 Coke, *Discourse of Trade*, p. 5; TNA, PRO 30/24/49, fo. 88.
51 While the English population had increased dramatically between 1550 and 1650, rising from almost 3 million in 1560 to 5.23 million in 1651, it stagnated and then declined to 5.06 million between 1651 and 1701. This decline was due to a combination of low fertility rates, higher mortality rates in low lying and urban areas with growing populations, and migration from the healthy countryside to the more pestilential cities. Political economists and pamphleteers had no concrete population figures, but there was a general sense within England that the country was becoming depopulated through the second half of the seventeenth century. See K. Wrightson, *Earthly Necessities: Economic Lives in Early Modern Britain, 1470–1750* (New Haven, 2000), pp. 159, 229–30.
52 R. Hakluyt, 'Discourse Concerning Western Planting', ch. 4, https://ebooks.adelaide.edu.au/h/hakluyt/voyages/v13/planting/complete.html Accessed 1 January 2016; For an historiographical overview see Swingen, *Competing Visions*, pp. 2–16, 19–20, 28–30.
53 Coke, *Discourse of Trade*, 8, original emphasis.
54 W. Petty, *Political Arithmetick* (1690), p. 88; T. McCormick, *William Petty and the Ambitions of Political Arithmetick* (Oxford, 2009), p. 231.
55 S. Bethel, *The World's Mistake in Oliver Cromwell* (1668), pp. 3–8.
56 Coke, *Discourse of Trade*, p. 11.
57 Bethel, *The Present Interest of England* (1671), preface.
58 Coke, *Discourse of Trade*, p. 12; see also Bethel, *Interest of Princes*, p. 83.
59 Coke, *Discourse of Trade*, p. 13.
60 Petty, *Poltiical Arithmetick*, p. 88.
61 TNA, CO 389/2, fo. 8.
62 *Ibid*.
63 C. McLean Andrews, *British Committees, Commissions, and Councils of Trade and Plantations, 1622–1675* (Baltimore, 1908), appendix 3.
64 Coke, *Discourse of Trade*, p. 36.
65 TNA, CO 389/2, fo. 8.
66 *Ibid*. Political economists who favoured empire estimated that the trade to the American colonies alone was worth over £1 million, and the doubling of customs duties over the course of the 1670s, from £46,767 in 1671–72 to £114,883 in 1682–83, bears this out: TNA, SP 9/2, p. 39; Spurr, *England in the 1670s*, p. 134.
67 N. Zahedieh, *The Capital and the Colonies: London and the Atlantic Economy 1660–1700* (Cambridge, 2010), pp. 262–4.
68 TNA, SP 9/2, p. 39.
69 This contrasted with the more conservative Whigs, who argued that there was no need to infiltrate Spanish colonial trade because Spain's decline in manufacturing meant most goods came from England, France, and the Netherlands, and smuggling was rampant: TNA, SP 94/57, fo. 17; S. J. Stein and B. H. Stein, *Silver, Trade and War: Spain and America in the Making of Early Modern Europe* (Baltimore, 2000), pp. 71–94.
70 As African slaves took the place of indentured servants in the colonies, islands like Jamaica experienced both population growth – from 14,000 to 40,000 between 1670

and 1690 – and a major demographic shift, as the black population doubled from 15,000 to 30,000 and the white population decreased from 12,000 to 10,000, going from about 45 per cent to 25 per cent of the total between 1680 and 1690: Swingen, *Competing Visions*, p. 162.
71 Though pro-labour imperial promoters like Shaftesbury and Locke were initial investors in the Royal African Company, by the late 1670s participation in the Company by proto-Whigs in the RAC had faded, and Shaftesbury and Locke sold their shares.
72 *CJ*, X, pp. 382, 393.
73 Pettigrew, *Freedom's Debt*, pp. 23–9; Theibert, 'Making an English Caribbean', pp. 327–32.
74 A. Sidney, *Court Maxims*, ed. Hans W. Blom, Eco Haitsma Mulier and Ronald Janse (Cambridge, 1996), p. 79; Quoted in Elliott, 'Learning from the enemy', p. 42.
75 Bethel, *Interest of Princes*, pp. 84, 75.
76 *Ibid.*, pp. 76–7.
77 These were not stable positions; for many eventual Whigs these policies developed through the 1670s, as they turned against the Dutch War, the extension of the royal prerogative, and the monopoly trading companies, and ideas about the value of labour, manufacturing, and trade became associated with other Whig ideas under the purview of patrons like Shaftesbury and Locke.
78 Though few embraced the identification until after the Glorious Revolution. For an account of the crisis See Whitson, *Constitutional Development*, pp. 70–109.
79 BL, Additional MS 12,429, fos 75–85; Egerton MS 2,395, fo. 574.
80 BL, Additional MS 12,429, fos. 75–85; TNA, CO 1/19, No. 23; SP 94/53, fo. 174; CO 1/52, No. 35; BL, Additional MS 12,424, fos. 3–52; Thornton, *West India Policy*, pp. 67–123.
81 BL, Additional MS 12,429, fos 75–85; TNA, CO 1/19, No. 23; CO 1/52, No. 35; CO 1/52, No. 62.
82 This had been strongly opposed by the Spaniards, who feared that it would allow English ships to land on the islands and trade illicitly: TNA, SP 94/56, fo. 216; BL, Egerton MS 2,395, fo. 501; TNA, CO 1/49, No. 35.
83 TNA, CO 1/50, No. 91; CO 1/49, No. 66.
84 TNA, CO 1/54, No. 41; CO 1/49, No. 66; CO 1/58, No. 44 I-III.
85 TNA, CO 1/49, No. 66; CO 138/5, pp. 128–39.
86 TNA, CO 138/5, p. 3.
87 TNA, CO 1/49, No. 66; CO 1/51, No. 106.
88 D. Eltis, *Rise of African Slavery in the Americas* (Cambridge, 2000), p. 208; Davies, *Royal African Company*, p. 363. Planters in Barbados shared these concerns about the limited numbers of slaves imported by the RAC: E. Littleton, *The Groans of the Plantations* (1689), pp. 6–7.
89 TNA, CO 1/49, No. 66; CO 1/51, No. 106.
90 TNA, T 70/1, p. 24; T 70/1, p. 23.
91 TNA, CO 1/43, No. 148.
92 TNA, CO 268/1, pp. 81–7.
93 *Ibid.*
94 TNA, CO 391/3, pp. 231–2; Swingen, *Competing Visions*, pp. 208–10; TNA, CO 1/53, No. 2.

CHAPTER SEVEN

Legal geography and colonial sovereignty: the making of early English 'Bombay'

Philip J. Stern

In 1661, Charles II received an impressive wedding present from the Portuguese crown upon his marriage to Catherine of Braganza: to hold 'for ever' all 'the Port and Island of Bombay in the East Indies with all the Rights, Profits, Territories, and Appurtenances whatsoever thereunto belonging ... As also the direct and absolute Dominion and Sovereignty of the said Port and Island'.[1] Along with the co-acquisition of the town of Tangier, the so-called 'transfer' of Bombay is both a well-known and little-regarded story of sorts, often understood either as a single event – the simple *handover* of a colonial possession – or, more subtly, as another tempestuous moment in the centuries-long fraught relationship among Europeans in Asia, which marked the beginning of the rise of English and concomitant and incipient decline of Portuguese power in coastal western India.[2]

However, in reality, the nature and extent of English sovereignty at Bombay remained a complex matter of dispute, a work-in-progress that lasted for a decade, if not, in some sense, for a century. The ongoing struggles over this issue hinged not only on officials in Bombay, London, Goa, Lisbon and Bombay itself, but also the regional and geopolitics of Mughal, Maratha and Dutch expansion, as well as the critical intersection between maritime and territorial sovereignty. In the process, this story offers some lessons about the complications at the heart of European claims to colonial sovereignty. Laws in Asian European empires were just as overlapping and 'entangled' as in the Caribbean,[3] if not even more so, in an Asia that even Europeans understood as having a very different relationship to indigenous histories, people, traditions and even 'publics' that could not so easily be rendered in legal and political oblivion at the supposed transfer of possession. Like in other places around the globe, the sovereignty of Bombay was a work-in-progress, a process rather than a product. It conjured thorny and not easily resolved issues about the relationship between states and companies, centuries-old debates over the nature of property and jurisdiction, outward-looking claims to jurisdiction at sea and those more inward-looking notions of sovereignty over places, people and things on land. Most crucially and perhaps most obviously, as Lauren Benton and others have shown, European claims to authority in the extra-European world rested on contestable claims over uneven legal geographies and spaces, from rivers and mountains to ocean and sea lanes.[4] Yet the ongoing conflicts over the limits and nature of sovereignty within and without Bombay revealed a deceptively complex but fundamental question: *what* exactly *were* the port, island and premises of 'Bombay' in the first place? The enduring struggle to resolve that question – and the legal issues that defined attempts to do so – revealed the nested and interrelated role of land and sea, insular borders and extraterritorial authority, and the ways in which colonial authority rested not only on the assertions of treaties among European courts but the information, arguments and discordant polycentric claims to power derived from the constantly shifting terrain of European colonial sovereignty in early modern Asia.

Most of the attention in stories about the transfer has focused on the several years in which possession of Bombay was held in limbo, initially by the Portuguese viceroy, Antonio de Mello de Castro. Despite (or perhaps owing to) his outward voyage with the English fleet and having been appointed particularly for this purpose, Mello de Castro famously refused to turn Bombay over to the English designee, the Earl of Marlborough, and its first governor, Abraham Shipman. The English administrators, soldiers and others were consigned to the desolate rock of an island of Anjidiv, where over 300 of them – including Shipman – perished.

The viceroy's delays rested on two ostensible objections: first, that the English had failed to live up to their treaty obligations, not defending Portuguese interests vigilantly enough from the Dutch in the Indian Ocean; and second, that Marlborough did not appear to have the proper paperwork authenticating his claim.[5] Mello de Castro had his own concerns, perhaps presciently, about the damage handing over Bombay would cause to the strategic interests of the *Estado da India*, and itself needs to be seen in the context of his short-lived mission to 'rehabilitate' the Portuguese establishment in India more generally and his struggles at Goa against a range of forces, from local administrators to the Inquisition.[6] To the English, he certainly became the story's principal antagonist and villain. One English official regarded him as like 'ye Divell who raines furiously'; others were convinced he was being bribed by Bombay's Jesuits.[7] For his own part, the Portuguese viceroy protested vigorously that it was he who had received ill-treatment at the hands of the English.[8]

This is often where this story seems to end. Forced from Lisbon to hand over the island, and periodically in and out of power at Goa, the subsequent conflict between English and Portuguese officials in western India seems to be the jostling of two regional powers, one waning and the other waxing. Yet the controversy had not simply been over whether the English should have Bombay but what it was they were granted in the first place – a question which was hardly settled with the formal 'transfer'. Indeed, from the very first reports sent back from India in the early 1660s, English Crown officials were dismayed. Bombay was, it seemed, 'far inferior to what ... was represented' in the treaty negotiations. Samuel Pepys cried 'knavery' at the 'inconsiderableness of the place'. The confusions were so great that a story arose that the Lord Chancellor initially thought Bombay was located somewhere near Brazil; though this is likely apocryphal, he certainly sought out various opinions as to its geography,[9] and fretted that the whole affair spelled the ruin of the infant Anglo-Portuguese alliance. For its own part, Lisbon clearly regretted the decision, making periodic overtures through the 1660s and 1670s to buy the island back.[10]

The frustrations and misgivings in Europe were matched by ongoing dispute in Asia over what it was that had actually been 'transferred'. As the ensuing debates revealed, very little had been clearly settled on the issue. Even the very origins of the name of the place, 'Bombaim' – did it arise from an old Marathi usage (from which Mumbai is derived), a corruption of the (ungrammatical) Portuguese 'bom baía' of 'good bay', or the plentiful indigenous bummalo fish? – could not be settled. At its most liberal definition, the Portuguese comprehended the jurisdiction of Bombay to be simply the island called 'Bombaim', the southerly most inhabited island in the archipelago, which under the Portuguese had essentially been the hereditary property of eleven families under the governance of one family, headed at the time by the largest landholder, Lady Donna Inez de Miranda, or the 'proprietrix' of Bombay. A 1646 Portuguese manuscript atlas, which came into the possession of the English envoy to Lisbon in the 1670s, seemed to indicate as much, as the map of the area is identified primarily as 'Tana', with a much smaller Bombay island set off to the south on its margins.[11] An English official who looked into the matter in the Portuguese manuscripts in 1677 similarly found the description ambiguous, and could not conclude whether or not Bombay consisted jurisdictionally of more than the small two-mile wide island by that name.[12] In fact, some Portuguese officials in the 1660s offered an even more restrictive definition, suggesting 'Bombay' might in fact only be the town and fort on the southeastern tip of that island. Such a description of Bombay as itself an archipelago threw into question English authority over other villages as well, including Mazagon, where there were large Portuguese-held estates, and Mahim, on Bombay island's northwestern end. In 1665, the viceroy insisted Mahim was itself a separate island 'some distance from the island Bombay', as in high tides it – along with other parts of 'Bombay' – could be separated from its mainland.[13]

That the various jurisdictions and towns on the 'island' were separated at times by the flooding of salt marshes was not in dispute; Gerald Aungier, in his 'report' on Bombay in 1673, in fact described Bombay itself as resembling 'four small Islands' in the high tide, and John Fryer, the Company surgeon who visited Bombay around the same time, described the entire jurisdiction as consisting of seven islands comprising Salsette, of which Bombay was one.[14] The question, however, was which time of day one was to use to understand the nature of their relationship. Fryer included 'Canorein' (Salsette), Trombay and Karanja in his list, and the map published alongside his account – which was very similar to the map used by the Company in making its case to the English Crown – clearly represented Bombay as a coherent island. Conversely, the viceroy – who had his own map to prove his case – was quite clear about the importance of such logic; to accept the English low-tide definition of Bombay would call into question the distinction between Bombay and Salsette, and Salsette and much of the rest of Portuguese territory in the region; thus, 'in order not to lose the north, it will be necessary to defend Mahim'.[15] Perhaps even more crucially, the viceroy and others argued that while the English might have territorial possession of Bombay, it did not include absolute rights over the people on it or the waters surrounding it. The viceroy insisted the Portuguese be ensured customs-free trade at Bombay as well as Bandra – on the southwestern tip of Salsette, the larger island to Bombay's north – and the 'other the Creeks of *Salsett* though under the *English* Artillery'. He also demanded all Portuguese land tenures at Bombay remain in effect, rents and taxes fixed, and that the Portuguese retain unhindered fishing rights in 'the Bay and River, even in the Arm which enters and divides *Bombay* from *Salsett* by *Bundura* up into the Bay'.[16]

For Goa, the navigable waterway that divided Salsette from Bombay – and more locally, at its westward narrowing point, Mahim, on Bombay, from Bandra, on Salsette – seemed to be a substantial, tributary *river* that clearly distinguished the two territories. In fact, the viceroy argued to the English that all the islands of the archipelago were connected (and divided) by rivers. Indeed, their very names showed that these other places could not be considered 'Bombay': that there was a 'river of Trombay' or the 'River of Carinjah' was evidence that Trombay and

Karanja were themselves distinct jurisdictional spaces. And, as rivers, command over these dividing lines belonged to the Portuguese: first because the Portuguese still maintained by virtue of its papal dispensation that all 'Navigation' in the East Indies 'did solely appertain to the Crown of *Portugal*'; and secondly, and more subtly, that while the law of nations recognised liberty of passage on open rivers, these rivers, including the passageway to the mainland between the islands of Tannah and Karanja, 'made a Bar that is lock'd or shut up' – which thus could be claimed and controlled by a sovereign power.[17]

With limited forces at his disposal and allegedly some personal motives, Humphrey Cooke, by now English governor of Bombay, agreed to a pact with the viceroy, which acquiesced to this definition of Bombay, but his pact was quickly repudiated. Indeed, for several years prior, the English Crown, and (most of) its representatives in India had been arguing for a very different definition of the marriage treaty. The English envoy to Portugal had insisted that Lisbon immediately cede the entire territory 'exhibited formerly to His Majesty in the map', which had accompanied the treaty. The problem was that after extensive searching, many seemed to remember a map among the papers, but no one could remember where it had been put.[18] Though the absent map took on an authoritative status, combined with the assertions of memory and the testimony of Captain Arnold Browne, who had commanded the English fleet to India. Browne insisted Bombay had been 'most strangely represented' to Charles II as consisting of the territory stretching from the bay in the south as far north as Bassein, which he was surprised to discover was in fact an archipelago, of which Bombay was by far the smallest of the islands. However, both his local pilot and the 'antientest Commanders', he argued, confirmed the English ambassador's claims that the *jurisdiction* of Bombay was, aside from a number of rocky formations and smaller outposts in the archipelago, to '*conteine three intire Islands*': Thana, furthest to the north and controlling the passage to Portuguese Bassein and the mainland; Salsette, the large island to its south; and of course, the 'Island of Bombay which is next Southerly to Salsett and divided from it by a Navigable Channell'.[19] Gerald Aungier, the Company factor at Surat and later governor of Bombay who accompanied Browne on his survey of the island from aboard ship, also observed that the 'Bombay' the Portuguese were prepared to hand over was only about a fifth of 'w[ha]t was represented to' the king in the Portuguese map, in which Bombay, Salsette and Thana 'were included, all in one island & all under ye name and Royalty of Bombay'.[20]

Thus, the English insisted that 'Bombay' encompassed far more than what was commonly understood to be Bombay 'island'. While based at first on a sense of the original agreement, as well as reported historical local usages and traditions, these arguments also came to rest on contestable definitions of the archipelago's maritime geography. To Henry Gary, English deputy governor and later briefly governor at Bombay, the value of Bombay was actually not to be found in Bombay itself, an island 'soe inconsiderable that it is not worth making of a tenn dayes Voyage for it'.[21] Indeed, he observed:

> that which our People understand to bee Bombain, in regard of the sound of the word Bombain, which they render (though falsely) good bay wch indeed would bee soe were it called Bombaya is Bay of att least 60 miles in circumference whose entrance is and begins at the Westermost part of the said Island of Bombain in which lyeth ye Islads vize of Carenja Ithados Olifantis or Island of Alleptr Ithados Patteceos or Island of Water Mellous and other Rocks of Little or noe Utility, and Trombay the Uttmost Limmits of this large Bay Easterly reaching over alllmost as far as Tanna.

Thus to Gary, it was not the fort but the *port* of Bombay that was 'of greate Consequence', and despite the nomenclatural misunderstanding, the value of Bombay island was dependent upon its sovereignty, and thus ability to command customs, on the seas surrounding it.[22]

On the basis of this understanding of Bombay, Cooke's pact was promptly repudiated in England and by his successors in India: the Crown's last governor, Gervase Lucas, and then the first East India Company governors, George Oxinden and Gerald Aungier. The Company's possession of Bombay in 1668 was itself the product of a boundary dispute of sorts, having reportedly accepted it of the Crown to 'prevent' ongoing 'misunderstandings' between Company and royal officials in India.[23] They were also clearly aware the conflict would continue. Among Aungier's recommendations for the new government of Bombay was Simon Serron, 'a person well read in the civill and Imperiall Lawes, and formerly Syndic and Procurator for the King of Portugal at Basseen'.[24]

The East India Company in turn seemed to have an even more robust vision of their 'island' than the Crown. Bombay, its leadership insisted, consisted of the entire archipelago, but focused their arguments, as the viceroy had, on the nature not of the land but the waterways, passageways and bottlenecks from which one controlled not just access to land but also the movements of people.[25] The Company disputed that the region consisted of a system of rivers. English officials had maintained that the body of water that divided Bombay island from Salsette was not a river but a less substantial channel; Fryer, for his part, regarded it as a mere 'stream'.[26] More broadly, the Company seemed to see not a system of rivers, but a bay filled with small islands. Since jurisdiction over a bay was meaningless if ingress and egress was limited, this in turn allowed them to make claims on even the most outlying islands, including Thana and Karanja. As the Bombay council observed, appealing to London for diplomatic help in June 1672: 'the dispute will chiefly lye in the latitude of the words (Portus et Insula Bombay), whether the King of Portugall in transferring his royall right and sovereignty to the King of England of the whole Bay, did not there and thereby transfer the same right of dominion over all the Islands therein, and allso over those small streights and passages which make it'.[27]

Thus, these were not rivers that divided the islands but 'small streights and passages' that united them. Dismissing out of hand the argument by virtue of the papal bulls as simply 'quite worn out', they confronted the viceroy's distinction between open and closed rivers by denying that the passage between Thana and Karanja was in fact a river: as 'the Sea it self flowes in', it was part of the bay that 'enters and makes the port of Bombay'. And if control of 'Bombay' implied control of its port, and control of its port implied control of the bay, the passages among the islands obtaining to the bay were subject to English sovereignty, as one of 'the Islands which stand in this Port ... which are surrounded by the Waters thereof, and which cannot be approached but through this Dominion of his Majesty's'. The alternative was to imagine that 'those Islands' could 'give Law to the Port', which would be tantamount to 'admit[ting] the exercise of two different Sovereignties in the one and the same place'. The Company also rejected Goa's argument about the importance of the names of the rivers, again, disputing not the names but their status as rivers: they were, the Company argued, more like 'the subdivision of Streets in the same Towne'. To think otherwise would be to suggest that 'a Vessell should not bee said to bee in Falmouth or Milfordhaven because shee Road in some *Creek* thereof, that went by another Name, though supplied from the Water of the Common Bas[i]n'.

Not that the Company rejected the nomenclatural logic; they simply substituted their own. Mahim belonged to Bombay, they insisted, because before the Portuguese, Mahim had actually been the name of the whole area; conversely, now the whole was simply 'comprehended in the name of Bombaim, as the Denomination is taken usually from the Greater part'. And if Mahim obtained naturally to Bombay, Salsette obtained to Mahim, as traditionally southerly Salsette, the Company insisted, citing Portuguese tax records, had been governed from the customs house and judicatory at Mahim. The Company's sense of geography was thus defined by a distinctly political history: though dismissed a decade earlier as so insignificant as to warrant open breach with the Portuguese, Bombay was now accounted to be, by nature, a

'Capital Place' and as such 'gives Denomination to the Port'. Therefore, its 'dignity', position, history and greater population rendered the 'neighboring Shores' in 'naturall dependance and Subserviency' to it.

Among themselves, Company officials admitted this entire matter was a question of judgment: 'We doe not know by what infallible signes and markes to chalke out the Boundaries of the Harbor of Bombaim', the London court wrote, 'but it seemes part of an argument that it extends to all the Bay of Water within.'[28] One part of that argument was derived from a sense of historical usage, and another part from more abstract notions of the law of nations. The controversy ultimately boiled down to whether the English had been given 'a thing expressly granted' – that is, merely 'Bombay' – or what was 'not expressly denied but presumptively ought to be understood as included in the right of the waters and territories dependent on the grant of the port & island of Bombaim taken jointly together'.[29] The Portuguese-controlled forts in the region offered no protection or security of navigation to Bombay or its ships, so any duties levied on English ships were unjust; indeed, it was Bombay, the logic went, that served as 'a Frontier and a Buckler on the Sea to All these Inner parts'.[30]

Company leadership continued to insist on the jurisdiction assumed to be in the original lost map, despite the fact that English officials were still looking for it, in vain, almost two decades later.[31] Moreover, more recent maps patronised or at least tacitly approved of by the Company clearly figured Mahim as a contiguous part of mainland Bombay and 'its small dependencies'.[32] If the Portuguese insisted at high tide Mahim was separate from Bombay, the Company countered with the obvious fact that at low tide one could 'walke dry' between them.[33] They also acted on this geographical assertion, collecting customs and taxes not only at Bombay but also at Mahim and smaller ports on the south-western coast of Salsette[34] and by seizing a few fishing vessels from nearby Portuguese settlements, which had 'claimed by ancient Custome the priviledge of fishing in the open sea and in several bays and Creekes belonging to' Bombay. The goal, the Bombay council reported to London, was to 'dispute their said priviledges and secure your right'.[35] Meanwhile, the Portuguese disputed these definitions in practice by entrenching themselves on Thana and Karanja, levying duties and demanding passes for ships, especially ones flying English or Company colours, desiring passage to the mainland.

Portuguese claims over movement on the water thus allowed them not only to 'cripple' Bombay's trade and supply lines – especially much-needed timber – to the main.[36] It also rendered ambiguous the sovereignty over Bombay's port. Just around the new year, 1675, a Portuguese ship en route to Trombay entered Bombay harbour, refusing to strike its flag, the captain insisting he 'rode in the King of Portugals channel'. Company officials of course took this as a sign that he 'designed to deprive his Ma[jest]ie of the Royalty of this his Port Bombay as also that of Trombay which of due right belong unto him'.[37] The following year, the Portuguese Captain General of the North sent about 1,500 men to threaten to take Mahim and destroy Bombay, in retaliation for Bombay's deputy governor's protection of a trading vessel from the Malabar coast that had been in conflict with a Portuguese man of war off Diu.[38] Importantly, when a Portuguese delegation arrived to negotiate a settlement, they immediately turned to disputing the Company's possession and occupation of Mahim itself; Lisbon too was reportedly incensed at the Company for occupying Mahim, 'that they had unjustly possessed themselves of and still kept places that noe way belong'd to them, that noe more was granted to his Majty but Bombaim and its Port'. The Company, the prince reportedly insisted, was 'a Company of thieves that deserve to be hang'd'.[39] For its part, the Company ignored these issues while also refusing to turn the ship or its crew over, citing both the particular diplomatic entanglements it implied – its obligations to the Zamorin of Calicut to honour the pass – as well as the more universal principles at stake: Bombay was a free port, and to turn the ship over would be a violation of the hospitality required of the Company by the law of nations.[40]

Thus, even two decades into English 'possession' of the island, neither maritime nor territorial jurisdiction were clearly settled. The Company consistently recognised the critical relationship between the two. The command of the sea implied rights of dominion on land:

> The Sea where it is mastered, seemes to carry and Convey with it a Right of Dominions, withersoever it goes. The first conquest of those Islands were made from the Sea, and where the Sea overflows any Territory of the neighboring Land, all that space of Sea (and in Virtue thereof all the Land below it) belongs to that Prince, who had the Soveraignity of the Sea before, so alsoe New Islands riseing up in the Waters of any Prince, doe become his Right, as doe all Islands standing in his Seas without inhabitation belonging unto him just as Wrecks in the Sea ... soe while the Question is so probable whither his Majestie should not have the soveraignity of [the] whole, how absurd is the practice to make him a Tributary in Part.

Defining Bombay as an *island* was thus critical to insisting upon the dominion over the seas surrounding it. In turn, owning Bombay was pointless and absurd – 'nothing but a poore limited and expensive spot of Ground to support' – if that dominion did not include free navigation to and from it, and the rights to commerce at sea to allow it to flourish. '[W]ill they', the Company asked, 'give us a port and forbid us the Use of that Land which makes it a port?'[41] In the Company's estimation there was no conceivable way the sense of the original treaty could have implied otherwise, if it had indeed been offered in good faith in the first place.

Thus, almost two decades after the marriage treaty, the precise nature of the 'transfer' of Bombay continued unsettled and ambiguous. By the late 1670s, Anglo-Portuguese relations in India were extremely tense, especially as they intersected with a variety of other conflicts in the region, including the ongoing jostling between the Sidi and Maratha fleets. The matter was also beginning to affect diplomacy back in Europe. On the East India Company's urging, Charles II ordered Francis Parry, the envoy to Portugal, to communicate that if the exactions at Thana and Karanja did not stop, he would give them permission to 'resist force p[er] force' (which he in fact had already done); the envoy, for his part, seemed to think the entire dispute over the jurisdiction was simply a matter of 'pride and peevishness', and that it was probably in Portugal's interest simply to hand over all their territories in India to the English and get out of the game altogether.[42] Still, whatever the reasons, the interlocutors in the ongoing debate drew upon a range of political and legal arguments, including pre-Portuguese practice on the island, intervening entanglements with Mughal, Maratha and other regional powers, as well as abstract principles of the law of nations, including references to vaguely analogous European political geography; the maritime controversies between Denmark and Sweden over passage between the Baltic and North Seas, and the duties paid at Elsinore, seemed to obtain particularly, but neither side could agree on even what that meant, the Company rejecting the analogy between that instance and the 'poor Narrow inconsiderable Channell' over which the Portuguese claimed dominion.[43] All of these arguments hinged on even more fundamental questions of what Bombay was in the first place. In turn, the definition of both territorial and maritime geography impacted the claims to sovereignty on and over various territories, the people on them, and the waterways within and between them.

Importantly, Portuguese assertions of rights to navigation had not only called into question English and Company control of Bombay, but more fundamentally kept the door open for Goa and Bassein to continue to 'pretend dominion over the Portugueses and other Subjects remaining' in that jurisdiction, even on the parts of the archipelago where English jurisdiction over the *territory* itself was never even in dispute.[44] Such claims were abetted by the island's Jesuits, who not only continued to support claims of extraterritorial spiritual jurisdiction over the Catholics at Bombay, but whose major landholdings were to be found precisely in the outlying, disputed districts; indeed, some English officials strongly suspected them of having bribed, or at least influenced, Mello de Castro into his initial refusal to turn over the island.[45] Thus, by repudiating Cooke's settlement with the viceroy over the definitions of the maritime and territorial dimensions of the island, Lucas and his successors also opened a space in which the English government could redefine on a more individual level the entire foundation for subjecthood on the island, and particularly the validity of existing private and public land tenures. Famously ordering large amounts of land confiscated throughout Bombay island, Lucas intended to launch a legal investigation of titles as well as to 'keepe the people in good order and obedience'.[46]

Such a move was an attempt to demonstrate definitively to Portuguese officials that the English rejected the promises Cooke had made to secure Portuguese land tenures and fix rents. It can also be seen, at least in part, as an attempt to establish a new relationship between English government and its new subjects. In questioning the title of some of the largest plantations, or *fazendas*, Lucas was affirming English juridical power over the more traditional seigniorial authority of large landholders like Bernadino de Tavora and Dona Inez de Miranda. Meanwhile, attacking the Jesuits' lands was a means to undermine their continued claim to an extraterritorial spiritual jurisdiction that linked Bombay to Goa and the wider Portuguese world. It was not coincidental, however, that the centre of their power rested in landholdings that spanned Mahim and Bandra. Lucas was thus laying a claim not just to jurisdiction over the Jesuits but over the disputed parts of 'Bombay' they occupied; moreover, the land confiscations opened the possibility of reshaping the political and economic geographies of the island more generally, making possible the building new houses and farms, part of a project of attracting new, presumably loyal and productive, settlers from Gujarat and beyond.[47]

By the time the Company assumed government on the island in 1668, very few titles had been confirmed or restituted. Oxinden and Aungier both continued in the project, with the ultimate goal of cultivating and protecting the colony of Bombay foremost in mind. It was perhaps no coincidence that the engineer appointed to design buildings on Bombay Fort was also appointed surveyor general to look into the rights for property on the island and to produce a map of the surveyed lands.[48] Aungier's council received petitions on a number of subjects, including many about the lands Lucas had seized; the response was evidently so overwhelming that in early 1670, he increased the size of the governing council – adding two customs officers, the minister and two military officers – to deal with them.[49] By 1671, the Company's government had examined the titles of a number of estates and farms, with 'several parcells where encroachments & alienations have bin made & royall priviledges imposed on are retain'd to your use'.[50] Importantly, however, their plan in the main was not to seize lands indiscriminately but to legitimate land titles so that they could be then bought back for the 'public' use. London authorised them to spend up to £1,500 to purchase land near the fort, cut down trees, remove the fishing villages to its outskirts and replace them with houses for merchants and new settlers.[51]

The inter-imperial dispute with the Portuguese over what was Bombay – both on land and sea – and the nature of English authority there was the premise for this investigation of land tenure. This provided an opening for the Company to overcome a critical ideological problem in planting colonies in Asia: namely, to try to create a *terra nullius* through law where one could not be argued to be found in nature. Like other colonies in the Atlantic, Bombay had been instructed to lay out a new city plan, based upon projects for rebuilding London after the fire. Key to this was encouraging settlement and immigration, which in turn raised the critical issue of extraterritorial authority. The Company was necessarily concerned not simply with how to resist Portuguese claims over residents on the island but also to somehow assert authority over new migrants, transforming them into residents and subjects. Bombay's government thus took a number of measures to assert the *territoriality* of their authority vis-à-vis Portuguese, Mughal, Maratha and other neighbouring polities, such as the council's pledge in 1673 to a five-year moratorium on suits against any settlers at Bombay for debts incurred elsewhere prior to their immigration to the island.[52]

Plans to strengthen the island's forts and encourage immigration and plantation by English, European and Asian migrants alike required reshaping its internal geographies, all articulated as being for the 'publique good' – which in turn continued to animate concerns at Goa over the flight of Hindu and Muslim residents (and key revenues, particularly in tobacco) to English jurisdiction.[53] Yet, at the same time, the investigation of tenures also became a venue in which a different kind of relationship between public participation and colonial authority could be defined. Those who refused to produce titles or have their ownership examined, certain Muslim inhabitants and of course the Jesuits, were deemed 'dangerous to ... government'.[54] Aungier and his council refused to even entertain the petitions of the Jesuit's agent, Gaspar Alfonço, unless he would actually come to Bombay and produce proof of their titles, and they wrote that it seemed the Jesuits 'had rather forfeit [their lands] then adventure their titles to publique examination'.[55] Only when they did come and promise to cease making any further appeals to London or Lisbon did Aungier even appoint the commissioners to inquire into the matter.[56]

Just as this was seemingly resolved, in 1672, rumours of a threatened Dutch attack led many, especially among the Portuguese community, to flee; again, the Company blamed the Jesuits as well as other large landholders, especially Alvaro Perez de Tavora, who held significant estates in Mazagon and had been recently been made captain of the Mazagon militia. Though pardoning most of the other absconders, the council was committed to making a 'publique example' of Perez. Not only had he abandoned his post as militia captain, an offense for which the Company's counsel in London believed he could be justly executed,[57] but perhaps even more critically, his resorting to Goa gave the viceroy yet another opening to press the case that the Catholics at Bombay were indeed still Portuguese subjects. His appeals to Goa and these claims from the viceroy prompted the Bombay government to issue a proclamation requiring all inhabitants to take an oath of allegiance to the English king and of fidelity to the East India Company, and prohibiting 'addresses by way of complaint to any forreign Prince or State whatsoever'.[58]

Like the Jesuits, only when he stopped pressing his case as a matter of right at Goa, Lisbon and London, and instead admitted guilt and begged the Company's 'tenderness and compassion' were his estates restored.[59] Even then, the Company rejected Perez's claims that the rights to his lands also included rights over its labourers, as this a 'considerable privilege of sovereignty', which should not be devolved 'to a subject as Alvaro Perez is'. Otherwise, Bombay wrote to the Company in London, 'all others of the like nature would be pretenders to the same privilege, and then you might account your power and authority only under an empty name to extend no farther than the walls of your Fort'.[60]

The Perez issue impacted the diplomatic wrangling over the wider sovereignty of Bombay, as delays in resolving this question of property seemed to be the argument in Lisbon as to why there was apparently no great rush to settle the issue of Mahim.[61] The land tenure investigations were deeply significant at Bombay as well, raising as they did a second meaning of the term 'public': what were the proper forms of active public participation necessary to recognise and secure the Company's colonial sovereignty? In requiring people to prove their rights to land, the Bombay government conjured a realm of public petitioning, forum and debate, which blended languages of rights in land with those of the indulgence and caretaking of good government. This was reflected most clearly in the ways in which the majority of land tenures were actually settled, since Perez and the Jesuits were in a sense exceptional. As early as 1663, over 200 Portuguese, Muslim and Hindu inhabitants of the island had petitioned Charles II to dispossess revenue farmers in various 'districts' of Bombay of their power, they being 'men powerfull, arrogant, and Exorbitant violators, Eccesiastiques as well as Civil'.[62] Some of those landholders, in turn, petitioned the Bombay government to restore what they claimed to be traditional municipal rights of *encabezamiento*, to collect rents and taxes on their own holdings.[63] Part of the argument for Bombay's traditional rights on Salsette were derived from the protests of those who used to hold the farms to collect those rents and customs.[64] Other merchants on the island petitioned directly to the Company to defend them against the duties charged at Thana and Karanja, and even offered the Company a 'tribute' in exchange for that protection.[65]

In July 1674, the Company's government came to an agreement with appointed representatives of the Portuguese community on the island about the terms on which land could be secured.[66] The opening lines of the ensuing document declared its origins not in government but in the 'disquiet' among landowners about the unsettled state of affairs. Even if only a convention and a conceit, the agreement insisted that it arose when the 'people thought fit, of their own free motion, by mutual assent, in a public *declaration and manifesto* to propose [the settlement] to the Governor in Council'. Aungier and his council called 'A general assembly of the *chief representatives of the said people*', 120 of the 'eminents of the Povo [or people] in behalf of the whole Povo of the Island', which included a number of Luso-Portuguese inhabitants, including the Attorney General's assistant, the Jesuits' agent, Alvaro Perez, and other major landholders. From this followed twelve articles, which essentially agreed to an annual quit-rent in exchange for confirmation of their rights in land. Following this, another *'General assembly'* was convened *'whereunto all the people in general interested in the affair* were invited to appear', and even a second almost town-hall-type meeting to hear supposed objections to the agreement, 'whereupon the Povo in general said they ... were thoroughly satisfied therewith and of the justice thereof'.[67]

Fixing land tenure thus served to eradicate, at least in theory, the ambiguity of Cooke's agreement with the viceroy and represented an attempt to fix the legal geography of Bombay, both locally as well as in its wider inter-imperial context in the region. It was also a way of establishing a particular type of loyalty to and belonging in the Company's colonial polity, less as a blind imposition and more through a form of active and engaged participation with that government. The 'povo' had certain rights of petition and assembly, as well as security in land; by petitioning the Company and paying it rent, in turn, they confirmed a certain jurisdiction and authority over them that made it near impossible for Goa to continue its claims to religious and political jurisdiction at Bombay. This was hardly democracy in action, nor did it recognise an unmitigated right to self-rule. In some respects, it re-inscribed existing hierarchies, premised as it was upon the notion that there were principal residents literally and figuratively rooted and vested in the island. From this followed Aungier's even more famous attempts to organise the island into particular districts and divisions, employing a variety of legal concepts: the Anglo-Saxon hundred, the South Asian *pakhadi* (which Aungier saw as analogous to a parish), and extant forms of Portuguese dispute resolution, particularly the *vereadores*, local administrators and judges, who acted somewhat like local JPs. After Bombay's incorporation in 1727, the island's Mayor's Court – like the one created at Madras several decades earlier – served as an even more robust site for political participation, particularly as regarded rights over land and other forms of property.[68]

While reaffirming private property and a certain scope of participatory and petitionary politics, other clauses in Aungier's so-called 'convention' also reflected the continued importance of that first concept of public good. The agreement authorised the Company to redirect early revenues from the taxes on the island's inhabitants towards the purchase of Old Woman's Island, a small point off the southwestern coast of Bombay, from estate holders there 'for the security and defence of this whole Isle'. Meanwhile, it asserted a more blanket right to all the coasts of the island, 'to be disposed of in necessary occasions for the public ... in regard that in all kingdoms of the world the ground on the water side from the distance of forty yards at least from high water marks belongs as a Sovereign right and privilege to the Kings or Princes thereof'. It also confirmed the intention to take 'a survey to be taken of the whole island ... that the lands and estates of each person be measured'; reaffirmed the Company's rights to seize land with proper compensation if necessary for defence or development; and most importantly, confirmed the obligation of military service, in the form of a militia, that had existed under Portuguese rule to that of Crown and Company.[69]

Such an obligation of land in return for military service was less akin to a feudal tenure than it was to its translation into the early modern notion that service to the polity, particularly in the form of a militia, was a fundamental duty and obligation of a subject and a form of political participation in itself. The Company was offering a clear signal of the end of Portuguese claims on the island's subjects, while also even expanding its rights over those subjects and their land, which under the Portuguese had been held largely as independent feudal land tenures. It was also in a way an implicit limitation on the property rights of both new and old subjects. Thus, in the aftermath of the Mughal invasion of Sion and Mazagon in 1689, Bombay's government again confiscated much of its private property, with the intention of reinstating those who 'had bin faithful' and for those who had been 'bad' to serve as an 'Example to be degraded & loose theirs'.[70] Again, the Company used the opportunity to dispossess the Jesuits, who were accused of encouraging Portuguese inhabitants to flee the island; once again as well, the priests did not help matters by trying to rally Portuguese officials at Diu and Goa to pressure the Company into a full-scale restoration, even by force if necessary.[71] The Company sought to take away a good deal of this land, 'They being Inhabitants of Bombay Island & formed into ye Meletia thereof were as all good Subjects are engaged to defend their Countrey and Estates as well as the Garrison Souldiers the neglect whereof was their great Crime.'[72] Thus, again in the 1690s, Bombay's government seized the opportunity to redistribute land to those who would 'set heartily about improving there estates & making them true to [the Company's] interest'.[73]

> Also like two decades earlier, these confiscations generated petitioning, which both signalled a form of participatory politics while also reaffirming in their language and very existence the Company's authority. This was, of course, a limited notion of a public sphere. Those who insisted on right, like the Jesuits, found their cries fell on deaf ears, while Goa took the opportunity to threaten all out war should their lands not be restored.[74] Those who stressed loyalty and service were more successful, like Rama Comotin, a *saraf* and former tax farmer who had sustained a leg injury by friendly fire from a company mortar during the siege,[75] who ultimately received title to sell, lease or farm rice fields on the southern tip of the island, which had formerly belonged to Muslims accused of aiding the Siddi's invasion.[76] A collective petition from the inhabitants of Mahim directly challenged their alleged disloyalty, insisting they had remained on the island and fought as 'people humble vassals Subjects & obedient to the most Honorable Company & to the General whom God keep & that he may commiserate the Miserys of these People.'[77] Conversely, a great many of the Portuguese inhabitants, finding themselves unable to convince the council of their loyalty, increasingly abandoned arguments of the injustice of the seizures in favour of appealing to the Company's mercy for their 'miserable' situations.[78]

Importantly, and in turn, the conflict between the Company and the Mughals which gave rise to these petitions and pleas was deeply connected to the now decades-old controversy with the *Estado da India* over Bombay. From the very start, the Company imagined that if the *Estado da India* could be seduced into taking the opportunity of a Company war with the Mughals to seize upon their continued claims over English possessions in the region, this would prove to be a prime opportunity for the Company either to take Salsette in its entirety or simply intimidate Portuguese officials through force of arms into ceding their claim over 'those adjacent Islands to Bombay which belong to Bombay & were formerly dependences upon Bombay (especially Salsett) and ought to have been delivered to his Majesty when Bombay was surrendered'[79] – some almost forty years earlier.[80] This conflict with the Portuguese continued through the eighteenth century. In 1705, Bombay requested copies of the 'lands, farms, and rents' established under the Company's early government at Bombay as well as a copy of Charles II's marriage contract and letters patents to the Company.[81] In 1707, the Company threatened to suspend Catholic worship at Bombay if the Portuguese would not return a resident who had gone to Salsette, reportedly in pursuit of a mythical treasure mine, who had been seized by officials and sent to be brought before the Goan Inquisition.[82]

By 1716, the Bombay government still found itself demanding the 'Compas rights to ye Customs of Salset Tannah & Carinjah & to require them to observe the Treaty of Marriage', though also proposed they could end the conflict by simply making an offer to purchase Salsette.[83] Later that year, supposedly at the instigation of a Jesuit at Bandra, the Portuguese fired on English boats coming into the Mahim river 'even disputing with Us its sovereignty'. The conflict finally impelled Company Governor Charles Boone and João Fernandès de Almeida, the Captain General of the North, to negotiate a treaty which seemed to settle the matter: relieving both sides of customs duties, allowing free passage in 'all Streights, Rivers & Creeks', permitting the *kolis* of Bandra their fishing rights in the River of Mahim, and most importantly confirming the Company's rights to the customs at Mahim and, by the Company's interpretation, therefore 'most Villages of ye Isle of Salset', including Trombay.[84] As the Bombay council wrote, they were 'of opinion Salset is part of ye Sovereignty & Dominion of Bombay', repeating the now decades-old arguments that the island was traditionally called 'Mahim', and fell under Mahim's authority to collect customs in both 'ye Jentue & Portugeeze time'.[85] This was supposedly confirmed by a map made for Boone by a *banian* (trader) at Bombay that asserted Salsette had fallen traditionally under Bombay's jurisdiction to collect taxes. 'Whether that entitles to ye Land wch did belong to ye K. Portugal', the Bombay council wondered, 'is submitted to the Civilians', but the Company's directors were further stymied by the fact that this map, despite several claims from Bombay to have sent it – as had become the habit – also managed to go missing.[86]

By the early 1720s, the treaty notwithstanding, matters were hardly resolved. The Portuguese insistence on 'their Kings having the Royal Patronage' to appoint priests on the island independent of Company government only intensified after the Bombay government expelled the

Jesuits from the island, in an attempt to place the jurisdiction of Catholic churches under other parties, such as French Carmelites.[87] Portuguese officials continued to lobby in Europe on behalf of Luso-Indians on the island – citing Cooke's agreement with the viceroy as their foundation, and even began separate negotiations for peace with Kanhoji Angre, which English officials interpreted as an attempt to forge an alliance to undermine Bombay's authority over its littoral. There was another aborted attempt to purchase the island back,[88] as well as renewed blockades of the passage between Mahim and Bandra, firing on ships and even, in 1722, firing on Mahim, damaging the church there.[89] The Company responded to the restriction of free passage at sea with a proclamation requiring those with estates on the island to take to arms, at the risk again of forfeiture of title to their land; the fort at Mahim also returned fire in the 1722 incident.[90] Ultimately, it would be neither the English nor Portuguese that would settle the issue of sovereignty at Salsette, but rather the Marathas, who took the island from the Portuguese in 1737. By 1762, the Company had opened negotiations to make a purchase of the island from the Marathas. Yet, even then, Company lawyers felt obliged to consult the Crown's Attorney General first on the legality of such a move. He offered his legal opinion that its conquest by a South Asian territorial and maritime power was what firmly determined it to no longer be possibly considered Portuguese dominion.[91]

Meanwhile, the Bombay government continued in active attempts to remake the physical geography of the region: stop up flooding and breaches, drain the marshes and connect the various parts of Bombay more regularly. As Samuel Sheppard noted in 1933, these efforts were the early stirrings of 'the signs of Bombay being converted from seven islands into one', a process of 'that great epic or reclamation which has been in progress for two and a half centuries and of which the end is not yet in sight'.[92] With this in mind, it is of course worth concluding with one simple observation. Among the colonial legacies one can find in modern Mumbai is this somewhat obvious fact: it is, after several centuries of debate, at least unambiguously no longer an island – a question of physical geography that had, in a sense, been anticipated by legal geographies centuries earlier.

Notes

1 *Materials towards a Statistical Account of the Town and Island of Bombay (Bombay Gazetteer)* (3 vols, Bombay, 1893) I, p. 5.
2 G. Ames, 'The role of religion in the transfer and rise of Bombay, c. 1661–1687', *HJ*, 46:2 (2003), 317–18.
3 Along with the others in the forum, see E. H. Gould, 'Entangled histories, entangled worlds: the English-speaking Atlantic as a Spanish periphery', *AHR*, 112:3 (2007), 764–86.

LEGAL GEOGRAPHY AND COLONIAL SOVEREIGNTY

4   Most notably, see L. Benton, *A Search for Sovereignty: Law and Geography in European Empires, 1400–1900* (Cambridge, 2009); C. Tomlins, 'The legal cartography of colonization, the legal polyphony of settlement: English intrusions on the American mainland in the seventeenth century', *Law & Social Inquiry*, 26:2 (2001), 315–72; C. Tomlins, *Freedom Bound: Law, Labor, and Civic Identity in Colonizing English America, 1580–1865* (Cambridge, 2010).
5   TNA, CO 77/8, fo. 225v; SP 89/6, fos 185–6.
6   G. Ames, *Renascent Empire? Pedro II and the Quest for Stability in Portuguese Monsoon Asia, ca. 1640–1683* (Amsterdam, 2000), esp. pp. 46–7; Ames, 'Transfer', 319.
7   BL, Additional MS 40,698, fo. 42.
8   TNA, SP 89/5, fos 151–2.
9   See, e.g., P. Cadell and J. Page, 'The acquisition and rise of Bombay', *The Journal of the Royal Asiatic Society of Great Britain and Ireland*, 3–4 (1958), 113–21.
10 TNA, SP 89/7, fo. 145; TNA, SP 89/13, fo. 142.
11 P. Barretto de Resende, *Livro do Estado Da India Oriental Repartido en tres partes* (Lisbon, 1674); BL, Sloane MS 197, fos 222–3.
12 TNA, CO 77/13, fos 110–13.
13 F. C. Danvers, *The Portuguese in India: Being a History of the Rise and Decline of Their Eastern Empire* (2 vols, London, 1894), II, p. 356; Ames, 'Transfer', 336; S. A. Khan, *Anglo-Portuguese Negotiations Relating to Bombay, 1660–1677* (Oxford, 1922), p. 479.
14 BL, IOR/E/3/34; IOR/H50, fo. 207; J. Fryer, *A New Account of East-India and Persia* (1698), p. 61.
15 Danvers, *Portuguese in India*, II, p. 356.
16 *A Description of the Port and Island of Bombay* (1724), pp. 12–14.
17 *Ibid.*, p. 18.
18 Khan, *Anglo-Portuguese Negotiations*, pp. 454–5.
19 TNA, CO 77/8, fo. 231; BL, IOR/E/3/27, fo. 141v; Khan, *Anglo-Portuguese Negotiations*, pp. 442–3.
20 BL, IOR/E/3/27, fo. 146v.
21 TNA, CO 77/9, fo. 70; CO 77/9, fos 46–7.
22 TNA, CO 77/9, fos 70–1.
23 BL, IOR/E/3/87, fo. 75.
24 Quoted by C. Fawcett, *The English Factories in India, Vol I. (New Series) (The Western Presidency)* (Oxford, 1936), p. 4.
25 See Benton, *A Search for Sovereignty*.
26 Fryer, *New Account of East India and Persia*, p. 70.
27 BL, IOR/H/50, fos 19–20.
28 TNA, CO 77/13, in Khan, *Anglo-Portuguese Negotiations*, p. 538.
29 TNA, CO 77/13, fo. 104.
30 TNA, CO 77/13, in Khan, *Anglo-Portuguese Negotiations*, pp. 533, 536.
31 TNA, CO 77/13, fo. 106.
32 TNA, CO 77/13, fo. 47; CO 77/13, fo. 99; Khan, *Anglo-Portuguese Negotiations*, p. 503.
33 TNA, CO 77/13, fo. 103.
34 BL, IOR/E/4/449, p. 20; Fawcett, *English Factories in India*, p. 118; BL, IOR/B/37, fo. 12.
35 BL, IOR/E/3/36, fo. 149.
36 Fawcett, *English Factories in India*, pp. 22, 57.
37 TNA, CO 77/13, fo. 12v; Fawcett, *English Factories in India*, pp. 113–14.
38 TNA, CO 77/13, fo. 75.
39 TNA, SP 89/14, fo. 28.
40 Fawcett, *English Factories in India*, pp. 145–8.
41 TNA, CO 77/13, in Khan, *Anglo-Portuguese Negotiations*, pp. 537–8.
42 BL, Additional MS 34,333 fo. 28; Additional MS 35,101 fo. 141; BL, IOR/E/3/87, fos. 159, 166.

43 TNA, CO 77/13, fos 67–8; TNA, CO 77/13, in Khan, *Anglo-Portuguese Negotiations*, p. 536.
44 TNA, CO 77/13, fo. 47; Khan, *Anglo-Portuguese Negotiations*, p. 505.
45 TNA, CO 77/9, fos 46–7.
46 BL, IOR/H/49, fo. 21.
47 Ames, 'Transfer', 332–4, 336 (Table I).
48 Fawcett, *The English Factories in India*, pp. 77, 110.
49 *Ibid.*, pp. 1–2, 4.
50 BL, IOR/E/3/32, fo. 10; IOR/E/3/32, fo. 14.
51 F. Warden, 'Report on the landed tenures of Bombay', *Transactions of the Bombay Geographical Society from June 1838 to February 1840*, 3 (Bombay, 1840), 8–9.
52 Fawcett, *English Factories in India*, p. 78.
53 Ames, *Renascent Empire?*, pp. 80–3.
54 BL, IOR/H/49, fo. 7; IOR/E/3/32, fos 10, 14; Ames, 'Role of religion', 332.
55 BL, IOR/E/3/32, fo. 10; IOR/E/3/32, fo. 14.
56 BL, IOR/H/50, fos 5–6.
57 BL, IOR/E/3/88, fo. 92v.
58 BL, IOR/G/3/1, pp. 62–3.
59 E. B. Sainsbury (ed.), *A Calendar of the Court Minutes, etc., of the East India Company* (11 vols, Oxford, 1907–38), XI, pp. 9–11, 13, 49, 51–2, 71, 79, 97–9, 115, 125–6; BL, IOR/H/50, fo. 86; Fawcett, *English Factories in India*, p. 64.
60 See Sainsbury (ed.), *Court Minutes*, XI, pp. 244–6; BL, IOR/H/51, fos 149–50.
61 TNA, SP 89/14, fo. 31.
62 TNA, CO 77/9, fos 64, 221; Khan, *Anglo-Portuguese Negotiations*, pp. 451, 473.
63 BL, IOR/G/3/1, pp. 17–18.
64 BL, IOR/H/60, p. 77.
65 BL, IOR/G/3/1, p. 59.
66 Warden, 'Report on the landed tenures', 11.
67 G. Forrest (ed.), *Selections from the Letters, Despatches, and Other State Papers Preserved in the Bombay Secretariat* (2 vols, Bombay, 1885–7), II, appendix C, original emphasis.
68 M. Fraas, 'They have travelled into a wrong latitude: the laws of England, Indian settlements and the British imperial constitution, 1726–1773' (Duke University PhD dissertation, 2011), pp. 48, 227.
69 BL, IOR/G/3/1, pp. 101–2; Forrest (ed.), *Selections*, II, p. 386.
70 BL, IOR/E/3/48, fo. 232.
71 BL, IOR/B/40, fos 103–4; IOR/H/36, fo. 99; IOR/H/36, fo. 99; IOR/H/36, fo. 97; IOR/B/40, fo. 19; IOR/E/1/3, fo. 388; IOR/E/1/3, fos 390–1.
72 BL, IOR/G/3/4, fo. 23.
73 BL, IOR/E/3/50, fo. 244.
74 BL, IOR/E/3/49, fo. 73.
75 BL, IOR/G/3/3, no. 3, fo. 31.
76 BL, IOR/G/3/10a, n.p.
77 BL, IOR/G/3/4, fo. 25.
78 BL, IOR/E/3/50, fos 251, 232–6.
79 BL, IOR/E/3/91, fo. 49.
80 *Ibid.*, fos 297, 262.
81 BL, IOR/E/4/449, p. 20.
82 *Ibid.*, pp. 78, 80.
83 BL, IOR/H/60, p. 21.
84 *Ibid.*; J. F. Judice Biker (ed.), *Collecção dos tratados, convenções, contratos, e actos publicos celebrados entra a coroa de Portugal e as mais ptencias desde 1640 até ao presente* (30 vols, Lisbon, 1856), II, pp. 278–80.
85 BL, IOR/H/60, pp. 21–2.
86 *Ibid.*, pp. 22, 23; IOR/H/60 no. 21, p. 108; IOR/E/3/99, fo. 205.
87 BL, IOR/E/3/101 fo. 120; Ernest R. Hull, *Bombay Mission-History, with a Special Study of the Padroado Question* (2 vols, Bombay, 1927), I, esp. part III.

88 S. Halikowski Smith, *Creolization and Diaspora in the Portuguese Indies: The Social World of Ayutthaya, 1640–1720* (Leiden, 2011), p. 29.
89 BL, IOR/H/60, p. 25.
90 Warden, 'Report on the landed tenures', 43.
91 BL, IOR/L/L/6/1, fo. 82.
92 S. Sheppard, 'Introduction', in John Burnell, *Bombay in the Days of Queen Anne, Being an Account of the Settlement* (London, 1933, repr. New Delhi, 1997), p. xviii.

CHAPTER EIGHT

Compensating imperial loyalty, 1700–1800

Julian Hoppit

The great and *chief end* thereof, of Mens uniting into Commonwealths, and putting themselves under Government, *is the Preservation of their Property*. To which in the state of Nature there are many things wanting.
John Locke[1]

... let it go forth to the world, that the parliament of Great Britain will protect their subjects and their property.
Lord North[2]

Governments expect loyalty from their people, with treason laws often providing an ultimate sanction.[3] What, though, should happen when people are loyal but their government fails to protect lives and property? Where the government itself is lost, the question is irrelevant. But what if it survives, at least in reasonably good working order and the people lack the sanction of the ballot box? Locke gave no answer to that question. However, providing compensation was one practical response made in Britain in the seventeenth and eighteenth centuries. For example, in 1663 £60,000 was awarded to royalist officers for hardships and losses following defeat in the Civil Wars; compensation of nearly £8,000 was paid following the Scottish judicial murder of officers of the English ship 'The Worcester' in 1704; Preston received £4,730 because of losses in the Jacobite rising of 1715; Charles Dingley got £2,000 for the riotous destruction of his Limehouse sawmill in 1768; and around £100,000 was provided, the majority via local rates, to cover losses sustained in the Gordon riots in London in 1780.[4]

Such efforts were not confined to the domestic sphere. Indeed, in practice governments find it much more difficult to protect people and property in a colonial than in a metropolitan context. At the edge of empire, imperial powers compete with indigenous people, rival empires, predators and free riders. They are unlikely always to succeed in those encounters, exposing colonists to risks of significant losses. It will, equally, be especially difficult for the imperial centre to help the needy at the imperial margin. Yet as at home, sometimes the government in London financially compensated its imperial people when it failed them, notably the white islanders of Nevis and St Christopher's (St Kitt's) in the West Indies after a French attack in 1706, and the propertied Loyalists to the Crown after Britain admitted defeat at the conclusion of the American war in 1783. This chapter explores these two cases, both to show a hitherto little noticed aspect of imperialism in practice, and also to shed light on some of the assumptions and principles that structured the making, maintenance and loss of empire that deserve more attention. What is found is a complex world for the management of some of the risks of imperialism, not least to maintain confidence about its sustainability. Brute force and the flow of people, goods, laws and institutions were, of course, the very stuff of empire, but it was also sustained by belief, a belief which sometimes required exceptional payments to sustain.

This chapter is in three sections. The first two consider the case studies at its heart. In the third, the wider issues involved are investigated, and related to other types of compensation paid as part of eighteenth-century British imperialism.

On 20 April 1706, in the midst of the War of the Spanish Succession, Sir Christopher Hedges, the Secretary of State for the south, wrote confidently to the governor of the Leeward Islands that worries of an impending French attack there were 'groundless'.[5] How wrong he was. Reports were already on board ship to London that in February and March French forces, including privateers, had raided two of Britain's islands, St Christopher's and Nevis, withdrawing as quickly as they had arrived; plunder, not territory, was their aim. By a French report, they were 'pillag'd and ravag'd', crops and houses were burned, many slaves and some plantation equipment taken as booty. Such was the destruction that the same French report claimed that 'those 2 Islands cannot in 10 Years be restor'd to the Condition they were in'.[6] Much the same account was submitted to the Board of Trade by English officials in the West Indies.[7] There is no doubt that much had been destroyed or seized, including many slaves. Immediately the official mind was concerned that this threatened a radical rethinking among the islanders of the very viability of Britain's colonial empire in the Caribbean. The white islanders were said to be 'dispirited ... despairing; they think themselves neglected, if not abandon'd, and a great many have already declar'd they will live soe precarious noe longer, and are preparing to seek for settlements and security elsewhere'.[8]

Soon enough, the white islanders sought aid from London. In May they petitioned the queen, asking for her compassion and exemption from the navigation laws and 4.5 per cent customs duty charged to finance local administration.[9] Separately they reported to Hedges that their losses were £1m, and that terms they had agreed under duress with the French required surrendering a further 1,400 slaves or £42,000 in October. Because so many slaves had already been seized, they saw no prospect of meeting this and that consequently they would 'be forced to desert the Island, as some have already done'.[10] The government's immediate response was to send to the islands five shiploads of supplies and to assert its commitment to the protection and resettlement of the islands.[11] Giving up the islands was never part of the government's strategic thinking.

Welcome though such succour and commitment must have been, it did not amount to much. Nevis was especially hard hit, leading to terrible disease. In December it was reported that 'The pestilence is so great at Nevis, that half the population are dead or dying'; its exports to Britain fell by 80 per cent between the three years before and after the raids.[12] It was probably the plight of Nevis in particular which prompted the white islanders to submit a petition to the House of Commons on 5 March 1707. Direct losses were now put at above £500,000, quite apart from the destruction of a valuable trade. Again it was noted that the islands might be abandoned unless significant help was forthcoming.[13] A select committee of thirty-four MPs considered the petition, quickly reporting that the case had been proven, believing that their losses had been 'computed at a very moderate Rate'. Deference to the Crown's authority led the Commons to address Queen Anne requesting an enquiry into the losses, and hoping that she might use public funds to help secure the islands again, with the aim of their resettlement. A positive response quickly followed, commending the compassion of the House of Commons, though noting that the islanders were 'justly entitled to their Care, by the large Returns they make to the Publick'.[14] The Board of Trade was ordered to investigate the losses on the two islands. An elaborate administration was erected: unpaid commissioners from among the white islanders, supported by two paid secretaries sent out from London, took evidence of detailed losses upon oath. Elaborate this may have been, but the Attorney General was already concerned that this system, depending so heavily upon interested parties, would mean that 'the losses will be estimated as high as may be'.[15]

The commissioners worked quickly, reducing claims only slightly. London received their reports in June 1708, but not until January 1709 did Lord Treasurer Godolphin summarise them to the queen: £355,351 had been lost, 61 per cent on Nevis, 39 per cent on St Christopher's. Over 600 individuals were concerned, around 110 of them women, including fifty-four female planters. Probably all were white; the sufferings of the seized slaves are absent from the official records.[16] In the interim further charitable supplies were sent to the islands to be distributed to the people 'in proportion to their wants'.[17] On 1 February Godolphin's summary was presented to the House of Commons to ponder. The following month they requested and received the detailed returns of the commissioners, suggesting that they were shocked by the scale of the reported losses and sought the information to allow them to reduce the amount. In early April it was proposed in the Commons that £154,000 should be provided to those who had or were going to resettle on the islands. But after debate this total was reduced to £103,003, aiming to recompense the sufferers for one-third of their losses.[18] Because the details of this debate have not survived it is unclear why this sum was decided upon, though it is clear that with the end of the parliamentary session only two weeks off, there was no time to legislate the necessary monies. This prompted the islanders to exhort Parliament to act; after all it was now more than three years since the French raids. Moral pressure was exerted: 'The poor Inhabitants of those Islands have been encouraged to continue there, under great Hardships, in the comfortable Hopes of the said Bounty.' But they also employed wider financial and economic arguments, that previously they had sent to Britain 12,000 hogsheads of sugar yearly, but now only 2,000, 'besides what is lost by not Exporting such large Quantities of Manufactures, and Employing so many Ships as formerly'.[19]

In fact it was to be two years before Parliament legislated the supply to pay the islanders to resettle, buried deep in an act for licensing and regulating hackney coaches.[20] But with the money now supposedly to hand, difficulties were encountered about ensuring that it went to those intended. Various nice questions emerged, such as whether someone who had left Nevis in 1706 but then resettled in St Christopher's, or vice versa, was eligible for compensation. In late 1712 oaths were taken regarding resettlement, with the first payments, all made in the form of interest bearing debentures, being issued from March 1713.[21] Still there were complications, requiring five further acts to settle matters, the last in 1727, twenty-one years after the islands had been overrun.[22] In 1730 forty-three of the debentures had still not been cashed, though only £285 was involved.[23]

Despite such delays and complications, the state had constructed a mechanism to compensate those it judged to be real sufferers on an imperial margin. This was a wholly new effort, though some of the issues had been encountered in working through the land settlements in Britain and Ireland after the Restoration in 1660, requiring not just considerable monies to be found, but an elaborate administration with various checks and balances to ward against fraud.[24] Yet the problem that was being addressed was very far from novel. Predations, by rival colonial powers and pirates, had been common in the Caribbean for almost half a century. In Dunn's words, this had 'taught the island planters to flee rather than fight, to accept frequent demolition of their property as a fact of life, and to lobby for compensation from the home authorities'.[25] Perhaps the attacks in 1706 were more destructive than before, but they were certainly not different in kind to previous experiences.

Several factors probably led to the state's innovative response to the raids on St Christopher's and Nevis, though want of direct evidence makes firm statements impossible. Possibly the islanders were now more skilled than ever at putting their case in London, that this marked an important stage in the development of the West Indian interest in London. Contests over the monopoly of the Royal Africa Company over the past decade had helped to mobilise West Indian interests in important ways.[26] Certainly the islands' colonial agents worked closely with the Board of Trade, a body which also occasionally consulted with those merchants and planters from the islands who happened to be in London.[27] They appreciated that this body, now a decade old, was pivotal in colonial government. Yet if the white islanders deferred to its authority, they skilfully spread their fire, exhorting the Crown, executive and Parliament to act. Even so, if such activities were important, they succeeded because the state was willing and able to respond to those calls.

There appears to have been a very real sense that the islands might be abandoned. Officials quickly sensed the possibility, and the islanders made frequent mention of it. After all, the disastrous failure of the Scottish Darien scheme less than a decade before was fresh in the mind, with compensation, a major part of the 'equivalent', agreed in the fifteenth article of the Union treaty in December 1706.[28] The strategic consequences of abandonment of the two islands might be grave, making British interests elsewhere in the Caribbean more vulnerable. And if Britain lost the Caribbean then France could concentrate more of its resources on the European conflict.

Central government may well have felt reasonably confident about considering compensation in 1706. If expenditure on war was high, revenues were reasonably strong, the alliance was strong and the war was going well. It is notable that just as compensation was being considered for the islanders, land and money was being lavished on the duke of Marlborough to build Blenheim Palace. But once the principle of compensation had been conceded the war took a turn for the worse with defeat at Almanza in April 1707. The increasing burdens of war meant that payment of compensation was deferred. As Oldmixon put it in 1708, "'Tis not likely so great a Sum should be given them, while the *British* Empire is at such prodigious yearly Expences to maintain the War ... What may be done for them in time of Peace, will come easily; till then we fear they must look on their Losses as a Debt.'[29]

Quite why the state decided specifically to offer compensation is unclear. It may be telling that another option it might have pursued, issuing a charity brief, was now losing some of its former purpose and scope. For example, a brief for £11,000 had been raised in 1691 following a French attack on Teignmouth and Shaldon in Devon, but briefs of this type, as well as for the redemption of captives, disappeared after 1700, partly because of heightened statutory regulation in 1705.[30] The only sign of charity for the islanders was in New England where about £700 was raised.[31] With state-sponsored charity now out of favour for such causes, compensation was perhaps the obvious alternative. Not, of course, that it was quite the same thing.

Charity differs from compensation in important respects, notably as between a gift and a right. Recall that Queen Anne thought that the white islanders were 'justly entitled' to parliamentary care. If this was not elaborated upon, and evidence for the reasoning behind the decision to provide compensation in 1706 or 1707 has not yet been found, it might have had various meanings. Clearly the expectation of compensation was meant to provide not only funds but a type of collateral so that the colonists would invest once again in the imperial project. Alternatively, the compensation can be viewed as a type of insurance payment, a post hoc mitigation of some of the risks of empire at this particularly perilous stage of its development. Another important aspect was the grant of compensation confirmed that the white islanders were British citizens, with all that entailed.[32] One interesting aspect of this was that compensation raised in effect the issue of virtual representation, showing as one analyst put it that Parliament was 'equally diffusive of their Bounty to all Her Majesty's Subjects in general ... they thought it not enough to give ear to the Complaints of those whom they more immediately represented, but took it as a Duty incumbent upon them, to remedy the Grievances of, and provide for, the Necessitous, how remote soever they might live from Places they serv'd for'.[33]

Whether the compensation given to the colonists on these two islands was effective is a moot point. From one perspective it looked inadequate. Initially the white islanders put their losses at £1m, then at half that, before proving them at over £300,000, only for the Commons to decide to cover only one-third of this, or one-tenth the original estimate.[34] Arguably, however, it was the government's decision on 21 March 1707 to tie material help to levels of loss that was critical by giving the white islanders the confidence to plan ahead. What is clear is that St Christopher's recovered soon enough, and, aided by the French ceding their half of the island to Britain at the peace in 1713, then expanded to become, according to Sheridan, 'the richest colony in the British Empire by the eve of the American Revolution'.[35] Nevis, the smaller of the islands, did less well.

Compensation should not be judged in solely material terms however, for it had contributed in a novel way to the political and economic culture of empire. A precedent had been set. However, one consequence was that the government in London was made fully aware for the first time of the private costs of empire. If it knew well enough how much it spent on its armed force and colonial administration, the market value of the private efforts of its citizens in the Americas had previously only been glimpsed through some trade statistics or asserted in wild speculations. Now, though, the costs of private property on two small islands had been detailed precisely, down to the last slave seized, crop burned and house ransacked. And if such losses were in any way representative then the value of private property across Britain's empire must have been many times higher. On the one hand that was cause for celebration; Britain's imperial economy was even more valuable than had previously been thought. On the other there was more to lose than ever, while the concession of the principle of compensation raised the spectre of further failures leading to even greater claims on the public purse. Perhaps some wondered if Britain could afford its empire on such terms. In fact, military successes avoided that scenario in the imperial setting until after the loss of the Thirteen Colonies when, once again, some of the risks and reciprocities of empire came back to haunt the metropole.

During the American war, American states had often seized the property of Loyalists, who numbered tens of thousands, while one interested party claimed that many hundreds of Loyalists had 'been *assassinated and murdered in cold blood'*.[36] If the treaty of Paris that ended the war in 1783 made some provision for the return of the seized property, this never had the slightest chance of success. Additionally, after the war Loyalists found it impossible to recover debts contracted in America before the war, yet were sometimes pursued by Americans for debts they had contracted but now lacked the property to repay – the states were meant to pay the debts from the property they had seized. Unsurprisingly, while some Loyalists remained in America, many moved elsewhere, including some 7,000 to Britain. All looked to Britain for material succour. About 40,000 acres of land was provided, mostly in Canada, to help many, while charitable efforts led to the establishment of Sierra Leone to home black Loyalists. But some propertied Loyalists sought financial aid for their loss of property, mounting a powerful case in London that is worth detailing a little, at the risk of repeating points made by Norton in her important study of 1974.[37]

During the war payments were made in London by the government to some Loyalists on an ad hoc basis, totalling £40,280 a year to 315 persons by the autumn of 1782, an average of £128 each. This led Shelburne, the Prime Minister, to complain that the sum had become 'enormous; some limit is necessary, and a judgement to be formed by some impartial person or persons of their claims'.[38] He appointed two MPs, Wilmot and Coke, to look over these cases to seek economies and some rationalisation. Working unpaid but with an office and clerical assistance at the Treasury, by January 1783 they had cut the annual bill by one-third. Even so, this was merely tidying up irregular developments and with the peace preliminaries having been signed in November 1782 the question of what the British government should do for the American Loyalists as a whole was unavoidable.

Sir Adam Ferguson told MPs that 'in the cause of the Loyalists were involved the honour, the justice, the gratitude, and ... the policy of the nation'.[39] Not all agreed with this, but crucially, the American Loyalists argued early and hard that they had not merely a claim but a right to compensation. Some calls were private initiatives, but a committee was also instituted that mounted a concerted campaign to obtain compensation, generating a sophisticated case in support.[40] A pamphlet from 1783 noted the statutory requirement for subjects 'to serve their prince against every rebellion, *power,* or *might*: That, whatsoever may happen in the fortune of war against the mind of a prince, it is against all law and good conscience, that such subjects, attending upon such service, should suffer for doing their true duty of allegiance'.[41] The common law was also invoked, on the reciprocity of allegiance and protection. Moreover, it was also noted that in 1775, when the Crown had issued a proclamation to suppress the American rebellion, loyal subjects had been promised *'the protection which the law will afford to their loyalty and zeal'*.[42] Relevant precedents were similarly recalled, including the case of St Christopher's and Nevis, as well as those who had lost property during the two major Jacobite risings in 1715 and 1745. Early on these various strands were woven with theoretical threads from Grotius, Pufendorf, Burlamaqui and, especially, de Vattel to produce a potent general argument about the very nature of civil society and the right to compensation:

> There is no fundamental law of civil society more clearly established, or better understood, than that of *transcendental propriety*, or *eminent domain*. By this law, the supreme power of every State is authorised to take and dispose of the wealth and property of individuals, when it becomes *necessary* to the *public safety*. But the same law enjoins that power to make *full compensation* for the property taken or given up, to the owners of it, and obliges the society to furnish the means of doing it.[43]

Joseph Galloway, a key figure in this campaign, emphasised that the Loyalists' property 'was given up as the price and purchase of peace for their *fellow-subjects*'.[44] The Loyalists argued that the state was duty bound to defend its citizens and if, as in the treaty of Paris in 1783, it acknowledged a failure to do so and had surrendered up the property of some of its citizens to make the peace, then compensation was due by right.

If there was some opposition to the idea of compensating the Loyalists, because some laid blame at the Loyalists' door for the outbreak of war, it did not amount to much. By act, a commission of enquiry was instituted (three of whom went to North America to investigate).[45] At the initial deadline in March 1784 there were already over 2,000 claimants to more than £7m of property. In fact, much more work had to be done to file and consider all claims, with the delays leading to complaints of uncertainty and anxiety endured by some Loyalists.[46] The investigation concluded in 1790 when it was reported that there had been 3,025 claims for a total of £10,358,413. Some 2,291 (76 per cent) claims were allowed, though allowed losses were put at only £3,033,091 (29 per cent).[47] The total final bill, including payments made during the war and administration costs, was £3.5m.[48]

It is important to note that the allowed losses were less than the value of the allowed claims – and nor were unpaid pre-war debts included, put at nearly £5m in 1791. Wilmot, the leading commissioner, thought that it was natural for the Loyalists, not knowing what claims would be allowed or disallowed, to throw everything in for consideration.[49] But the reduction by 71 per cent of the value of the losses was strikingly different to the reductions made by the commissioners to St Christopher's in 1707 who disallowed only 6 per cent.[50] Fraud was likely a factor in part, but the huge cost of the American war was surely especially important. After 1783 the public finances were very straitened, with savings being sought at every turn. In 1786 Pitt warned that Parliament was not bound to make good the full loss of the Loyalists.[51] Two years later he plainly stated that the losses were so large that full compensation was unaffordable. Such pragmatism was placed alongside a wholly compatible principle: 'The American Loyalists, in his opinion, could not call upon the House to make compensation for their losses as a matter of strict justice; but they, most undoubtedly, had strong claims on their generosity and compassion.'[52] Pitt set out different levels of compensation for four different types of Loyalists: those who had been in America when the war began; those who had chosen to live in England during the war; those who had held 'places or exercised professions in America' and so had 'lost their incomes'; finally were the West Florida claimants. Only the last of these were certainly to be compensated in full, because Florida had been ceded to Spain, with sliding scales used to determine payments to the other three classes.[53] All were equally citizens of the British empire, but in this instance at least some were more equal than others.

Like Pitt, Burke believed that the Loyalists 'had no claim upon the House founded in strict right', but that it was bound by a sense of honour and justice, key terms that recur in the debates, to do what it could to help. Pitt's scheme he described as 'liberal and prudent'. Strikingly, he went on to claim that it would have done the Loyalists no honour had they been paid in full 'because it would have proved, that they had no real principle of loyalty to inspire their conduct, but that they had joined the side that they had joined, under a certain expectation of running no risk whatever, but of receiving back the whole of their property'.[54] To Burke, loyalty was not a marketable commodity and one of the reciprocities of empire was risk-sharing between the state and its citizens. Both had to bear the costs of failure. Fox, unsurprisingly, argued differently: that there was a strict right to compensation, but not to the full amount claimed. Critically, he noted that compensation as viewed by Pitt and Burke was effectively a 'matter of compassion'. To him, compensation involved rights.[55]

This level of abstract reasoning has not been found when the fate of Nevis and St Christopher's were considered. But then it was founded upon developing ideas of empire between 1763 and 1776 that reached a wholly new level. One unusual aspect of this appears to have been important in the case made by the Loyalists when they employed the ideas of de Vattel and others. That is, they hitched their case to natural law theorists. In fact, very similar points and references had been made to the Commons in 1765 by Grey Cooper, counsel of the duke of Atholl, regarding the proposed purchase by the Crown for £70,000 of the duke's rights of regality over the Isle of Man (to aid the suppression of smugglers based there). Cooper summoned up the Lockean idea that 'Government, into whose-ever hands it is put, was intrusted with this condition, and for this end, that men might have and preserve their property.' Yet such preservation was not absolute, for 'it is one of the conditions under which civil property is held in all societies, that the owners may be forced to part with it to serve the necessities, or even the convenience of the state'. Crucially, however, though Cooper granted that the powers of Parliament were extensive he was sure that they were limited by its own sense of moderation and equity, as well as by the 'laws of God and nature'. His invocation of natural law theory was telling, as perhaps were his quotations from, among others, Grotius and Pufendorf.[56]

The similarities in the reasoning and referencing of Cooper and Galloway are too striking to have been mere coincidence. Though Cooper's speech was immediately judged exceptional and was soon in print, perhaps it resonated in the colonies because on exactly the same day that he spoke Martin Howard of Newport, Rhode Island, published a pamphlet similarly noting the distinctive status of the Isle of Man (and the Channel Islands) within, yet somewhat apart from, the British state. Howard was a Loyalist, ending his days in London, coming into contact with Galloway there in 1779 at the latest.[57] It seems likely that Galloway followed up on Howard's thinking about virtual representation and the case of the Isle of Man, coming across Cooper's case in the process. Cooper was then recalled in 1783 when, if the circumstances were very different, deep concerns remained over what commitments or contract existed between state and citizen in the making, maintenance and loss of empire.

If Cooper was an important source for Galloway and the Loyalists, he explicitly drew from a variety of intellectual traditions, notably that of natural law. Grotius was generally acknowledged as a particularly important fount for that tradition, but the publication of de Vattel's *The Law of Nations* in French in 1758 and in English in 1759 expressly considered some of the key practical issues raised by the American case: the rights of citizens when the nation submits to a foreign power; the right to security; the duties of nations when making a peace; and, critically, the alienation of property in order to make a peace. To de Vattel, such alienations were reasonable sacrifices to preserve the state, but were to be treated as alienations of property under the principle of eminent domain, that is 'the state is bound to indemnify the citizens who are sufferers by the transaction'.[58] Cooper and Galloway both followed de Vattel closely.

It was also the case, however, that the question of compensation had been raised as relations between Britain and her American colonies deteriorated after 1763. At the time of the repeal of the Stamp Act in 1766, the Commons addressed the Crown about obtaining compensation for those who had suffered in America at the hands of rioters the previous year. The presumption was that such payments should come from revenues raised there, not Britain. This led to governors being officially asked to seek such compensation from the colonial assemblies. Unsurprisingly, the assemblies were unenthusiastic, with Massachusetts initially denying that justice required such compensation. Pressure from its agent led it to yield somewhat, passing a bill to compensate, but also to pardon the rioters. The money was paid, though the Privy Council disallowed the pardons.[59] The question was raised again with the destruction of East India Company tea at Boston in December 1773. The following March Lord North insisted that Boston should be held to account, calling up precedents from Britain, including restitution for the destruction of property in Glasgow in 1725 during opposition to the malt tax. North's reasoning was challenged in the Commons and by Americans, and no payment for the destroyed tea was ever made.[60] In the two decades before helping the Loyalists became pressing, the compensation question had, then, been raised with regard to the rights of regality of the Isle of Man, the Stamp Act riots, Dingley's sawmill (which was connected to the Wilkes disturbances), the Boston tea party and the Gordon riots. Compensating American Loyalists, then, formed part of a wider attempt to negotiate security in an age of increasing popular unrest.

There were of course important differences between the two cases just outlined. In the first, while the white islanders sought aid, it does not appear that they claimed it as a right, perhaps because they could return, and quickly. They had mainly lost moveable not fixed property and so with some new investment their lives could be rebuilt along familiar lines. Moreover, they had been the victims of a failed campaign, not a failed war. Indeed, Britain was victorious in 1713, gaining the whole of St Christopher's. Its enhanced authority would stand it in good stead against its main rival, France, for a generation. By contrast, much of the property of the American Loyalists, both moveable and fixed, was lost to them forever; they were refugees, the West Indians in 1706 were not. For many, returning to the communities they had left was impossible. Similarly, they had backed the losing side in what began as a civil war but turned into an international war in which Britain was isolated, defeated and diminished. They claimed, however, compensation as a right.

Despite such important differences, both cases raised similar questions about the relationships between propertied colonists and imperial government. At heart was the issue of the division of responsibilities for losses between individual colonists and their governments, both colonial and imperial. The losses plainly did not arise from risks that were then insurable given the nature of available insurance provision, while the sums involved took it well beyond the capacity of charitable aid. From one perspective, it might have been expected that the imperial government would have fully met the costs of its failure to defend the colonists, but in both cases this was too costly to contemplate. But neither did the government absolve itself from any responsibility, in both cases shouldering a sizeable if minority share of the costs with the colonists, viewing them as citizens fully deserving of its care. This partial compensation was one means by which the imperial government demonstrated that colonial empire might be a public–private partnership in which the state had to do more than merely provide military might, political and legal authority and the navigation system. In doing so, it recognised the colonists as citizens of the empire, certainly under the care of the Crown, but who could justly make demands on the public purse via Parliament – though perhaps this was less of an option in proprietary colonies whose owners were notionally responsible.

Compensation was obviously vitally important to those who had lost property, but it influenced perceptions more widely of the reciprocities and risks involved in imperialism. Put another way, questions of national honour or dishonour mattered, affecting confidence in the imperial project. If an imperial government abandoned colonists when it had failed, then colonists, actual as well as potential, might feel that a Hobbesian dystopia was much too close for comfort.[61] Or, using North and Weingast's formulation, the imperial government had to commit in a way that was credible if Britons were individually to risk their lives and fortunes at the imperial margins.[62] Arguably it mattered hugely that having failed in both cases, the imperial government tried to make good some of the losses. There is a striking contrast here with the French state's repudiation of its debts to its former citizens in New France after 1763, this despite giving explicit undertakings at the peace. In 1765, David Hume, *chargé d'affaires* in Paris, noted how this questioned the trustworthiness of the French government, a stain the ancien regime found almost impossible to remove in its final decades. By 1769 those debts totalled £2.6m and forlornly their owners looked to their new British masters for payment.[63] How different the case of the American Loyalists was.

Clearly compensation was an exceptional type of governmental action. It was nowhere prescribed, while as has been seen, both Pitt and Burke specifically denied that it was provided to satisfy a right. This was contested, notably by Galloway, but the principle was not conceded. The reasons for not yielding are unclear. One point may have been that the imperial government might have believed that it was absolved from formal responsibility if it had made a reasonable effort to defend its colonists and their property. But surely crucial were the costs involved. Over £3m was paid to the American Loyalists, some thirty times the figure of compensation paid out after the Gordon riots of 1780, which, in turn, dwarfed all other payments of compensation within Britain following a failure by the government to defend property in the island. A crucial consequence of the two cases studied here is that they brought home vividly to Britain just how much wealth was bound up in empire. Dealing with the costs of its defence was of course a vital factor in the evolution of empire in the period, but the potential costs of compensation should defence fail set practical limits to some of the rights of colonists.

As has been noted, in part compensation was paid in these cases because they involved non-insurable risks. Such considerations obviously grew as empire, their economies and the destructive power of weaponry developed. Two twentieth-century examples help provide some context for the findings of this chapter. In 1941, the War Damages Commission was established essentially as an insurance scheme to cover the risks of wartime destruction within the UK, its costs being shared between property owners and taxpayers. This recognised the unavailability of commercial insurance in a new era of aerial bombing. After the Second World War, by contrast, the imperial government was generally keen to use language such as 'emergency' rather than 'war' to describe armed colonial independence efforts, in part so as not to invalidate commercial insurance cover for property, thereby keeping potentially huge liabilities off public finance balance sheets.[64] Such considerations were less significant in the eighteenth century because the insurance market was still relatively simple (mainly marine and fire) and inaccessible to many. The cases considered in this chapter are, therefore, those of a particular stage of imperial development, where the value of property had somewhat outstripped the means for its protection or insurance.

A final piece of context is to note that compensation sometimes intruded into Britain's eighteenth-century empire by other routes. In 1729 seven of the eight proprietors of Carolina surrendered their rights to the Crown, for some £22,500 in compensation. Similarly, when the Royal Africa Company was wound up in 1752, just over £100,000 was paid in compensation. And in January 1739 the Convention of Pardo signed (though quickly ignored) between Britain and Spain required the latter to pay British merchants £95,000 as compensation for Spanish attacks on their property in the Americas.[65] Taken with the two cases considered in this chapter, these instances make clear the occasional importance of significant payments to the negotiations by which parts of empire developed in the eighteenth century. At issue in all were property rights, whose definition, ownership and security were absolutely essential to the very nature of empire.⁶⁶ As they show, such rights were never settled and secure. How could they be, given the complex ways in which the British empire evolved, and the competition its colonists frequently faced?

Greene has argued that 'Throughout the British Empire, both at the center and in the peripheries, constitutions were customary. That is, in the best English constitutional tradition, they were all the products of evolving usage.'⁶⁷ Usually such changes are identified by considering moments of tension. The cases explored in this chapter provide a rather different perspective upon the negotiations and choices central to British eighteenth-century imperialism. It helps to point up the ways in which empire was bound together not only by migration and trade, the navigation system and brute force, but by expectations that are often hidden from view. Expectations, of course, do not come ready made; they bear the weight of the past, of experience as well as hope; and they change slowly and quietly. These two instances of compensation contribute to such change in important ways. But they also solidified expectations to the extent of raising the question of whether empire rested on a quasi-contract between the metropolitan government and its white colonists. In compensation we get an important insight into imperial constitutionalism in practice.

Notes

1 J. Locke, *Two Treatises of Government*, ed. Peter Laslett (Cambridge, 1991), pp. 350–1, original emphasis.
2 Speech in the House of Commons, 14 March 1774, in W. Cobbett (ed.), *The Parliamentary History of England* (36 vols, London, 1806–20), 1771–4, col. 1165. Hereafter this series is Cobbett, *Parliamentary History*.
3 L. Steffen, *Defining a British State: Treason and National Identity, 1608–1820* (Houndmills, 2001).
4 P. R. Newman, 'The 1663 list of indigent royalist officers considered as a primary source for the study of the royalist army', *HJ*, 30:4 (1987), 885–904; BPP, 1868–9, XXXV, pp. 39, 41, 71, and 163; G. F. E. Rudé, 'The Gordon riots: a study of the rioters and their victims', *TRHS*, 5th series, 6 (1956), 100.
5 *CSPC 1706–1708*, p. 116.
6 *Daily Courant* (18 May 1706 old style), reprinting in translation a report from the *Paris Gazette* (22 May 1706 new style), p. 251.
7 *CSPC 1706–1708*, pp. 76, 103, 117–119; *Journal of the Commissioners for Trade and Plantations, from April 1704, to February 1708–9* (London, 1920), pp. 258, 260, 268, 270, 277.
8 *CSPC 1706–1708*, p. 136. This case has not been explored previously by historians. Notably, it is ignored in N. A. Zacek, *Settler Society in the English Leeward Islands, 1670–1776* (Cambridge, 2010). She notes the raid, p. 223, but does not discuss the issue of compensation, being preoccupied with the troubled tenure of Parke as governor, 1706–10.
9 *CSPC 1706–1708*, p. 138.
10 *CSPC 1706–1708*, pp. 141, 146–7. The French originally seized from Nevis, the most badly hit of the two islands, 3,187 slaves from a total of 6,023.

11 *CJ*, XVI, p. 79; *CSPC 1706–1708*, pp. 186–7.
12 *CSPC 1706–1708*, p. 329; C. Whitworth, *State of the Trade of Great Britain in its Imports and Exports, Progressively from the Year 1697* (1776), pp. 61, 71; R. B. Sheridan, *Sugar and Slavery: An Economic History of the British West Indies, 1623–1775* (Barbados, 1974), p. 150; *CSPC 1706–1708*, p. 146. St Christopher's population probably declined only slightly, while its exports to Britain recovered quickly.
13 The petition is *To the Honourable the Knights, Citizens, and Burgesses, in Parliament Assembled. The Humble Petition of Several Proprietors of Plantations in the Islands of Nevis and St. Christophers in America, and Merchants Trading to the same* ([1707]). ESTC wrongly suggests a date of 1705 for this.
14 *CJ*, XV, pp. 323, 331, 347, 354. The Earl of Sunderland was now Secretary of State for the south and actively involved in dealings with the Leeward Islands. G. M. Townend, 'The political career of Charles Spencer, third Earl of Sunderland, 1695–1722' (University of Edinburgh PhD dissertation, 1984), p. 67.
15 *The Case of the Sufferers of Nevis and St. Christophers* ([1714?]), p. 1; *CSPC 1706–1708*, p. 504.
16 Details of the claims have survived for St Christopher's but not Nevis. There the total claimed was £132,333, which the commissioners reduced by £8,492, or 6.4 per cent: TNA, CO 243/2/6. Eventually 669 claims were paid, but some individuals had more than one claim: CO 243/8. Some 585 individual oaths were sworn, though this may be incomplete. Both the debentures and the oaths provide full names, which island, and whether the person was a planter or an inhabitant.
17 *CSPC 1706–1708*, pp. 738; *CSPC 1708–1709*, p. 91; *CJ*, XVI, p. 79.
18 *CJ*, XVI, p. 79, 178, 190. The calculation of one-third is clear from calculations inserted at the rear of TNA, CO 243/8.
19 *The Case of the Poor Distressed Planters, and Other Inhabitants of the Islands of Nevis, and St. Christopher's, in America* ([1709?]).
20 9 Anne, c. 23, § 88.
21 *Journal of the Commissioners for Trade and Plantations, from February 1708–9 to March 1714–15* (London, 1925), pp. 383–400, 417.
22 10 Anne, c. 34; 5 George I, c. 32; 8 George I, c. 20; 13 George I, c. 3; 1 George II, sess. 2, c. 8.
23 TNA, CO 243/8, loose insert at rear. Four debentures were still outstanding in 1744.
24 L. J. Arnold, 'The Irish Court of Claims of 1663', *Irish Historical Studies*, 24 (1985), 417–30; G. Tallon (ed.), *Court of Claims: Submissions and Evidence* (Irish Manuscripts Commission, Dublin, 2006); J. Thirsk, 'The Restoration land settlement', *JMH*, 26:4 (1954), 315–28; J. Habakkuk, 'The land settlement and the Restoration of Charles II', *TRHS*, 5th series, 28 (1978), 201–22.
25 R. S. Dunn, *Sugar and Slaves: the Rise of the Planter Class in the English West Indies, 1624–1713* (London, 1973), p. 118.
26 T. Keirn, 'Monopoly, economic thought, and the Royal African Company', in J. Brewer and S. Staves (eds), *Early Modern Conceptions of Property* (London, 1995), pp. 427–66; W. Pettigrew, 'Free to enslave: politics and the escalation of Britain's transatlantic slave trade, 1688–1714', *W&MQ*, 3rd series, 64:1 (2007), 3–38.
27 Generally on the role of agents, L. M. Penson, *The Colonial Agents of the British West Indies: a Study in Colonial Administration Mainly in the Eighteenth Century* (London, 1924).
28 Investors in the Darien scheme were reimbursed both for their initial investment, plus 5 per cent annual interest, a total return of 142 per cent. D. Watt, *The Price of Scotland: Darien, Union and the Wealth of Nations* (Edinburgh, 2007), ch. 17.
29 J. Oldmixon, *The British Empire in America* (2 vols, 1708), II, p. 218.
30 W. A. Bewes, *Church Briefs, or Royal Warrants for Collections for Charitable Objects* (London, 1896), pp. 293, 297; T. L. Auffenberg, 'Organized English benevolence: charity briefs 1625–1725' (Vanderbilt University PhD dissertation, 1973); 4 & 5 Anne, c. 14.
31 *A Modest Enquiry into the Grounds and Occasions of a Late Pamphlet, Intituled, a Memorial of the Present Deplorable State of New-England* (1707), p. 13.

32 See J. P. Greene, 'Liberty, slavery, and the transformation of British identity in the eighteenth-century West Indies', *Slavery and Abolition*, 21:1 (2000), 1–31, especially 6–7.
33 W. Pittis, *The History of the Present Parliament. And Convocation* (1711), pp. 168–9.
34 Eventually, islanders collected £99,361 in debentures. TNA, CO 243/8.
35 Sheridan, *Sugar and Slavery*, p. 160.
36 [J. Galloway], *Observations on the Fifth Article of the Treaty with America: and on the Necessity of Appointing a Judicial Enquiry into the Merits and Losses of the American Loyalists* (1783), p. 9.
37 P. J. Marshall, *Remaking the British Atlantic: The United States and the British Empire after American Independence* (Oxford, 2012), pp. 46 (n. 55), 156–8, 182–5; M. B. Norton, *The British-Americans: the Loyalist exiles in England, 1774–1789* (London, 1974). For a flavour of the cases for financial compensation see H. E. Egerton (ed.), *The Royal Commission on the Losses and Services of American Loyalists 1783 to 1785 Being the Notes of Mr. Daniel Parker Coke, M.P. One of the Commissioners during That Period* (Oxford, 1915).
38 J. Eardley-Wilmot, *Historical View of the Commission for Enquiring into the Losses, Services, and Claims, of the American Loyalists* (London, 1815), p. 17. This provides a good insider's account of the work of the compensation commission.
39 *Parliamentary Register*, 9 (1782–3), p. 210.
40 As an example of a personal appeal, see *A Narrative of the Transactions, Imprisonment, and Sufferings of John Connolly, an American Loyalist* (1783). Fraudulent claims became a problem. One was from J. F. D. Smyth, who mentioned the cause in *A Tour in the United States: Containing an Account of the Present Situation of that Country* (Dublin, 1784), pp. 287–8.
41 *Collections with Regard to the Case of the American Loyalists* ([1783]), p. 1 quoting 11 Henry VII, c. 1. This pamphlet refers, p. 3, to the 'provisional treaty' of Paris, and so may even have been published late in 1782.
42 *Collections of American Loyalists*, p. 1.
43 *The Case and Claim of the American Loyalists Impartially Stated* ([1783]), pp. 19–20. In the Anglophone world the concept of 'eminent domain' developed in colonial America but not Britain. For a telling discussion, see S. Reynolds, *Before Eminent Domain: Toward a History of Expropriation of Land for the Common Good* (Chapel Hill, NC, 2010). I am grateful for the advice of Susan Reynolds on this point.
44 *The Claim of the American Loyalists Reviewed and Maintained upon Incontrovertible Principles of Law and Justice* (1788), p. 68. Galloway's activities in Britain are dealt with only briefly by his various biographers.
45 23 George III, c. 80. Many more acts were needed to keep this commission going until its work was completed. For details see Eardley-Wilmot, *Historical View*.
46 *Parliamentary Register*, 20 (1786), p. 409–10; *St James' Chronicle* (14 September 1786).
47 *CJ*, XLV, p. 358.
48 P. Colquhoun, *A Treatise on the Wealth, Power, and Resources of the British Empire* (London, 1814), p. 216.
49 Eardley-Wilmot, *Historical View*, p. 63.
50 TNA, CO 243/6
51 *Parliamentary Register*, 20 (1786), p. 241.
52 *Parliamentary Register*, 23 (1787–80), p. 539; Cobbett, *Parliamentary History*, 1788–9, col. 610.
53 *Ibid.*, cols 610–12.
54 *Ibid.*, cols 614–15.
55 *Ibid.*, cols 615–16.
56 Cobbett, *Parliamentary History*, 1765–71, cols 24–5.
57 Grey's speech is in *State of the Proceedings in the House of Commons, on the Petition the Duke and Duchess of Atholl, Against the Bill 'For the More Effectual Preventing the Mischiefs Arising to the Revenue of Great Britain... from the Illicit and Clandestine Trade to and from the Isle of Man'* ([1765]); [M. Howard], 'A letter

from a gentleman at Halifax' [in fact, Newport, Rhode Island] in Merrill Jensen (ed.), *Tracts of the American Revolution, 1763-1776* (Indianapolis, 1967), p. 69; Norton, *The British-Americans*, pp. 162–4.

58 Emer de Vattel, *The Law of Nations*, ed. B. Kapossy and R. Whatmore (Indianapolis, 2008), pp. 208–9, 288–9, 448, 657–9, quotation at p. 659.

59 L. H. Gipson, *The British Empire before the American Revolution* (15 vols, New York, 1965), XI, pp. 16–24; P. D. G. Thomas, *British Politics and the Stamp Act Crisis: The First Phase of the American Revolution, 1763-1767* (Oxford, 1975), pp. 181–3, 199, 251.

60 Cobbett, *Parliamentary History*, 1771–1774, cols 1163–5, 1170, 1180, 1189–92; J. G. Marston, *King and Congress: the Transfer of Political Legitimacy, 1774–1776* (Princeton, 1987), p. 71.

61 T. Hobbes, *Leviathan*, ed. C. B. Macpherson (Harmondsworth, 1977), p. 186.

62 D. C. North & B. R. Weingast, 'Constitutions and commitment: the evolution of institutions governing public choice in seventeenth-century England', *JEcH*, 49:4 (1989), 803–32.

63 J. Y. T. Greig (ed.), *The Letters of David Hume* (2 vols, Oxford, 1932), I, pp. 405–6; Joël Felix, 'Finances, opinion publique et diplomatie: le Committee of Canada Merchants et la question du remboursement par la France des «billets du Canada» de propriété Britannique, 1763–1775', in Jean-Pierre Jessenne, Renaud Morieux and Pascal Dupuy (eds.), *Le Négoce de la Paix: Les Nations et les Traités Franco-Britanniques (1713-1802)* (Rouen, 2008), pp. 127–64; J. F. Bosher, *The Canada Merchants, 1713-1763* (Oxford, 1987), ch. 10.

64 I am very grateful for the help of David French here. Strikingly, there is no history of the War Damages Commission. Richard Fisher suggested that I consider the case of bombing in the Second World War at a meeting of the RHGS.

65 *CJ*, XXI, p. 426; BPP, 1868–9, XXXV, 129, 133; C. Jenkinson, *A Collection of all the Treatises of Peace, Alliance and Commerce between Great Britain and Other Powers* (3 vols, 1785), II, pp. 341–2.

66 Best discussed in P. J. Marshall, 'Parliament and property rights in the late eighteenth-century British empire', in Brewer and Staves (eds), *Conceptions of Property*, pp. 530–44; see also J. Hoppit, 'Compulsion, compensation and property rights in Britain, 1688–1833', *P&P*, 210 (2011), 93–128.

67 J. P. Greene, *Peripheries and Centre: Constitutional Development in the Extended Polities of the British Empire and United States, 1607-1788* (New York, 1986), p. 65.

CHAPTER NINE

Sheffield's vision: the American Revolution and the 1783 partition of North America

Eliga H. Gould

'As a sudden revolution – an unprecedented case – the independence of America has encouraged the wildest sallies of imagination.' Today, few Americans have heard of Lord Sheffield, the Anglo-Irish peer who wrote these words in 1783, and even fewer, it is probably safe to assume, have read the work that they introduce. Yet for a time, Sheffield's *Observations on the Commerce of the American States* was one of the most influential British statements on the American Revolution.[1] For readers in the former colonies (of whom there were quite a few), much of what Sheffield had to say would have rung true. Americans, Sheffield noted, were an industrious, enterprising people, as ready to work for their livelihoods as they had been to fight for their liberty. Given the right conditions, there was no reason why they should not prosper. But praising the late rebels was not why Sheffield wrote. Instead, his concern was with what the war's end meant for the British empire. Taking aim at pro-American merchants and politicians, many of whom advocated a speedy resumption of business as usual, Sheffield reminded his readers that Americans were 'no longer... British subjects'. To allow them to continue trading with the empire as if nothing had happened would be foolhardy. The sooner people accepted that fact, the better.[2]

More than 200 years after Sheffield wrote, the American Revolution remains almost as important to British history as it is to the history of the United States. As is true of American history, the aspect of the revolution that British historians generally emphasise is not the peace that ended the war but the democratic era – what R. R. Palmer famously called 'the age of democratic revolution' – that the revolution helped inaugurate.[3] There are good reasons for this preference. Although most Britons experienced the fighting in America at one remove, key groups in England, Scotland and Wales drew inspiration from American ideas of popular sovereignty, seeing in the erstwhile colonists' revolt a cause to be celebrated, if not an example to be followed.[4] Significantly, the revolution's British critics often acknowledged the appeal of such principles as well. Faced with boasts about how the former colonists had perfected British liberty, British conservatives responded with libertarian claims of their own, embracing humanitarian causes like the abolition of slavery and noting the thousands of Indians, African Americans and Loyalists who clearly preferred the freedom that only Britain could provide. In a sense, the American Revolution gave Britons a mirror with which to weigh the relative merits of their own government, pro as well as con. As would happen with France after 1789, much of the exchange took the form of a comparative argument over liberty – who had it, who did not and who had the best claim to the freedom that was the birthright of English people everywhere. In the competition that resulted, each nation served as the other's antithesis, while having little direct contact.[5]

In terms of the relationship between Britain proper and the United States, there is much to recommend such a perspective. As Sheffield's *Observations* reminds us, however, the American Revolution was also a defining moment in Europe's century-long scramble for America, one that had started with the Peace of Utrecht in 1713 and that would persist through the first quarter of the nineteenth century.[6] For that reason, the revolution was, among other things, a moment of imperial partition. In anticipation of the partitions that accompanied Britain's decolonisation during the twentieth century – notably the partition of Ireland in 1922 and the division of British India and British-controlled Palestine after the Second World War – one consequence, as Sheffield correctly perceived, was to ensure that Britons and Americans would remain entangled with each other in the hemispheric neighbourhood that they still shared. No less important, the revolution altered Spain's borders as well, creating a transcontinental dominion that briefly stretched from the Pacific Northwest to the Florida Keys and that contained thousands of people (red, white and black) who had once been subject to British rule and who, it was well known, were less than ardent in their allegiance to their new rulers. In the conflicts that resulted, partisans sometimes replayed the Anglo-American rivalry over liberty. But for the British and the other people affected by the empire's partition, including people in what became the territory of Spain and the United States, the questions that really mattered concerned how to make peace. In a region where governments were weak, where borders were shifting and ambiguous, and where the forces that had once bound the new territories and their inhabitants together were often as powerful as the ones that drove them apart, making peace turned out to be no simple matter, and that fact weighed heavily on people throughout North America. For this reason alone, the issues that Sheffield found so 'unprecedented' are issues that historians would do well to make part of how we understand the American Revolution today.[7]

In order to understand the American Revolution as it appeared to Sheffield, the first thing to grasp is that the treaty of 1783 was an act of partition that Britain, acting in concert with France, Spain and the United States, imposed on all of North America, including those parts that had remained loyal to George III. Although historians sometimes speak of Britain and its empire as though they made up a single, coherent polity, the British empire that the peacemakers carved up in 1783 was as fragmented as it was diverse. Probably the most important fissure was the divide that separated Britain proper – namely England, Scotland and Wales – from George III's colonies and overseas dependencies. In the years leading up to the revolution, this fissure was obviously a conspicuous part of metropolitan relations with the colonies that became the United States, but tensions between core and periphery also affected British subjects and allies who sided with the Crown. During the Revolutionary War, Loyalists – white as well as black – complained bitterly about the high-handed behaviour of the king's officers. In many localities, the British army's requisition system was a particular source of discontent, with commissaries seizing horses, wagons and provisions at below-market rates, and sometimes paying nothing at all. Loyalists also resented Britain's decision to keep many of the enclaves that it controlled under military law, instead of restoring civil government. 'Usage like this', wrote Chief Justice Thomas Jones of the impact on Long Island, which Britain occupied for most of the war, 'was a cruelty, an injustice, and such an act of dishonesty, as [the predominantly loyal inhabitants] had little reason to expect'.[8] For their part, British authorities often regarded Loyalists like Jones with almost as much suspicion as they did the rebellion's patriot leaders. In the bitter recriminations with which the British greeted the final defeat at Yorktown, one oft-heard allegation was that the war's outcome might have been different had the king's forces placed greater trust in Americans who refused to give up their allegiance to the Crown.

These tensions between core and periphery featured prominently in the peace treaty that the ministry of Lord Shelburne negotiated during the fall of 1782 and that Parliament ratified the following spring. Although Britain sought to protect Americans who had fought for the king – in what Maya Jasanoff has called a new paternalistic 'spirit of 1783' – Loyalists had good reason to feel betrayed.[9] The terms of this betrayal were especially stark in Indian country, where Britain's peace commissioners transferred millions of acres to the United States and

Spain without so much as mentioning the land's native proprietors. The peace also bore hard on the Loyalists, black as well as white. In the case of the black Loyalists, Sir Guy Carleton, commandant of the British garrison at New York, managed (for the most part) to blunt treaty provisions that obligated Britain to return former slaves to their patriot masters; however, for the tens of thousands of British Americans, well-born as well as humble, who lost everything that they owned, it was clear that Britain had promised more than it could deliver. While recognising an American obligation to return or pay compensation for property seized from Loyalists, the treaty only required that Congress 'recommend' compensatory measures to the states. Because the states were free under the Articles of Confederation to do as they pleased, this placed Americans under no obligation to do anything at all. Not surprisingly, when the settlement's terms were made public in Britain, the Shelburne ministry was widely criticised for abandoning the Loyalists to the Union's 'different provinces', as Thomas Pitt lamented when the House of Commons debated the treaty on 17 February 1783.[10]

The result was a peace settlement in which Britain and the other three contending powers carved up the British empire as it had stood in 1776, often with only minimal attention to the wishes of the ceded territory's inhabitants. In many places, Britain's former subjects and allies responded by accommodating (often grudgingly and reluctantly) the new reality. At the West Florida trading post of Manchac, across Lake Pontchartrain from New Orleans, the Irish merchant John Fitzpatrick and his common-law French creole wife remained loyal during the war's early years but 'turned Spaniards' after forces under Bernardo de Galvéz invaded in 1778. When Fitzpatrick died in 1790, he was a subject of Spain's Charles IV, though he retained friends and family throughout the empire.[11] Elsewhere, people relocated or resisted – or did both. In East Florida and the short-lived province of New Ireland in eastern Maine, both of which served as Loyalist sanctuaries during the war and which Britain hoped to keep once the war was over, thousands left for areas that were still under British control. In Saint Andrews, New Brunswick, the port that the New Irelanders founded on the eastern shore of Passamaquoddy Bay, houses to this day bear plaques with two sets of dates: one giving the year, usually 1779, when the structure was built in Castine (or Bagaduce), Maine; the other 1783 or 1784, which was when the building was disassembled, placed on a barge and shipped 150 miles down the coast to the new international border.[12] And not everyone was that fortunate. When the last British ships left East Florida in 1785, the beach was strewn with lumber from structures that the departing families could not take with them.[13]

Whatever the particulars, the numbers affected by the British empire's 1783 partition were enormous, and they dwarfed anything that Europeans in the New World – as opposed to Indians and African Americans, who knew dispossession and removal all too well – had ever before experienced.[14] This upheaval in turn forced people everywhere to grapple with four interrelated consequences. From the standpoint of the sovereigns most directly concerned, namely Britain, Spain and Congress and the states in the new American Union, the most important of these involved fashioning institutions that would bring order to a region where war and violence were still the norm. Although we do not usually think of the state and federal charters that Americans crafted in such terms, the quest for peace was an important part of constitution-making in the early United States – and it ultimately played a crucial role in the Constitutional Convention that met in Philadelphia in 1787.[15] Sheffield, for one, was keenly aware of this international dimension, noting the Union's weakness under the Articles of Confederation and advising the British government not to be over-hasty in its efforts to negotiate a commercial treaty with the former colonies. 'No treaty can be made with the American states that can be binding on the whole', wrote Sheffield, and he predicted that unless Americans devised a new federal charter, their Union might soon break apart.[16] Significantly, more than a few Americans agreed. In his *Circular to the State Governments* on resigning the command of the Continental Army in 1783, George Washington warned that without a strong national government, Americans would find themselves in a 'state of nature', warring among themselves and vulnerable to European manipulation.[17]

Nor was the need to fashion new governing institutions a phenomenon exclusive to the British colonies that became the United States. For Britain and Spain, the two European powers whose territorial borders changed under the settlement that ended the war, America's problems usually took a back seat to problems in Europe, yet both governments embarked on ambitious, institution-building projects in the colonies. In Britain's case, the most urgent task involved establishing sanctuaries for dispossessed Loyalists. Two of these, Nova Scotia and the Bahamas, were old colonies that had been peripheries of New England and the Carolinas, respectively, before the revolution but that assumed a new strategic and economic importance as thousands of British Americans moved in and put down roots. In two other colonies – New Brunswick, which was part of Nova Scotia until 1784, and Upper Canada, which Parliament took from Quebec in 1791 – Britain carved new sanctuaries out of older colonies with sparse European populations. And in 1787, black Loyalists planted several new settlements on the

Sierra Leone River in West Africa. Whatever the enclaves' genesis, the authorities in charge often tried to eradicate any vestiges of the republicanism that had powered the American movement for independence in 1776; however, the British were also mindful that if the empire was to recover, its subjects would need to be treated at least as well as citizens of the United States. In this spirit, Sheffield recommended adhering to the promise not to levy colonial taxes that Parliament had enacted in its effort to reconcile with Congress in 1778, and he criticised East Florida's assembly (before the colony was ceded to Spain) for approving a perpetual tax on foreign trade, with the proceeds to be placed at Parliament's disposal.[18] 'Whatever makes mankind most easy and contented', wrote Sheffield of Britain's policies toward its remaining colonies, those, surely, were 'the best means to fix them, and render them averse to changes'.[19]

Despite abandoning Native Americans in the treaties with Spain and the United States, Britain also continued to cultivate ties to Indians in the territory of both powers, and to look for ways to revive and formalise the relationship. In what became the Northwest Territory of the United States, responsibility for Indian trade and diplomacy remained in the hands of the British Indian Department in Montreal. Meanwhile, the Nassau-based Scottish firm of Panton, Leslie, which secured an exclusive trading license from Spanish authorities in East Florida in 1784, helped preserve Britain's influence among the powerful Creek and Seminole nations on the Gulf Coast into the second decade of the nineteenth century. Although Native Americans never forgot their betrayal in 1783, Britain's uncertain friendship came to look like the best hope for independence to the generation of native leaders who came of age during and after the revolution, and Indians continued to make common cause with British military and colonial authorities through the War of 1812. During the 1840s, the Métis Creek George Stiggins wrote that his people had an almost 'magnetic predilection for the British'. 'Many old men of the present day', Stiggins recalled, 'expiate on the candid, honest, and liberal disinterestedness of the British as friends to the Indians... [and] remark with wrath the contrast between the latter and the Americans.' For anyone who knew anything about the history of Indian country over the previous six decades, whether in the British empire or the United States, Britain's continued presence was an established fact.

By and large, the Spanish authorities who replaced Britain in East and West Florida followed a similar strategy. Although historians tend to describe Spain's North American empire as 'porous and precarious', in the words of David Weber, vastness alone made the dominion that Madrid acquired in 1783 a force to be reckoned with.[20] In Indian country, the Spanish initially opted for a kind of Hispano-British consortium, using the services of Panton, Leslie to arm and encourage the Creeks and Cherokees in the decade-long war that they waged against American settlers in territory that Spain disputed with the United States. During the 1780s, the Métis Creek leader Alexander McGillivray, son of a French-Creek mother and the South Carolina Tory merchant Lachlan McGillivray, emerged as a lynchpin of this arrangement, acting as a silent partner with William Panton of Panton, Leslie while accepting a Spanish pension and earning a reputation among Bourbon officials as 'nuestro mestizo'.[21] But Spain also created its own confederacy, eventually negotiating the Treaty of Fort Nogales (1793) – on the site of modern Vicksburg, Mississippi – with the Cherokees, Chickasaws, Choctaws and Creeks. On the strength of these ties, Spain was able to establish a military presence deep in territory also claimed by the United States. In 1794, Spanish soldiers built Fort Confederación some 200 miles up the Tombigbee River from Mobile, followed in 1795 by Fort San Fernando de las Barrancas at what is today Memphis, Tennessee.[22]

Like Britain, the Spanish also worked to secure the allegiance of English-speaking settlers who might otherwise seek to rejoin the British empire or, many observers feared, join the United States. Here again, following the lead of contemporary Spaniards, historians have tended to emphasise Spain's vulnerability in the face of what Juan Gassiot, an official in Sonora, Mexico, described in 1783 as the 'active, industrious, and aggressive' people who had just gained their independence from Britain.[23] Writing in 1790, shortly before he stepped down as governor of Spanish East Florida, Vicente Manuel de Zéspedes warned that the 'insatiable appetite of the English' had become even stronger 'among the present inhabitants of the United States'.[24] Eventually, history would prove both men right. During the first two decades of the Union's existence, however, it was often Spain that encroached on the United States. Exploiting inconsistencies in the British peace treaties with Spain and Congress, Madrid claimed a northern border for West Florida that included the southern portion of modern Alabama and Mississippi, and it barred American ships from the lower Mississippi River, which British colonists had navigated before the revolution. Spanish officials also reached out to disaffected Americans in the trans-Appalachian west, offering land on generous terms in Louisiana and the Floridas to those who were willing to move and fanning secessionist plots as far inland as Pittsburgh.[25] Probably the most notorious double-dealer in this entangled history was the former Continental Army officer and Kentucky adventurer James Wilkinson, but Wilkinson was hardly alone. The roster of people who gave Spain's advances at least a passing nod reads like a who's who of the early United States and includes such luminaries as Daniel Boone, Zebulon Pike, Aaron Burr, William Blount and Andrew Jackson.

In attempting to strengthen their hold on their respective parts of North America, Britain, Spain and the United States each acted in what they took to be their own interest, and they often did so in a self-consciously comparative and competitive manner. Inevitably, though, the main participants in the British empire's 1783 partition were also forced to collaborate. Sometimes, the collaboration was implicit. In the case of the US Constitution, one of the strongest arguments deployed by the document's Federalist authors was that in a neighbourhood dominated by Europe's colonial powers, Americans had no choice but to create a central government with comparable military and fiscal capacities and that other governments would view as a worthy treaty partner.[26] Conversely, Britain and Spain both realised that they would need to grant colonists in the Union's vicinity many of the rights that the states' own citizens enjoyed. In Louisiana and Florida, the change was particularly striking, as Spanish officials suspended the once non-negotiable requirement that the colonial subjects of Europe's Most Catholic Majesty all be Catholic and allowed English-speaking Protestants to settle in Spanish territory and become Spanish subjects. Although the change in policy was less apparent, British officials acknowledged the new reality as well. In the short-lived province of New Ireland, where Britain attempted to create an anti-republican government in 1780, Parliament had the sole right to legislate and raise taxes, members of the upper house were appointed by the Crown and served for life, and landholding was to be concentrated, with most inhabitants working the land as tenants. When New Brunswick was chartered four years later, however, Britain gave the province's white male inhabitants the same rights of self-government that British settlers had possessed in the colonies that became the United States.[27] With anything less, it was feared, people might conclude that life on the American side of the border was better.

In other matters, Britain, Spain and the United States collaborated explicitly and deliberately. Not surprisingly, such collaboration was particularly conspicuous in Anglo-American relations. Despite the widespread use of military law in the wartime enclaves that the British army controlled, Britain, for one, showed a keen awareness throughout the Revolutionary War of the need to uphold the laws and charters of the rebellious colonies as they had stood before 1776. This was ultimately one of the main reasons for New Ireland's failure. Backed by Lord George Germain and his undersecretary William Knox, and supported by some of the principal Loyalists from Massachusetts, including Thomas Oliver, Daniel Leonard and Henry Caner, all of whom hoped to secure places for themselves, the scheme involved turning the eastern third of Maine into a new colony. The problem was that Maine was a district of Massachusetts. When the charter reached the desk of Alexander Wedderburn, the King's Attorney General, in 1780, Wedderburn ruled that even though the Bay Colony's government had been inoperative since 1775, the Massachusetts charter of 1691 was still legally binding and could only be changed by act of Parliament, which New Ireland's backers did not have. During the Anglo-American peace talks two years later, when Britain made one last bid to secure the Loyalist enclave for the Crown, John Adams used the same logic to ensure that Castine and the Penobscot remained part of both his native state and the United States.[28]

Although Anglo-American relations after 1783 usually turned on questions of international as opposed to municipal law, such interactions did not end with the war's conclusion. Under the treaty of 1783, Britain and the United States pledged to cooperate on an array of issues, including the restoration of enemy property, the repayment of pre-war debts, the evacuation of posts in each other's territory, and the return of fugitive slaves. As Carleton's evacuation of the black Loyalists from New York and the states' failure to compensate the white Loyalists showed, these pledges were often honoured in the breach, and that failure was the occasion for renewed conflict into the mid-1790s. Gradually, though, a new international regime emerged for managing relations between the two English-speaking nations. Some of this was the result of formal diplomacy, notably the so-called Jay Treaty (1795), which settled most of the questions that the treaty of 1783 had failed to resolve. But Britons and Americans also collaborated informally in a number of areas, notably the management of Indian relations in the Northwest Territory and trade between US ports and Britain's colonies in the Caribbean and the Canadian Maritimes. As Sheffield's *Observations* suggests, Britain turned commerce into a particular sticking point, with Parliament refusing to make concessions to American ships and goods under the Navigation Laws and the Crown refusing to negotiate a commercial agreement, yet American firms repeatedly found ways to get around Britain's restrictions, often with the assistance of merchants in Britain and the colonies. For Captain Horatio Nelson, who commanded the Royal Navy's station in the Leeward Islands during the mid-1780s, it was more than he could bear 'to see American ships and vessels with their colours flying in defiance of the laws... landing and unloading in our ports'.[29]

Spain's relations with Britain and the United States followed a similar trajectory, with bouts of renewed conflict mixed with periods of compromise and collaboration. Because of the territorial extent of

Spain's North American empire, the resulting interactions spanned the entire continent. For the most part, Spain proved willing to allow its differences with the United States to remain unsettled until the wars of the French Revolution intervened in the early 1790s. With Britain, on the other hand, the 1783 partition of the British empire brought the two powers into conflict from one end of North America to the other. The most serious confrontation occurred in the Pacific Northwest, where British and American merchants had established a brisk trade in sea otter pelts during the final years of the Revolutionary War. In 1789, a Spanish naval captain detained two British ships at Nootka Sound on Vancouver Island, which Captain James Cook had visited in 1778, causing an international crisis that for a time looked as though it would lead to war. But there were tensions elsewhere in the war's aftermath, notably over the British settlements that Spain had tolerated (often barely) on Honduras Bay and the Mosquito Coast since the seventeenth century. In the dispute over Honduras Bay and the Mosquito Coast, which had been the site of fighting between Britain and Spain during the war and which received a significant number of Loyalist refugees once the war was over, the two governments resolved their differences in 1786 with a convention that conferred Spanish recognition on the British settlers on Honduras Bay (modern-day Belize) while requiring Britain to evacuate the Mosquito Coast.[30] The Nootka Convention of 1790 struck a similar compromise in the Pacific Northwest, with Spain allowing British ships to trade as far south as the northern border of California and both powers agreeing to abandon the disputed harbour.[31]

Taken together, the institutional arrangements that Britain, Spain and the United States adopted in the revolution's aftermath – both for their own subjects and citizens and in their relations with each other – are a reminder of the extent to which the British empire's partition created new forms of connection and entanglement, and not just within the empire's pre-1783 borders but throughout much of North America as well. Although the general outlines of a new continental order gradually began to emerge, this entangled history ensured that the peace that took hold during the late 1780s and early 1790s remained notable for its fragility and tenuousness. Moreover, the same fragility characterised the institutions that people everywhere created to bring order to the chaotic world in which they found themselves, and it did so whether the new institutions took the form of treaties between sovereign powers or informal accommodation on the part of people who had not been represented at the peace talks in Paris. Either way, the entanglements that resulted from the partition of 1783 encroached on all of North America's governments, keeping the borders that they erected porous, forcing each to fashion institutions with an eye to what others were doing, and limiting everyone's freedom of manoeuvre. And that, in turn, ensured that peace would remain one of the great desiderata for all of North America's people, existing alongside – while occasionally eclipsing and always complicating – the quest for liberty that still frames scholarship on the revolutionary era.

Compounding these weak and vulnerable institutions, the British empire's partition had three other consequences, each of which served to entangle Britain's former and current subjects still further and which also affected their search for peace. The first involved the all-important question of maritime trade. In terms of actual effects, it can be tempting to argue that the revolution had no impact at all on international commerce. This was particularly true of France, which disavowed all territorial ambitions in North America when it entered the war in 1778 and instead hoped to supplant Britain as the former colonies' main trading partner. Considered as a matter of formal policy, the gambit succeeded, with Louis XVI and Congress each granting the other most-favoured nation status and France opening several of its ports in the West Indies to American ships and goods. From a practical standpoint, however, the new agreement achieved little. Although American exports to both France and the French Caribbean did grow – Saint-Domingue, in particular, became one of the largest markets for US goods during the late 1780s and early 1790s – most of what the Union imported still came from Britain. Moreover, British and American merchants continued to work closely together, often with Loyalist factors as intermediaries, while commerce between France and America languished.[32] During the Paris peace talks in 1782, the Scottish diplomat Caleb Whitefoord told one of the French commissioners that while America might someday be a great empire, it was certain 'from a similarity of Language, Manners, and Religion, that Great Empire wou'd be *English*'.[33] In matters of trade, Whitefoord knew whereof he spoke.

If North America's trading patterns appeared unchanged from what they had been before the revolution, the British empire's partition nonetheless created new sources of conflict over the regulation of that trade. As the agreement between France and the United States indicated, one of the most dramatic changes involved the emergence of free trade as a serious instrument of policy, as opposed to an idea whose proponents were mainly academics like the Scottish political economist Adam Smith and French philosophes. Sheffield displayed a keen awareness of the implications in his *Observations*. Dismissing as 'rash theory' the suddenly fashionable critique of mercantile regulation, he used the pamphlet to defeat the Shelburne ministry's proposal to suspend the Navigation Acts for the former colonies and allow Americans to continue trading as they had before the war.³⁴ Yet in a number of instances, Britain embraced – and was a beneficiary of – the new ideas. In 1786, capitalising on the same Physiocrat-induced naiveté that informed French relations with the United States, the government persuaded Versailles to open France's heavily protected domestic markets, flooding them with cheap, well-made British goods.³⁵ Eventually, in pursuit of what Ronald Robinson and John Gallagher would call the imperialism of free trade, the British did the same with Spain and Spanish America.³⁶ In the latter case, Napoleon and the collapse of the Spanish Bourbons played a role in opening new markets, but Britain also benefited from having treaty partners whose belief in free trade was so 'doctrinaire', as Stanley Elkins and Eric McKitrick have written, 'that they had little idea what a bad bargain they were making'.³⁷

(The point here is that Sheffield defended the Navigation Act, not as an instrument of economic protection, but as a bulwark of Britain's merchant marine and the vital role that it played in sustaining British naval power. The post-1783 Anglo-American debate over 'mercantilism' was first and foremost a debate over shipping rights, one predicated on the shared conviction that British manufacturing was more than a match for rival producers in the United States. During the 1790s, the Corn Laws occasionally intruded, with Parliament's determination to protect the market share of great aristocrats and landed gentlemen serving to keep cheap grain from the Ohio Valley out of British markets, but such considerations were always secondary, in British minds – slightly less so to Americans – to the need to safeguard the Royal Navy. In this sense, Sheffield's defense of mercantilism owed little to zero-sum thinking and was instead consistent with Whig political economic theory and an expansionist understanding of both Britain's domestic economy and its overseas trade.)

No less important, the end of the Revolutionary War expanded the scope for smugglers and illicit traffickers of all descriptions, many of whom pursued their own version of free trade, with or without the permission of authorities in the jurisdictions where their business took them. As it happened, the mid-1780s produced a crippling cycle of droughts and hurricanes in the West Indies, which British officials repeatedly used to waive the prohibition on ships and goods from the United States. Captain Nelson's outburst against American vessels that visited the Leeward Islands, 'with colours flying in defiance of the laws', was aimed, at least in the first instance, at the royal governors who authorised the trade, not the former rebels. As they had done before the American Revolution, however, merchants of all nations also traded across the new international boundaries without legal sanction, and they adopted a variety of ingenious schemes to avoid detection. One widely used device was for British and American firms to enter into partnerships with each other, which enabled their ships to carry the papers – and display the flags – of both nations. When entering ports in the British Caribbean, ships engaged in such ventures invariably displayed the Union Jack, while on the return voyage, they often raised the Stars and Stripes, especially if there was any danger of being stopped by a Royal Navy warship looking for able-bodied seamen to impress into the vessel's crew. For the participants in such arrangements, it could be maddeningly difficult to say exactly what their nationality was. But that of course was the point.

Although nothing could match seaborne trade in terms of what European governments with interests in America cared about, the British empire's partition also revived – and in many areas intensified – the contested borders and borderlands that had long characterised large stretches of North America. Some of this was the result of ambiguity in the provisions of the various treaties that brought the Revolutionary War to a close. In the case of the peace treaties that Britain negotiated with Spain and the United States, the two documents used different latitudes to demarcate the northern border of what became Spanish West Florida. The result was to give each government an equally valid claim to a hundred-mile wide strip extending from western Georgia to the Mississippi River. Elsewhere, the new borderlands were internal and emerged within the new nations that the peace settlement created. Probably the best known of these was Vermont, which was claimed by both New Hampshire and New York and which declared independence from both during the war. Although the Congress resolved the dispute in 1791 by admitting the self-proclaimed republic as the Union's fourteenth state, the most direct route to foreign markets for many Vermonters, especially those like Ethan Allen and his brothers who farmed the rich bottomlands along Lake Champlain, ran north to the St Lawrence River. With that in mind, the Green Mountain Boys kept channels open throughout the 1780s to British officials in Quebec.

No matter where they were situated, the borders that the British empire's partition created frequently cut across what had been coherent social, political and economic networks and communities, and they divided people with long histories of interacting as subjects and allies of the same government. For George III's French subjects, the post-1783 redrawing of colonial borders was a particularly heavy blow, as the creation of New Brunswick and Upper Canada split Acadian and French Canadian families and communities that had already endured the effects of partition and displacement after the peace that ended the Seven Years War a generation earlier. In some cases – my own Acadian ancestors are a case in point – families turned the new jurisdictions to their advantage, using the French and English versions of their last names (Dubois *dit* Wood, Doucet *dit* Sweet, or Gould *dit* Doiron) to petition for land grants twice, sometimes doing so on both sides of the new borders. But North America's post-1783 boundaries unsettled the property rights of many others, and they left countless people stranded. And they gave displaced groups everywhere an incentive to recreate the ties that the boundaries had sundered. In what would become the states of Michigan, Wisconsin and Illinois, the British maintained a diplomatic and commercial presence into the 1820s, and Native Americans continued to travel to Montreal in order to collect the yearly 'annuity', namely, broadcloths, hats and silver ornaments, with which the British rewarded their Indian allies. Similar cross-border connections ensured that Passamaquoddy Bay and the St Croix River, which divided Maine and New Brunswick, would become the site of a brisk trade in illicit goods of all descriptions. Wherever such ties persisted, they tended to weaken the authority of the governments that the Revolutionary War created, and they were often sources of continued conflict.[38]

The final area where the end of the Revolutionary War complicated the quest for peace was in the protean loyalties of the people whom the empire's partition displaced. Historians have often described the demographic upheaval that accompanied the revolution as a matter of choosing between belonging to one national community or another – whether British, Spanish or American. There are, of course, good reasons for doing so. For the tens of thousands of Loyalists who left the lands that Britain ceded at the war's end, exile was the result of a conscious decision not to give up their allegiance to king and country, and many went on to distinguished careers in the service of the empire.[39] In some cases, though, exile weakened those loyalties, as refugees moved from place to place and as they found themselves abandoned by the government – or governments – for which they had fought. Although they often had no choice but to accept Britain's advances, Native Americans tended to be especially bitter over their betrayal, and they showed considerable flexibility, entertaining British overtures even as they kept channels to the Spanish and Americans open. Loyalists could also be surprisingly protean in their allegiance. This was especially true of people who lived and worked in the liminal maritime and territorial spaces that the empire's partition created, whether as seaborne merchants or Indian traders. In Florida and the Ohio Valley, Loyalist merchants were notoriously autonomous, with many taking Indian wives and joining Indian nations. If anything, the former slaves who founded Sierra Leone were even more independent-minded. Although historians usually describe the settlement as a British 'colony', both the black Loyalists who settled there and many of their white backers initially thought of it as a 'nation'. These aspirations kept the district in turmoil and triggered a brief settler rebellion in 1799.

In each of these areas – maritime trade, the creation and proliferation of borderlands and the movement of displaced peoples – the partition of the British empire at the end of the Revolutionary War unleashed forces every bit as powerful as the drive to fashion new institutions. At times, of course, governments benefited from the entanglements that these forces engendered. Noting the influx of American settlers into Spanish Florida and Louisiana, many of whom hoped to add both to the United States, Thomas Jefferson, for one, predicted in 1791 that the migration would eventually allow the Union to gain 'peaceably, what [might] otherwise cost us a war'. Although neither Britain nor Spain – nor France – could draw on comparable settler populations, they repeatedly sought to do the same thing in reverse, making common cause with Indian nations in US territory and reaching out to disaffected groups. Responding in 1794 to a proposal from Harry Innes, a federal judge in Kentucky, to open New Orleans to boats and goods from his state, Governor Manuel Gayoso of Spanish Natchez did not rule such a step out; however, he advised Innes that Kentucky would first need to 'separate from the Union'. 'Acquaint us with your proceedings', wrote the Spaniard: 'when things are come to an estate of maturity, push on the grand object of your Independancy and... send Commissaries properly authorized to treat the business with us in a more positive manner.'[40] As the Irish adventurer John O'Fallon observed shortly after arriving at Lexington in 1790,

> It is a fact well known and acknowledged throughout this *Western Country*... that the Inhabitants thereof can derive no *Commercial* or *political* advantage whatever by their being Subjected to *Congressional Supremacy*... [T]heir *last hope* of ever rising into any consequence as a people must be founded on confederating, independently,... on the Stipulation of a general Market or *free trade* at New Orleans... with that European power who shall hold it.[41]

As these remarks suggest, the upheaval caused by the British empire's partition continued to feed rivalries between North America's main imperial powers. Often, though, the people affected preferred to go their own way and make peace on their own terms, and they left a legacy of unilateralism that was destined to have a long life indeed. Along the border that Americans shared with New Brunswick and the Canadas, the imagined communities that such groups created tended to be short-lived and soon vanished from the historical record. Today, few people outside of New England have heard of the Indian Stream

Republic or the Aroostook War of 1838, both of which involved border disputes with British North America. In the Floridas, on the other hand, the Creek and Seminole Indians and Anglo-American settlers who remained after the 1783 handover experimented with one nationalist project after another. By far the most colourful was the State of Muskogee, which the white Loyalist William Augustus Bowles established in 1799 as an independent Creek nation in East Florida, replete with its own laws, flag and army and navy, but it was by no means the only one. In 1810, a group of Anglo-Americans, some from Loyalist backgrounds and all nominally subjects of Spain's Ferdinand VII, seized the Spanish citadel at Baton Rouge and made West Florida the second Spanish American colony (after Venezuela) to declare independence.[42] Although US forces quickly took control, deposing the republic's president, nullifying its constitution and dividing its territory between what became Louisiana, Mississippi, Alabama and Florida, the memory of America's first 'lone star state' refused to die. During the 1830s, the Republic of Texas took the West Florida flag, which displayed a white star on a blue background, as the model for its own standard, and the Irish songwriter Harry Macarthy eventually turned the 'Bonnie Blue Flag' into a popular symbol of the Confederacy with a popular song by the same name.[43]

To invoke the start of the American Civil War, of course, is to travel a long way from the peace treaty that carved up the British empire in 1783. Yet the latter event was no less an act of partition (albeit a failed one) than the former. Together, the two partitions place bookends on either side of the Union's early history, and they remind us that partition has – or at least ought to have – a place in the British, Spanish and Anglo-American history of the American Revolution at least as central as the familiar quest for liberty. They also remind us that while peace and liberty often go together, they can also work at cross purposes, especially when one person's search for peace is the cause of another person's war. This has long been a theme in Indian history and the history of slavery, but it deserves to be one in the revolution's general history too.[44] In the case of Britain and the American Revolution, the government of George III decided to make peace in 1782, not because the British cared about what peace would mean to the king's subjects and allies in North America, but because there was no longer support in England, Scotland and Wales for continuing to resist the former colonies' struggle for independence. Not surprisingly, although the treaty acknowledged the suffering of the Loyalists, the peace that resulted was one calculated first and foremost to serve the interests of Britons who lived in metropolitan Britain.

In so doing, the British effectively achieved two things. First, they ensured that Britain would continue to function as a metropole for all of the colonies and overseas possessions that had been subject to George III in 1776, including the colonies that became the United States. For Americans in the revolution's aftermath, one of the great unanswered questions would be when the United States finally achieved the independence that Congress had declared in 1776. Was it the Jay Treaty (1795), the War of 1812, the Monroe Doctrine (1823), the Texas Annexation between 1845 and 1848 or the American Civil War? Although Britain's dominion after 1783 was informal and exercised through the soft power of culture, trade and diplomacy, it often felt very real to citizens of the United States. The second consequence of Britain's actions at the conclusion of the Revolutionary War was to condemn the empire's former and current American subjects to a much longer cycle of war and conflict. That cycle was destined to have a profound impact on everyone involved, including people who lived in the colonies that became the United States. That of course is what partitions have usually done. The one that accompanied the American Revolution was no exception.

Notes

1 J. Holroyd, Viscount Sheffield, *Observations on the Commerce of the American States* (revised edition, originally published 1784; New York, 1970), p. 1.
2 *Ibid.*, p. 134n.
3 R. R. Palmer, *The Age of the Democratic Revolution: A Political History of Europe and America, 1760–1800* (2 vols, Princeton, 1959–1964).
4 For the revolution's British sympathisers, see, especially, J. Sainsbury, *Disaffected Patriots: London Supporters of Revolutionary America, 1769–1782* (Kingston, Ont., 1987). See also K. Wilson, *The Sense of the People: Politics, Culture, and Imperialism in England, 1715–1785* (Cambridge, 1995).
5 L. Colley, *Britons: Forging the Nation, 1707–1837* (New Haven, 1992). See also E. H. Gould, *The Persistence of Empire: British Political Culture in the Age of the American Revolution* (Chapel Hill, NC, 2000); S. Conway, *The British Isles and the War of American Independence* (Oxford, 2000).
6 The argument here builds on E. H. Gould, *Among the Powers of the Earth: The American Revolution and the Making of a New World Empire* (Cambridge, Mass., 2012).
7 For entangled history generally, see E. H. Gould, 'Entangled histories, entangled worlds: the English-speaking Atlantic as a Spanish periphery', *AHR*, 112:3 (2007), 764–86.
8 T. Jones, *History of New York during the Revolutionary War, and of the Leading Events in the Other Colonies at That Period*, ed. E. F. de Lancey (2 vols, New York, 1879), I, p. 331. For the British army's fraught relations with civilians on Long Island, see J. S. Tiedemann, 'Patriots by default: Queens County, New York, and the British army, 1776–1783', *W&MQ*, 3rd series, 43:1 (1986), 35–63.
9 M. Jasanoff, *Liberty's Exiles: American Loyalists in the Revolutionary World* (New York, 2011), pp. 11–13.
10 *Debate of the Commons of Great-Britain on the Articles of Peace. Monday, Feb. 17, 1783* (1783), p. 6.
11 M. F. Dalrymple (ed.), *The Merchant of Manchac: The Letterbooks of John Fitzpatrick, 1768–1790* (Baton Rouge, LA, 1978), p. 307.

12 J. S. Leamon, *Revolution Downeast: The War for American Independence in Maine* (Amherst, Mass., 1993), pp. 174–81.
13 Jasanoff, *Liberty's Exiles*, p. 109.
14 For the Loyalists' dispossession and removal as a 'diaspora', see K. Mason, 'The American Loyalist diaspora and the reconfiguration of the British Atlantic world', in E. H. Gould and P. S. Onuf (eds), *Empire and Nation: The American Revolution in the Atlantic World* (Baltimore, 2005).
15 Gould, *Powers of the Earth*, pp. 130–4. See also D. M. Golove and D. J. Hulsebosch, 'A civilized nation: the early American constitution, the Law of Nations, and the pursuit of international recognition', *New York University Law Review*, 85:4 (2010), 932–1066; D. C. Hendrickson, *Peace Pact: The Lost World of the American Founding* (Lawrence, KS, 2003).
16 Sheffield, *Observations*, p. 199.
17 G. Washington, *A Circular Letter from His Excellency General Washington, to the Several States* (Annapolis, MD., 1783), p. 12.
18 Sheffield, *Observations*, p. 177 and n.
19 *Ibid.*, p. 179.
20 D. J. Weber, *The Spanish Frontier in North America* (New Haven, 1992), p. 272.
21 G. B. Nash, 'The Hidden History of Mestizo America', *Journal of American History*, 82:3 (1995), 941–64.
22 Weber, *The Spanish Frontier in North America*, pp. 282–5.
23 K. McCarty (ed. and trans.), 'The Sonoran prophecy of 1783', *Journal of the Southwest*, 32:3 (1990), 318. For the modern interpretation, see Weber, *The Spanish Frontier in North America*, ch. 10.
24 J. A. Lewis (ed. and trans.), 'Cracker – Spanish Florida style', *Florida Historical Quarterly*, 63:2 (1984), 190.
25 Gould, *Powers of the Earth*, pp. 122–4, 135.
26 D. Higginbotham, 'War and state formation in revolutionary America', in Gould and Onuf (eds), *Empire and Nation*, pp. 54–71.
27 Leamon, *Revolution Downeast*, pp. 175–6, 180.
28 *Ibid.*, pp. 176–80.
29 Nelson to Lord Sydney, Nevis, 17 Nov. 1785, quoted in G. C. Bjork, 'The weaning of the American economy: independence, market changes, and economic development', *JEcH*, 24:4 (1964), 551.
30 St J. Robinson, 'Southern Loyalists in the Caribbean and Central America', *South Carolina Historical Magazine*, 93:3/4 (1992), 205–20.
31 Weber, *The Spanish Frontier in North America*, pp. 285–9.
32 S. M. Elkins and E. McKittrick, *The Age of Federalism: The Early American Republic, 1788–1800* (New York, 1993), pp. 70–3.
33 Quoted in E. H. Gould, 'A virtual nation: Greater Britain and the imperial legacy of the American Revolution', *AHR*, 104:2 (1999), 481, original emphasis.
34 Sheffield, *Observations*, p. 1.
35 Elkins and McKittrick, *The Age of Federalism*, pp. 71–2.
36 J. Gallagher and R. Robinson, 'The imperialism of free trade', *EcHR*, 6:1 (1953), 1–15.
37 Elkins and McKittrick, *The Age of Federalism*, p. 72.
38 See, for example, A. Taylor, *The Civil War of 1812: American Citizens, British Subjects, Irish Rebels, and Indian Allies* (New York, 2010).
39 Jasanoff, *Liberty's Exiles*, pp. 12–14.
40 M. Gayoso to Judge Harry Innes, Natchez, 27 July 1794, in *AHA Annual Report for 1945* (4 vols, Washington, 1947), IV, part 3, pp. 330–1.
41 O'Fallon to Miró, Lexington, 16 July 1790, *AHA Annual Report for 1945*, III, p. 360, original emphasis.
42 See discussion in Gould, *Powers of the Earth*, pp. 192–5, 201–2.
43 J. M. Coski, *The Confederate Battle Flag: America's Most Embattled Emblem* (Cambridge, Mass., 2005), pp. 2–4.
44 For the implications as it relates to Indian history and the history of slavery, see Gould, *Powers of the Earth*, pp. 210–8.

CHAPTER TEN

Legal pluralism and Burke's law of nations

Jennifer Pitts

> We have shown you that those people lived under the Law, which was formed even whilst we, I may say, were in the Forest, before we knew what Jurisprudence was ... And we contend that Mr. Hastings was bound to know and to act by these Laws.
>
> Edmund Burke, 1794[1]

In 1786, the House of Commons voted to impeach Warren Hastings, the former Governor General of Bengal, before a committee of the House of Lords, for 'unwarrantable criminal practices' that threatened the well-being of the natives of India, the fortunes of the East India Company, and the honour of the British nation and the Crown.[2] Edmund Burke, the chief manager of the prosecution, was widely hailed as a humanitarian during the early stages of one of the greatest political dramas of eighteenth-century Britain, as the British public grew increasingly anxious over the Company's practices of widespread bribery and corruption, aggressive war making and mistreatment of Indian rulers. By the time Hastings was finally acquitted in 1795, he was regarded as the victim of Burke's vindictive and monomaniacal crusade. For a long time scholarship continued to read the trial for evidence of Burke's motives and psychology; more recent scholarship has recovered a compelling moral and political theory from Burke's India speeches.[3]

This chapter is an effort to read the impeachment trial of Warren Hastings as a fertile moment of what might be called the politics of legal pluralism. Burke himself understood the impeachment as a peculiar and potent form of global legal encounter, and by the end of the trial, he had come to characterise his dispute with Hastings as at bottom a controversy about law.[4] Burke regarded the trial as a mobilisation of British law, through the rarely used mechanism of impeachment, to rein in and check the abuse of British power abroad – abuse that had been facilitated, he maintained, by the limitations, the parochial nature, of Britain's domestic laws themselves. Burke had insisted throughout the trial that Hastings and the East India Company were obligated by a dense network of laws. Arguing that 'all power [is] limited by law', Burke again and again enumerated the array of applicable laws: British laws and statutes; the law of nature and the law of nations; and local laws and customs, Hindu and Muslim.[5] Burke contrasted what he called this 'Table of Law' to the 'table of Law which this Prisoner has claimed', 'laws which he has laid down to himself' in defiance of the many systems of law whose authority he was obliged to recognise.[6] Hastings, in Burke's depiction, cast aside all these legal systems as irrelevant, on the grounds that European laws could not apply in India, and Indian laws effectively did not exist, since Asian societies knew nothing but arbitrary power.

Burke's speeches in the Hastings trial may be read with a view to understanding his views about the nature and the possibilities of law-governed interactions between Indians and the British, and perhaps more broadly between Europeans and those outside what Burke came to call the commonwealth of Europe. What we might call Burke's legal pluralism was an important means by which he articulated his understanding of a just global politics. Contemporary legal theorists have begun to apply the notion of legal pluralism, by which they mean the coexistence of multiple legal orders in the same space, to the international sphere.[7] After two centuries during which the field of international law had come to insist on a neat separation between two types of law – domestic law within states, and international law between states – legal thinkers seem recently to be discovering the possibility of a more diverse, capacious and messy global legal order.

The theorist William Twining, for instance, has recently urged a challenge to the common perception of law as monist, statist and positivist: that is, as imagining legal systems as internally coherent and mutually exclusive, and regarding law as the exclusive preserve of states, and as utterly distinct from other kinds of normative order.[8] This vision of law, made famous by John Austin in the 1830s, continues to be dominant. The rubric of legal pluralism, Twining and others suggest, may be a useful alternative, both empirically and normatively: in helping to supply more accurate depictions of how law actually operates in complex global interactions, and also in offering a vision of an international legal order (or orders) more accommodating of diversity and perhaps also more responsive to the claims of the most vulnerable. If the recent application of ideas of legal pluralism to international politics is fairly new, it is not entirely surprising, given that early theories of legal pluralism of the first decades of the twentieth century emerged out of studies of colonial societies. In those instances, however, the diversity of legal orders under study were contained within an overarching and hierarchical imperial structure. The new global legal pluralists find the approach useful precisely because no such hierarchy exists at the global level. In light of such innovations in the contemporary legal landscape, Burke's conception of the place of law in global interactions, particularly in its most mature articulation in his closing speech of the Hastings trial in 1794, is of particular interest. His efforts to make sense of and accommodate the interpenetration of a multiplicity of legal systems in India lend his impeachment speeches an affinity with the kind of legal pluralist thinking that Twining and others recommend. This chapter is thus a modest effort to contribute to the growing body of literature on the history of law and empire, which has been exploring the emergence of new kinds of jurisprudence in imperial spaces.[9]

Burke's speeches on India are instead often read as providing a theory of empire, a theory that is sometimes regarded as the forerunner of nineteenth-century liberal imperial theories. Robert Travers, for instance, has described Burke as the 'prophet of a reconstructed imperial sovereignty' in which Parliament would provide virtual representation for millions of Indian subjects.[10] Nicholas Dirks, in *Scandal of Empire*, likewise depicts Burke as the prophet of nineteenth-century reformist imperialism. It is true that Burke began very early to speak of Britain's 'empire' in India, while the East India Company was still a largely independent body, and before such a notion was common parlance in Britain.[11] He made use of distinctly constitutional language, speaking of Hastings's 'disfranchisement' of Asia[12] and describing the Company's acquisition of the diwani of Bengal in 1765 as the 'constitutional entrance of the Company into the affairs of India'.[13] Dirks describes the impeachment trial as an event that for Burke as well as later historians 'brought closure to the crisis over sovereignty that empire in India had posed'.[14] But Burke expressed no sense of closure at the conclusion of the trial. On the contrary, in one of his final comments on the trial less than a year before he died, he regretted that grief over his son's death had contributed to the feebleness of his 'endeavours to rescue this dull and thoughtless people from the punishments which their neglect and stupidity will bring upon them for their Systematick iniquity and oppression', and he charged a friend to 'make out the cruelty of this pretended acquittal, but in reality this barbarous and inhuman condemnation of whole Tribes and nations, and of all the abuses they contain. If ever Europe recovers its civilisation that work will be useful. Remember! Remember! Remember!'[15]

Burke was not, as Dirks suggests, immovably committed to the rescue and preservation of the empire. He held in an often quoted passage that all the 'circumstances' of corruption, misgovernment and British lack of sympathy for Indians 'are not, I confess, very favourable to the idea of our attempting to govern India at all. But there we are; there we are placed by the Sovereign Disposer; and we must do the best we can in our situation. The situation of man is the preceptor of his duty'.[16] The passage reminds us that Burke was not prepared to claim that British rule in India was categorically or inevitably unjust. But even at this relatively early period of his involvement with debates over India, when he was more optimistic that imperial injustice might be checked, he argued that if Britain could not stem its oppression of India, 'a ground is laid for their eternal separation', a prospect he contemplated without regret other than his dismay at the injustices that were precipitating such a break.[17]

Burke did not, in the end, articulate a precise constitutional solution for India. He argued that the sovereignty of Indian states should be shielded from encroachment or usurpation, but he also acknowledged a place for Warren Hastings as a British governor sent to 'protect' his Indian subjects.[18] He was aware that none of the readily available legal models – domestic or municipal law, imperial law, or law of nations – was adequate to the complexity and the novelty of the situation.

Burke's reflections on these questions point us toward a notion of international legality different from either existing models of the state or the vision of international law that was emerging in thinkers as different as Vattel and Bentham, and which would triumph in the nineteenth century.[19] Vattel's *Droit des Gens* of 1758 was the most influential articulation in Burke's time of the idea that states are equal, free and independent.[20] And Bentham's project of universal jurisprudence, of comprehensive codification, was a characteristically ambitious effort to subsume all law into a single unified framework.[21] This emerging paradigm rested on a strict separation between the internal law of independent states and an international law restricted to relations between sovereigns, and it saw these as exhaustive legal categories.

Burke departed from such models, in that he emphasised the multiplicity of legal orders within and among states, and so called into question any unitary notion of the state. This is particularly striking given Burke's avowed interest in Vattel's thought.[22] For all Vattel's influence on him, Burke complicated Vattel's view of perfectly independent sovereigns in his writings not just about India but also about Europe, where in response to the French Revolution he articulated his vision of a European Commonwealth or community, the 'grand vicinage of Europe', which was governed by a sort of 'Law of Neighbourhood'.[23] Burke saw the legal problems thrown up by both the Company in India and by Jacobinism in France as unprecedented, as impossible to encompass within traditional legal canons.²⁴ Those who regarded the war with France through the lens of simple interstate law were, he thought, mistaken. He similarly accepted the coexistence and interpenetration of multiple legal systems in India, without insisting, as Hastings and others did, that an authoritative hierarchy or code of jurisdictions, with Europeans as the ultimate arbiters, was required.

What is often emphasised about Burke's India speeches is his insistence that India was a law-governed place, not a scene of inveterately arbitrary government or oriental despotism. Burke himself made much of this point, stating it eloquently and indeed relentlessly throughout the trial. He had frequent recourse, in particular, to the passages in Hastings's opening defence before the House of Commons in 1786 claiming that Indians knew nothing but arbitrary rule, that, in Hastings's words, '[t]he whole history of Asia is nothing more than Precedents to prove the invariable exercise of Arbitrary Power'.²⁵ Burke's closing speech in the trial also dwelt on the arguments of the most senior and most combative of Hastings's defense counsel, Edward Law. Law had offered a history of India (using a great number of sources, almost exclusively European) to show that the country had known nothing but 'despotism and arbitrary power', with no 'system of law, the institution of something that would give security to property, peace and happiness to mankind. Not a trace of it!'²⁶

Some of Burke's most fertile legal thinking emerged in response to such claims. In rebutting Hastings's claim that Indians had 'no laws [and] no rights', Burke depicted Indian society as richly endowed with legal order. He appealed to a variety of normative orders in Indian society, from property and inheritance regimes, to 'hereditary dignities' and systems of 'honour and distinction'.²⁷ Whereas Hastings and his lawyers held that disorder was endemic in India, for Burke, order was evidenced in the society's multiple overlapping and mutually reinforcing normative systems, some of which were legal, and it was the British who represented the irruption of disorder. He suggested that India had a long history of functioning legal pluralism, disrupted by the British and their contempt for and ignorance of local structures of obligation.²⁸

This aspect of Burke's attack on Hastings, although it responded to Hastings's testimony, was arguably something of a caricature. Hastings later disowned the most notorious passages about Asian despotism in his testimony before the Commons as having been written not by himself but by his supporter Nathaniel Brassey Halhed, translator of the 1776 *Code of Gentoo Laws*.²⁹ (Burke noted that it was alarming that the man responsible for the *Code*, which he admired, had penned these 'horrible doctrines' about lawlessness in India.) But Hastings delivered the words, and as Burke pointed out, his defence lawyers continued to repeat similar arguments.[30] Still, Burke's insistence on arguments that Hastings himself had not actually drafted, and that stood in marked contrast to his own statements while Governor General about the sophistication of Indian laws, may have cast their disagreements in something of a false light.[31]

There were undoubtedly greater affinities between Burke and Hastings than Burke's rhetoric of excoriation – or, it should be added, Hastings's own defense – allowed. The adversarial context of the trial heightened the opposition between Burke and Hastings and effaced the points of similarity, as the defence was driven to exaggerate Indians' unreliability and Burke to overstate the stability of the pre-British order in Northern India. As an admirer of Indian civilisation, and a great patron of scholarship about it, Hastings wrote sensitively and powerfully about the virtues of Indian literature and about the obstacles to its proper appreciation in Europe.[32] The notorious passages about oriental despotism in his opening speech belied his more complex recognition of the desirability of accommodating Indian law. In a 1774 letter to the Lord Chief Justice, Lord Mansfield, Hastings, sounding very much like Burke during the impeachment, had criticised the view that Indians were 'governed by no other principle of justice than arbitrary wills, or uninstructed judgements', and had called Muslim law 'as comprehensive, and as well defined, as that of most states in Europe'.[33] Hastings saw himself as having undertaken to govern Indians as far as possible by their own laws, whether Muslim or Hindu.[34] Like the Orientalist Sir William Jones, he fought factions in Parliament that he believed intended to supplant Indian law with English law. The legal reforms that Hastings instituted in 1772, in which he established civil and criminal courts in Bengal, staffed in large part by Indians and reliant upon Hindu and Muslim precedent as Hastings understood it, were intended precisely to entrench Indian legal systems in the territory under British authority.[35] And in 1781 he established a madrassa in Calcutta to cultivate among Indian Muslims 'erudition in the Persian and Arabic Languages, and in the complicated system of laws founded on the tenets of their religion'.[36] Burke himself, in the course of criticising Hastings for opportunistically appealing to Muslim law when it suited his purposes, noted that 'the thing Mr Hastings values himself upon' was 'to keep the Law of England and the Law of Mahomet upon a just par'.[37]

Notwithstanding Burke's more extreme portraits of him, then, Hastings was undoubtedly attempting to further a *form* of legal pluralism in India. Still, Hastings's approach to British–Indian legal relations, though far more nuanced than it appeared in Burke's rendition and even

Hastings's own defense, represented a vision deeply at odds with the view that Burke came to hold by time of his 1794 closing speech in the impeachment trial. Three differences are worth highlighting between Hastings's formulation of a plural legal order in India, and Burke's approach in his closing speech: differences in the *characterisations* they offered of multiple normative orders; in the *reasons* they gave for recognising those different systems; and in the *structure* they thought a plural legal order should take.

First, Hastings characterised Indian legal systems as evidence of a cultural chasm between India and Britain.[38] For all his admiration of Indian civilisation, and his fostering of research into Indian law, Hastings often pointed to Indian laws and legal practices as evidence of the country's backwardness and stagnation, and as betraying the unreliability of Indian legal experts. His 1772 Judicial Plan for Bengal justified its reforms in part on the basis of the 'Litigiousness and Perseverance of the Natives of this Country', on the 'Chicane and Intrigue, which Passions amongst these People often work to the Undoing of their Neighbours'.[39] His letter to Lord Mansfield insisted, in a common trope of the time, that Hindu laws had 'continued unchanged from the remotest antiquity', an implicit contrast with Britain's more supplely evolving law.[40]

Second, the reasons Hastings gave for taking Indian laws into account were purely pragmatic: doing so would make it simpler, indeed was indispensable for making it even *possible*, for the British to administer a large territory and complex societies. The small number of British agents in India meant that the Company were reliant on local elites, who would only be willing to act according to familiar laws. A related argument was that Indians, who were peculiarly hampered by custom and religious strictures, were incapable of recognising the force of alien laws. Hastings, again like Jones, believed that unfortunate but deep-seated cultural limitations on the part of Indians made the preservation of local law imperative.[41] Moreover, he believed that in order to make local law viable and usable in the empire, it had to be fixed, codified and translated in authoritative editions, so that British officials could have direct access to authoritative law, rather than having to rely on native legal experts, whom he suspected of being corrupt and liable to mislead the court whenever it was in their interest to do so.[42]

Third, Hastings argued for a purely hierarchical form of recognition, in which British law and government was authoritative but could elect to make use of local laws when it was feasible or convenient.[43] He argued in his opening speech that British sovereignty over Indian provinces would become a burden instead of a benefit, unless 'the whole of our Territory in that Quarter shall be rounded and made a uniform compact Body by one grand and systematic Arrangement'.[44] He lamented 'the

Informality, Invalidity, and Instability of all Engagements in so divided and unsettled a State of Society; and ... the unavoidable Anarchy and Confusion of different Laws, Religions, and Prejudices, moral, civil, and political, all jumbled together in one unnatural and discordant Mass'. Hastings is often characterised as a late exemplar of the colonial order of corrupt Company officials superseded by an improving colonial state that is said to owe much to Burke's vision of a benevolent empire. These officials were replaced, it is often said, by a more orderly, and self-consciously improving, type of colonial official that conformed better to Burke's own vision of empire.[45] But it was Hastings's hierarchical version of legal pluralism, centred on the colonial state, which ultimately triumphed.[46]

Burke's understanding of Indian legal systems evolved dramatically during the course of his involvement in Indian affairs.[47] For all his castigation of Hastings's claims about Indian lawlessness, and his dramatisation of their differences, there are affinities between Burke's early views and the legal pluralism that, as we have seen, Hastings sometimes articulated. Burke's 1787 opening speech in the impeachment continues some of these themes but also gestures at the more interesting view Burke was to develop by the time of his closing speech as his voracious acquisition of knowledge about India continued and his hostility toward British conduct there deepened.

Although Burke in his early speeches drew on the Montesquieuian thought that peoples have different 'geniuses' that are reflected in their laws, with Asian societies tending towards despotism, he later emphatically rejected such a view.[48] In his 1779 speech on the *Policy of Making Conquests for the Mahometans*, for instance, Burke held that people's tendency to prefer rulers of their own religion and customs was especially exaggerated 'among those nations where there is not settled law or constitution, either to fix allegiance, or to restrain power'.[49] During the 1781 debates over the Bengal Judicature Bill, which Burke took a central role in drafting, he continued to adhere to a Montesquieuian account of the prevalence of and necessity for strong government in Asia. These early speeches proposed that the British should strive to improve the condition of the people and impose a superior legal order on India (though he insisted that the British had failed so far to do any such thing).[50] Even in his speech on Fox's India Bill, where he sought to render India familiar to his audience, to make it an object of their sympathy, Burke described the rights that were due Indians as those of which 'their condition is capable'.[51]

Along with this characterisation of Indian laws and society as flawed went the view that the *reasons* they should be recognised had to do with Indians' own limitations, and the belief that the appropriate *structure* for accommodating their laws was one in which British law was ultimately authoritative.[52] These relatively early speeches are scathingly critical of the Company's failure to respect treaties, and they call for good faith in the Company's external relations with independent princes, as well as good governance within its territories.[53] But their characterisation of Indian law falls short of the interpretive generosity and mutuality on which Burke later insisted.

Even in the opening of the impeachment trial, which begins to gesture at the more expansive vision of the closing speech over six years later, Burke described the 'gulf' between Indian and British laws as 'radicated in the very nature of the [Indian] people, and which you can never efface from them'.[54] He argued that the British must be 'conformable to their necessities and not our inventions', because 'to say that *that* people shall change their maxims, lives and opinions, is what cannot be'.[55] In contrast, he praised Britain for its unusually pluralistic legal heritage. Although Burke insisted here, as he did so often, on the narrowness and parochialism of British laws, he suggested that the pluralism of its legal traditions contained the potential for something more expansive and made possible a flexibility on the part of the British that could not be expected of Indians.[56]

By the time of the closing impeachment speech, Burke was suggesting an even more wide-ranging form of encounter between legal systems. On each of the points noted above – the characterisation of the relevant legal systems; the reasons for recognising the authority of a variety of systems; and the structure that a plural order would take – Burke, over the course of the trial, developed a distinctive and compelling version of legal pluralism that cannot be reduced to a theory of benevolent empire. His early vision of the British as a superior and supervisory power orchestrating the relations among the inferior laws and powers is one that fades by his closing speech, giving way instead to a less determinate pluralism.

First, then, Burke was far more insistent by this time on the limitations and failings not of Indian but of British legal traditions.[57] A Montesquieuian insistence on the deep-seated differences between British and Indians, and on the particular vices of Indian governance, had, by Burke's writings and speeches of 1794, given way to an insistence on the authority of Hindu and Muslim law. In contrast to Hastings, whom he accused of having 'ransacked all Asia for principles of despotism', Burke's strategy in the closing speech was to take, in his words, 'the largest and most liberal construction' of both Hindu and Muslim laws.[58] This meant, for him, reading them as being in conformity with the law of nations, and as having been established for the protection of the governed.[59] These laws, he argued, had a claim on

British attention because of their antiquity;[60] their technical sophistication; their place in a tradition of learned reflection and commentary; and because they served as the basis for a settled existence, especially a regime of property rights.[61]

Burke now dismissed Montesquieu's arguments as based on the gossip of 'idle and inconsiderate Travellers', and instead drew on Halhed's *Code of Gentoo Laws* (1776) for his account of Hindu law, and on Charles Hamilton's 1791 translation of the *Hedaya* for Muslim law.[62] Burke appealed to Halhed, for instance, to insist on the fineness – the 'nicest accuracy', as he said – of Hindu legal distinctions. The code, he argued, showed that magistrates were considered subject to the law and it enumerated judicial procedures that constrained the use of state power; 'there is not even a trace of arbitrary power in it'.[63] This use of Halhed, as Burke himself knew, was ironic, given Halhed's authorship of the notorious passages about Indian lawlessness in Hastings's defence speech. But Halhed's broad European audience read a variety of meanings into his text; so it is not surprising that Burke drew on it in a limited way to confirm views that Halhed himself contradicted during the trial. Halhed's own view of legal pluralism was more like that of his patron Hastings. He made clear, for instance, in his widely read preface to the Hindu law code that his intention in compiling and translating it was to make it possible to incorporate Hindu law in a unified system presided over by British law. Motivated by the advantages for Britain of territory in Bengal, he sought to increase Indian cooperation with British projects by adopting 'such original Institutes of the Country, as do not immediately clash with the Laws or Interests of the Conquerors'. The purpose was to temper British laws in Bengal with a 'moderate Attention to the peculiar and national Prejudices of the Hindoo'. Though these were often 'fanciful and injudicious', they were suited to the people, and because Hindu laws were interwoven with religion, they were particularly deeply entrenched.[64]

Second, as to the *reasons* for taking plural legal systems into account, Burke had come to insist that the British should respect Indian laws not because Indians themselves were incapable of moving beyond them, as Hastings argued and Burke had earlier done, but because those laws independently obligated the British. In addition to British law and the law of nations, Hastings 'was bound to proceed according to the laws, rights, laudable institutions, customs, privileges and franchises of the Country that he governs, and we did contend that to such laws, rights, privileges and franchises the people of the Country had a clear and just claim'.[65]

Most directly this was so for contractual reasons, as an implicit element of the agreement that, Burke claimed, underlay the Company's power in India. 'And we contend [he argued] that Mr. Hastings was bound to know and to act by these Laws. And I shall prove that the very condition upon which he received power in India was to protect these people in their Laws and known rights.'[66] It is perhaps striking that Burke continued to make such a strong claim that power is *conditional* on its being exercised for the benefit of the people, in the post-revolutionary closing speech as well. But the many parallels between Indianism and Jacobinism in Burke's mind include the thought that rebellion is the obverse of tyranny: just as Hastings, a tyrant in India, was a rebel against British authority, the Jacobin revolutionaries were proto-despots.

Intimations of the contractual argument had been apparent in the opening impeachment speech as well. There he described Hindu religious laws, for instance, as laws that 'either prohibit connexion or *oblige us* to a connexion very different from what we have hitherto used toward them'.[67] But it is worth noting that while sometimes he makes clear that he means these laws to impose obligations on the British *as governors*, elsewhere these are simply stated as constraints on Hastings's general 'relations with the people of that Country'. Burke's argument seems to rest on a notion of the sanctity of the rule of law itself, so that a structure of legal relations should be treated with respect, across polities as well as within them. The British were not operating in a legal vacuum beyond their own territory in India. One reason, in Burke's view, that these legal systems all had normative standing is that they had been worked upon and reformed over a long period of time: they should be presumed to be distinctive but valid approximations of what he called the eternal law.[68]

One of Burke's most often repeated charges was that the Company under Hastings, with a flagrant contempt for the law of nations, violated every treaty it made with Indian powers. Burke used the occasion of such charges to maintain that the law of nations applied 'with regard to all foreign powers', in India as well as in Europe.[69] And he argued that the British were obligated to extend the benefit of the doubt to powers that 'appear to be sovereign' or who had recently been sovereign. In contrast, that is, to Hastings and later Company officials, who sought to give themselves the greatest room for manoeuvre by hewing to a narrow standard of sovereignty that ruled out many non-European states on the ground that they were weak or not fully independent, Burke was expansive in his construction of the 'foreign powers' whose relations with the British must be governed by the law of nations.

In the closing speech, Burke framed the treaty violations not simply as a problem of bad faith or opportunism, but as the product of a dangerous legal theory. He rebuked Hastings for having questioned, in testimony before the Commons, 'the validity of any Treaty that can be made at present with India'. Here as elsewhere, Burke drew on elements of Hastings's testimony that highlighted a gulf between their views of legal relations between India and Britain, even though Hastings's practice as Governor General had been less obviously opposed to Burke's position. Hastings had certainly broken treaties for purposes of expediency, as Burke charged. But he did not altogether reject the idea of treaties with Indian rulers, as Burke suggested.

That sort of contempt for the very possibility of treaty relations with many Asian states, however, was to become common among British legal thinkers in the following century.[70] Here, as (arguably) in his portrayal of the French Revolutionaries in the *Reflections*, Burke exaggerated, but in a way that seems prescient, given later developments. Most nineteenth-century jurists were to argue that Europeans in Asia could not be bound by the law of nations since it was a product of Europe's particular history and other states could not be expected to know or abide by it. Many also claimed that cultural disabilities among 'barbarians', such as the lack of a capacity for reciprocity, made it absurd to hold Europeans strictly to their treaty obligations in Asia. Hastings did not articulate such a view in the stark terms that were to become common several decades later, though he gestured in that direction in the testimony cited by Burke.

Burke, in contrast, not only argued that Europeans were bound by the law of nations when they dealt with Asian societies. He also drew on Vattel, then the standard authority on the law of nations, as a means of interpreting and justifying the actions of Indian political agents. This was sensible because the law of nations, on Burke's account, was natural law that had been 'recognised and digested into order by the labour of learned Men'. Even if they were not familiar with European legal texts, Indian rulers could be expected to follow a similar logic; and Burke maintained that their own jurisprudential authorities had similarly articulated particular versions of natural law. He therefore invoked Vattel to defend Chait Singh, Raja of Benares, against Hastings's imputation that the Raja was 'guilty of a great crime' in fomenting a resurrection against the Company. Burke read the Raja's actions as reasonable in light of Vattel's theory of agreements between greater and subordinate powers. According to such authorities, Burke argued, Chait Singh in fact had done 'that which his safety and his duty bound him to do'.[71] Burke's suggestion seems to be that the British were obliged not merely to follow the law of nations in their dealings with Indian rulers, but also to attempt to construe those rulers' actions as if they might be in accordance with the same principles.[72] Once again, there was an obligation to presume a legitimate legal order that, though it might not match European law of nations in the particulars, was analogous to it and thus comprehensible to and obligating on Europeans. Burke's strategy was to presume and to seek agreement at the level of principle, to assume that the British are bound by the law of nations and to interpret Indian actions as if they might be as well. As to the *structure* of the pluralistic legal order, in contrast to the hierarchical and carefully orchestrated meshing of legal orders sometimes advocated by Hastings, Burke presented, in his closing speech, a more contingent, more fluid and more political form of legal pluralism.[73]

Finally, Burke envisioned British law itself being transformed by this global encounter. We find this in his repeated calls for an expansive approach to evidence and judicial procedure in the impeachment trial.[74] It was, of course, in Burke's interest in the trial to argue for the widest possible latitude in collecting evidence. But in this instance as in so many others, he capitalised on a line of argument that suited his immediate purposes to make a point of much broader theoretical interest. He had argued in his opening impeachment speech that rules 'formed upon municipal maxims' were inappropriate when what was at issue was justice for 'various descriptions of men, differing in language, in manners and in rites, men separated by every means from you'.[75] And he developed this line of argument most fully in his *Report on the Lords Journal* of 1794, where he argued that law would stagnate if it were to hew narrowly to existing doctrine. Law evolved and progressed by constant reference to both morality and society – by 'keep[ing] Pace with the Demands of Justice, and the actual Concerns of the World'.[76] Adherence to the strict letter of the law, he argued, was appropriate to simpler societies, but the extraordinary complexity introduced by empire and global commerce made a more flexible sense of equity imperative.[77] Burke himself arguably showed more contempt for legal forms in his closing speech than even his theoretical defense of flexibility in an impeachment trial would warrant. But this does not detract from the power of his legal imagination and the fruitfulness of the vision of law he developed over the course of the trial.

Burke insisted on the interdependence of our conceptions of law and of moral duty, arguing that when we think people have no rights, no property and no law, we invariably feel contempt for them, and sympathy becomes impossible.[78] It was important for Burke to insist on the coherence and respectability of Indian and Asian legal systems not simply for legal reasons, that is, but also for more broadly moral and political reasons. It is often, and rightly, emphasised that Burke's primary aim in the Hastings trial was moral suasion rather than legal conviction: that the British public, and posterity, were as much his audience as the Lords.⁷⁹ A central element of this project of persuasion was Burke's effort to prompt a reconception of *law* itself: more specifically, of the role of law in global commercial and political encounters. This meant soliciting from his British audience both a new respect for unfamiliar legal and normative systems and an unaccustomed sense of doubt about the adequacy of their own. As was typical of Burke, this was a project of both transformation and conservation, in the sense that he argued both that British legal traditions were parochial and inadequate to a global politics; and also that they contained the seeds of their own transformation.

I also want to suggest that Burke's reflections on the encounter of multiple legal systems were central to his more general project of chastening power. Unlike Hastings, who invoked multiple legal systems as means of authorising and channelling British power, Burke appealed to those systems as constraints on that power. He criticised the Company's use of legal structures and arguments to deny Indians recourse against abuses of power, and Company officials' efforts to arrange and appeal to plural legal orders in order to enhance their own power.⁸⁰ He warned of the danger of Hastings's opportunistic version of legal pluralism when he urged that the judges not judge Hastings 'by Laws and institutions which you do not know, against those Laws and institutions which you do know, and under whose power and authority Mr Hastings went out to India'.⁸¹ Whereas Hastings sought to use law, including Indian legal systems, in the service of the Company's projects of administration and revenue extraction, Burke emphasised the function of laws as constraints on the powerful, and as resources available to the vulnerable. And for all his vilification of Hastings as an individual, Burke was equally troubled by structural aspects of British involvement in India: above all, the inaccessibility to Indians of the main political processes by which the company's power was checked.⁸² Parliament's virtual representation of Indians, and its use of both legislation and impeachment, were one channel for the redress of abuses, though Burke had little faith in its adequacy, given his belief that the British people and their legislators had little knowledge of or interest in Indians.

Finally, although part of Burke's purpose may have been to reform imperial structures, as Nicholas Dirks and Richard Travers have recently argued, his conceptualisation of British–Indian relations cannot be reduced to that aim. Rather, in offering an account of the ways in which British actions in the world beyond Europe were constrained by a complex web of laws – including positive law of both British and Indian origin as well as natural law and the law of nations – Burke was articulating a distinctive vision of the international legal order. This was a vision that had its roots in the tradition of natural jurisprudence that formed the dominant discourse of European international law in the eighteenth century, but Burke attended far more closely than many of the canonical exponents of that tradition to its potential implications for engagements beyond Europe.[83] It was also a vision that was very soon to be superseded by an increasingly constricted notion of the international legal order as exclusively European in origin, a notion codified and entrenched by professional international lawyers in the nineteenth century and that continued to structure the international order throughout the twentieth.[84]

Notes

1 *Writings and Speeches of Edmund Burke* (9 vols, Oxford, 1981–2000), VII, p. 284. The editors of the volumes cited are as follows: I (T. O. McLoughlin and J. T. Boulton; V, VI, VII (P. J. Marshall); IX (R. B. McDowell).
2 *CJ*, XLII, p. 666, quoted by P. J. Marshall, *The Impeachment of Warren Hastings* (Oxford, 1965), p. 1.
3 Recent scholarship and criticism includes: F. Whelan, *Edmund Burke and India* (Pittsburgh, 1996); U. Mehta, *Liberalism and Empire* (Chicago, 1999); and D. Bromwich, *Burke on Empire, Liberty, and Reform* (New Haven, 2000).
4 See, e.g., *Writings and Speeches*, VII, p. 256. Mithi Mukherjee has analysed the dispute as being between Hastings's 'colonial' discourse of sovereignty, and Burke's 'imperial' 'supranational and deterritorialized discourse of justice', and she stresses Burke's turn to the discourse of natural law as an alternative to common law jurisprudence. See M. Mukherjee, 'Justice, war, and the imperium: India and Britain in Edmund Burke's prosecutorial speeches in the impeachment trial of Warren Hastings', *Law and History Review*, 23:3 (2005), 589–630. While I find much to agree with in Mukherjee's account, here I explore Burke's conceptualisations of these legal interactions as lying at the *intersections* of different polities, rather than his vision of the justice that is *internal* to empire.
5 See the epigraph to this chapter. Burke often offered to judge Hastings by various Asian laws: *Writings and Speeches*, VI, p. 465.
6 *Writings and Speeches*, VII, p. 282.
7 See P. Berman, 'Global legal pluralism', *Southern California Law Review*, 80 (2007), 1155–1237; S. Merry, 'Legal pluralism', *Law and Society Review*, 22:5 (1988), 869–96; S. Merry, *Colonizing Hawai'i: The Cultural Power of Law* (Princeton, 1999). For a historical analysis of various forms of legal pluralism in colonial contexts, see L. Benton, *Law and Colonial Cultures: Legal Regimes in World History, 1400–1900* (Cambridge, 2002).
8 He describes the dominant conception today as 'monist (one internally coherent legal system), statist (the state has a monopoly of law within its territory), and positivist (what is not created or recognised as law by the state is not law)'. W. Twining, *Globalization and Legal Theory* (London, 2000), p. 232.
9 See, e.g. A. Anghie, *Imperialism, Sovereignty, and the Making of International Law* (Cambridge, 2004); M. Koskenniemi, *The Gentle Civilizer of Nations: The Rise and Fall of International Law 1870–1960* (Cambridge, 2001); J. Greene, *Peripheries and Center: Constitutional Development in the Extended Polities of the British Empire and the United States, 1607–1788* (Athens, 1986); D. Hulsebosch, *Constituting Empire: New York and the Transformation of Constitutionalism in the Atlantic World, 1664–1830* (Chapel Hill, NC, 2005); M. S. Bilder, *The Transatlantic Constitution* (Cambridge, Mass., 2004); L. Benton, 'From international law to imperial constitutions: the problem of quasi-sovereignty, 1870–1900', *Law and*

History Review, 26:3 (2008), 595–619; L. Benton, 'Constitutions and empires', *Law and Social Inquiry*, 31 (2006), 177–98.
10 R. Travers, *Ideology and Empire in Eighteenth-Century India* (Cambridge, 2007), p. 220.
11 See, e.g.: *Writings and Speeches*, VI, pp. 94, 105ff. Burke even gestured at the ideal of a liberal empire when he noted that English treachery had led the people of India to consider 'the most despotic empires as more liberal than Britain': *Writings and Speeches*, V, p. 137. I explore this theme in 'Burke and the ends of empire', in D. Dwan and C. Insole (eds), *Cambridge Companion to Edmund Burke* (Cambridge, 2012).
12 *Writings and Speeches*, VII, p. 260.
13 *Writings and Speeches*, VI, p. 341.
14 Dirks, *The Scandal of Empire: India and the Creation of Imperial Britain* (Cambridge, Mass., 2006), p. 207.
15 T. W. Copeland et al (eds), *The Correspondence of Edmund Burke* (10 vols, Cambridge, 1958–78), IX, pp. 62–3.
16 *Writings and Speeches*, V, p. 404. He repeated the idea that the empire was an 'incomprehensible dispensation of the Divine providence into our hands', in his 1796 letter to French Laurence: Copeland et al (eds), *Correspondence*, IX, pp. 62–3.
17 *Writings and Speeches*, V, p. 383.
18 For the former, see his claim that Chait Singh, Raja of Benares, should have remained 'totally independent': *Writings and Speeches*, VII pp. 260–1.
19 Edward Keene has argued that as early as Grotius we can find a bifurcated notion of law and sovereignty, so that while sovereignty in Europe was seen as unitary and absolute, the prerogatives of sovereignty in Asia were seen by European theorists as divided between semi-sovereign Asian rulers and European states and their agents. See E. Keene, *Beyond the Anarchical Society: Grotius, Colonialism and Order in World Politics* (Cambridge, 2002).
20 See *Droit des Gens*, Introduction, §§14–21. In E. de Vattel, *The Law of Nations or the Principles of Natural Law*, trans. C. G. Fenwick (Washington, 1916), pp. 6–7; the law of nations is the 'science of the rights which exist between Nations or States, and of the obligations corresponding to these rights' (§3, p. 3).
21 In 1822 Bentham published a 'Codification Proposal, Addressed by Jeremy Bentham to All Nations Professing Liberal Opinions'; see J. Bentham, *'Legislator of the World': Writings on Codification, Law, and Education*, ed. P. Schofield and J. Harris (Oxford, 1998). See also his *Plan of the International Code*: J. Bowring (ed.), *Works of Jeremy Bentham* (11 vols, Edinburgh, 1843), III, pp. 200–1.
22 For Vattel's influence on Burke, see D. Armitage, 'Edmund Burke and reason of state', *Journal of the History of Ideas*, 61:4 (2000), 617–34.
23 *Writings and Speeches*, IX, pp. 248–51.
24 On Burke's insistent linking of 'Indianism' with Jacobinism, see S. Agnani, 'Jacobinism in India, Indianism in English Parliament', paper presented at 'Imperial Legacies', UCLA Center for 17th- and 18th-century studies, 26–27 April 2007.
25 See *CJ*, XLI, p. 696. Burke cited the passage at, e.g., *Writings and Speeches*, VI, p. 107 and VII, pp. 258–9.
26 E. A. Bond (ed.), *Speeches of the Managers and Counsel in the Trial of Warren Hastings* (4 vols, London, 1859–61), II, p. 537.
27 *Writings and Speeches*, VII, pp. 264–5.
28 Even the Muslim conquerors of India at the time of Muhammed, whom he characterised as cruel religious fanatics, 'left [he said] the ancient people in possession of their states; and left the ancient Sovereigns of the Country possessed of an inferior Sovereignty; and where the nature of the Country would permit it, they suffered them to continue in a separate state of Sovereignty from them': *Writings and Speeches*, VI, p. 308).
29 Burke ridicules this disavowal: *Writings and Speeches*, VII, p. 261. Lock notes that a witness, Major Scott, claimed that Hastings had not even seen parts of this testimony before reading them to the Commons: F. P. Lock, *Edmund Burke* (2 vols, Oxford, 2005), II, p. 182.

30 Burke ridiculed Hastings for forswearing that defence but then 'get[ting] his Counsel [Edward Law] to resort to it again and to shew that India had nothing but arbitrary power for its Government': *Writings and Speeches*, VII p. 262.
31 P. J. Marshall goes so far as to say that in these passages Burke was 'probably destroying a target of his own construction': *Writings and Speeches*, VI p. 267; but Hastings's defence contributed to the construct.
32 See, e.g., his letter to Nathaniel Smith introducing a translation of the Baghavad-Gita; in P. J. Marshall (ed.), *The British Discovery of Hinduism in the Eighteenth Century* (Cambridge, 1970), pp. 184–91. On Hastings's patronage of Orientalist research, see P. J. Marshall, 'Warren Hastings as scholar and patron', in J. S. Bromley and P. G. M. Dickson (eds), *Statesmen, Scholars, and Merchants* (Oxford, 1973).
33 G. R. Gleig, *Memoirs of Right Hon. Warren Hastings* (3 vols, London, 1841), I, pp. 399–404.
34 Robert Travers has described the legal reforms that Warren Hastings proposed in 1772 as an 'uneasy partnership of constitutional variation and natural law': Travers, *Ideology and Empire*, p. 105. Hastings declared that Company policy should be 'to let their laws sit as light on them as possible, and to share with them the Privileges of our own Constitution, where they are capable of partaking of them consistently with their other rights and the Welfare of the State': *Ibid.*, p. 106, quoting BL, Additional MS 29,303 fos 10–11v.
35 For recent accounts of some of the legal arrangements Hastings supervised, see Benton, *Law and Colonial Cultures*, pp. 133–49; and Travers, *Ideology and Empire*, pp. 100–40. On Hastings and Jones, see B. S. Cohn, *Colonialism and its Forms of Knowledge* (Princeton, 1996), pp. 60–72.
36 S. C. Sanial, 'History of the Calcutta madrassa', *Bengal Past and Present*, 8 (1914), p. 109.
37 See *Writings and Speeches*, VII, p. 455, in the course of a discussion of the Begums of Oudh; Hastings 'seizes the goods of these Ladies and at your Bar he justifies it upon Mahometan law'; the Lords 'have nothing but a quotation cut out with scissors out of the Mahometan law book'.
38 See Benton, *Law and Colonial Cultures*, p. 147.
39 For Hastings's 1772 'Plan for the Administration of Justice', See *Reports from Committees of the House of Commons* (16 vols, London, 1803–6), IV, pp. 348–51.
40 Gleig, *Memoirs*, I, p. 400; note that this was a view Burke shared in an earlier speech, when he called on the British to accommodate Indian law since British law was already pluralistic and flexible.
41 As Bernard Cohn has put it, Hastings held that British law was 'too technical, too complicated, and totally inappropriate for conditions in India': Cohn, *Colonialism*, p. 66. In a similar vein, Jones wrote to Burke that British law must not be imposed on India, for 'a system of *liberty*, forced upon a people invincibly attached to opposite *habits*, would in truth be a system of tyranny': G. Cannon (ed.), *Correspondence of Sir William Jones* (2 vols, Oxford, 1970), II, pp. 643–4; Cohn, *Colonialism*, p. 68.
42 See Cohn, *Colonialism*, pp. 60–72, where the similarities with Jones on this point are also made clear.
43 As Robert Travers has argued, 'In Hastings' view, 'Mughal legality... was provisional and subordinate to the reserved and absolute powers of sovereignty': Travers, *Ideology and Empire*, pp. 139–40.
44 *CJ*, XLI, p. 696 (note that this is in the same section of the speech apparently drafted by Halhed).
45 See Dirks, *Scandal of Empire*, p. 314, for a recent such claim.
46 Benton has criticised conceptualisations of 'plural legal orders as comprising a set of 'stacked' legal systems or spheres', which she argues pervades contemporary analysis of legal processes: L. Benton, 'Beyond legal pluralism: towards a new approach to law in the informal sector', *Social and Legal Studies*, 3 (1994), 223–42. Burke's version of legal pluralism, however, which presupposes and searches for commonalities among legal system, may fall foul of Benton's strictures in other ways.

47 On the dramatic change in Burke's views on India in the decade after Lord North's Regulating Act was passed in 1773 – from an anxiety to protect the Company from government interference to a conviction that the Company was so corrupt as to be incapable of governing India – See Marshall, *Impeachment*, ch. 1. The later shift I describe is more subtle but can be seen as a continuation of the earlier development.
48 *Writings and Speeches*, V, p. 140. On Montesquieu's influence in Burke's India writings, see C. P. Courtney, *Montesquieu and Burke* (Oxford, 1963), pp. 127–41.
49 *Writings and Speeches*, V, p. 113.
50 In the Bengal Judicature debates, his proposed response to the administrative wrangling between the Company administration and the recently formed Supreme Court was a strongly centralising one. A Supreme Court had been established in 1773 under the Regulating Act to check abuses by the Company, but constant wrangling between the administration and the court had brought the issue to the attention of Parliament. In the long term, he argued, Parliament ought to develop a judicial structure 'in which the sense of the people themselves might be collected, and a permanent system established, founded on their consent': *ibid.*, p. 142.
51 The bill was, he said, 'intended to form the Magna Charta of Hindostan': *ibid.*, p. 386.
52 The British had a duty to 'make some sort of compensation for the mischiefs inseparable from a foreign and commercial superiority, to keep a balance of justice and proportion in the several powers that were inferior to us': *ibid.*, p. 113.
53 *Ibid.*, p. 391.
54 *Writings and Speeches*, VI, p. 302.
55 *Ibid.* emphasis added. For a thoughtful and critical account of Burke's revisions to the shorthand notes of this speech, see Christopher Reid, *Edmund Burke and the Practice of Political Writing* (New York, 1986), pp. 127–33.
56 In his opening speech, he argued that the coexistence of multiple sources of law and obligation – religion, country, honour – in Britain, made the British particularly flexible: *Writings and Speeches*, VI p. 302.
57 See the arguments in the *Report on the Lords Journal* that commerce leads to a more expansive legal system, and that the British 'must not restrict the infinitely diversified Occasions of Men, and the Rules of natural Justice within artificial Circumscriptions, but conform our Jurisprudence to the Growth of our Commerce and our Empire': *Writings and Speeches*, VII, p. 168.
58 *Ibid.*, p. 257.
59 *Ibid.*, p. 287. Burke claimed that under Muslim law, the 'Sovereign's rights are undoubtedly sacred rights ... because exercised for the benefit of the people': *ibid.*, p. 284.
60 *Ibid.*, p. 285.
61 'That it is a refined, enlightened, curious, elaborate, technical Jurisprudence under which they lived, and by which their property was secured and which yields neither to the Jurisprudence of the Roman Law nor to the Jurisprudence of this Kingdom, formed and allowed to be, as it is, a basis and substratum to the manners and customs and opinions of that people, which is different': *ibid.*, p. 285. See also *ibid.*, pp. 267ff, where he describes a 'system of enlightened jurisprudence with regard to the body and substance of it as perhaps any nation ever possessed'.
62 *Ibid.*, p. 265ff. Courtney argues that in his closing speech Burke merely criticised Montesquieu's sources but continued to admire his method and his doctrine of *esprit général*. But Burke's closing speech is an indictment of the ideas of oriental despotism, and of Asian societies' extreme dependence on custom, that are central to Montesquieu's argument; his implicit critique of Montesquieu was far deeper than a quibble about sources.
63 *Ibid.*, p. 266. "[H]ere is a book which has in itself not only good and excellent positive rules, but a system of as enlightened Jurisprudence ... as perhaps any Nation ever possessed, which shews it was composed by men of great cultivated understandings': *ibid.*, p. 267.

64 N. B. Halhed, *A Code of Gentoo Laws* (1776), p. ix. Also note the Montesquieuian notion that readers should attribute 'any Opinions not reconcileable to our Modes of thinking' to different effects of climate (p. lxvi). On the *Code*'s reception, see Rosane Rocher, *Poetry and the Millennium: The Checkered Life of Nathaniel Brassey Halhed* (Delhi, 1983), pp. 54–60. For a nearly verbatim caveat about the failings of Muslim laws, see Charles Hamilton's preface to the Hedaya, arguing that 'however defective or absurd these may in many instances appear, still they must be infinitely more acceptable than any which we could offer; since they are supported by the accumulated prejudice of ages, and, in the opinion of their followers, derive their origin from the Divinity himself': C. Hamilton (trans.), *The Hedaya, or Guide* (1791), p. iv.

65 *Writings and Speeches*, VII, p. 282; see also *ibid.*, p. 257: 'with regard to his relation to the people of that Country, that he was obliged to act according to the laws, rights, usages, institutions and good customs, according to the largest and most liberal construction of them'.

66 *Ibid.*, p. 285. And then: 'every person exercising authority in any country shall be subject to the laws of that country or he breaks the very covenant by which we hold our power there: *ibid.*, p. 286. Note that Burke here is insisting that the basis of British power in India is not conquest but covenant; he calls Hastings 'no Conqueror, nothing but what you see him to be, a bad Scribbler of absurd papers', a fraudulent 'Bullock Contractor'.

67 *Writings and Speeches*, VI, p. 307, emphasis added. Note that he is speaking here only of the laws of their religion 'as relates to our government over them', rather than regarding their relations with Indians more broadly, including those with whom they had other sorts of political relations than those of direct governance.

68 As Mukherjee argues, Burke staged a 'convergence ... between two independent traditions of jurisprudence', the 'exclusively national' tradition of common law and the 'international discourse' of natural law: Mukherjee, 'Justice, war, and the imperium', p. 619.

69 *Writings and Speeches*, VII, p. 256; also: 'we do contend that the Law of Nations is the Law of India as well as Europe': *ibid.*, p. 291.

70 J. Pitts, 'Boundaries of Victorian international law', in D. Bell (ed.), *Victorian Visions of Global Order* (Cambridge, 2007).

71 *Writings and Speeches*, VII, pp. 290–2.

72 In the course of denouncing the Jacobins for having 'demolished' the jurisprudence that France shared with 'other civilized countries', Burke wrote: 'I have not heard of any country [except France], whether in Europe or Asia, or even in Africa on this side of Mount Atlas, which is wholly without' institutions dedicated the conservation of that universal jurisprudence: *Writings and Speeches*, IX, p. 240.

73 In his notes for the opening speech, Burke criticised Hastings for seeking to 'reduce all the religious establishment and Tenures of Land into one uniform mass ... and on that uniformity build a system of arbitrary power: *Writings and Speeches*, VI, p. 462.

74 He expanded on this theme in his *Report on the Lords Journals* of 1794, where he appealed to Lord Mansfield as one who had understood that the law must 'keep Pace with the Demands of Justice, and the actual Concerns of the World', that 'our Jurisprudence [must conform] to the Growth of our Commerce and of our Empire': *Writings and Speeches*, VII, p. 168.

75 *Writings and Speeches*, VI, p. 277n3.

76 *Writings and Speeches*, VII, p. 168. See Lock, *Edmund Burke*, II, pp. 470–4.

77 'as Commerce, with its Advantages and its Necessities, opened a Communication more largely with other Countries; as the Law of Nature and Nations (always a Part of the Law of *England*) came to be cultivated; as an increasing Empire; as new Views and new Combinations of Things were opened, this antique Rigour and over-done Severity gave Way to the Accommodation of Human Concerns, for which Rules were made, and not Human Concerns to bend to them': *Writings and Speeches*, VII, p. 163.

78 *Writings and Speeches*, VII, p. 264.
79 This is especially apparent, as Lock has pointed out, in Burke's nine-day closing speech: Lock, *Edmund Burke*, II, p. 468.
80 *Writings and Speeches*, VII, p. 452, where he deplores the fact that the 'express regulation made in Parliament for the redress of the Natives' was made 'an instrument for destroying the property real and personal of the natives'.
81 *Writings and Speeches*, VI, p. 347.
82 Arguing that the question of the Begums' entitlement to property could not possibly be judged by the Lords, Burke said: 'The parties are at a distance from you. They are neither represented by themselves nor any Counsel, Advocate, or Attorney, and I hope no house of Lords will ever judge upon the title of any human being, much less upon the title of the first women in Asia, shut up from you at nine thousand miles distance': *Writings and Speeches*, VII, p. 458.
83 Grotius is an important exception, and there is a large recent literature on Grotius's legal ideas about and involvement with Dutch imperial activities in Asia. See Keene, *Beyond the Anarchical Society*; P. Borschberg, 'Hugo Grotius, East India trade and the King of Johor', *Journal of Southeast Asian Studies*, 30:2 (1999), 225–48; M. van Ittersum, *Profit and Principle: Hugo Grotius, Natural Rights Theories and the Rise of Dutch Power in the East Indies, 1595–1615* (Brill, 2006). For a discussion of the broader tradition, see R. Tuck, *The Rights of War and Peace* (Oxford, 1999).
84 Pitts, 'Boundaries'; for a powerful account of both the early history and the twentieth-century consequences of this view, see Anghie, *Imperialism*.

INDEX

Acadia 28, 95
Adams, John 168
Addison, Lancelot 63–9
Africa 25, 27, 29, 95, 102, 103, 105, 112
Ahn, Doowan 47
Alabama 175
Albermarle, Duke of *see* Monck, George
Alfonço, Gaspar 132
Allen, Bob 31
Allen, Ethan 172
Almanza, Battle of (1707) 147
American Revolution and Revolutionary War 12, 30, Chapter 8 *passim*, Chapter 9 *passim*
   loyalists 12, 143, 148–55, 162–4, 167, 168, 173, 175, 177n14
Anglesey, Earl of *see* Annesley, Arthur
Anglo-Dutch wars 7, 38, 88, 91
Anglo-Scottish Union (1707) 51, 94, 146
Anglo-Spanish Treaty (1715) 48
Anjidiv 122
Anne, Queen of England 21, 23, 27, 28, 38, 44, 47, 48, 144, 147
Annesley, Arthur, 1st Earl of Anglesey 87
anti-popery 10, Chapter 4 *passim*, 82, 90, 92
anti-puritanism 10, Chapter 4 *passim*
Appleby, Joyce 43
Argentina 27
Armitage, David 31, 35n14, 78, 117n8
Aroostook War (1838) 175
Asiento 17, 25, 27, 28, 33, 36n55, 45, 48, 49, 105, 108, 112, 114
   see also slavery and the slave trade
Atholl, Duke of *see* Murray, William
Aungier, Gerald 124, 125, 126, 131, 132, 134, 135
Aurangzeb (Muhi-ud-Din Muhammad, Mughal emperor) 71
Austin, John 179

Bacon's rebellion (Virginia, 1676) 90
Bahamas 86, 103, 164
Bandra 124, 131, 137, 138
Bank of England 24, 44
Barbados 83, 120n88
Barbary corsairs 84
Barrier Treaty (1709) 19, 46
Bassein 125, 126, 130
Bateman, Sir James 24
Baton Rouge 175
Baxter, Richard 88, 89
Bayly, C. A. 30–1
Beale, John 80, 84, 90
Beckford, Peter 113
Beeston, William 113
Bengal 72, 178, 180, 187, 195n50
Bentham, Jeremy 181, 193n21
Benton, Lauren 13, 53, 194n46
Bermuda 86
Bernier, Francois 57
Bethel, Slingsby 109, 112
Blenheim, Battle of (1704) 17, 18
Blenheim Palace 147
Blount, William 167
Board of Trade (England) 19, 23, 33, 34, 53, 93, 144, 146
Bolingbroke, Viscount *see* St John, Henry
Bombay 11, 103, Chapter 7 *passim*
Bonaparte, Napoleon 42, 171
Boone, Charles 137
Boone, Daniel 167
borders Chapter 7 *passim*, 161, 164, 169, 171, 172–3
Boston (Massachusetts) 82, 87, 88, 94, 153
Botero, Giovanni 41
Boulanger, Nicholas 57
Bowen, Huw 5
Bowles, William Augustus 175
Bowrey, Thomas 25, 55n37
Boyle, Robert 83, 84
Boyle, Roger, 2nd Earl of Orrery 21, 22
Braddick, Michael 5
Bray, Thomas 93

[198]

INDEX

Breen, Tim 30
Brenner, Robert 2
Browne, Arnold 125
Buckingham, Duke of *see* Villiers, George
Buenos Aires 24, 25, 28, 29, 46, 49
Bulman, William 10
Burke, Edmund 13, 151, 154, Chapter 10 *passim*
Burlamaqui, Philip 149
Burr, Aaron 167
Byng, Sir George 25, 36n46

Cain, Peter 3, 5
Calcutta 183
California 169
Calvert, Sir George 77
Cambridge (England) 86
Canada 47, 91, 149, 164, 168, 172, 174
Caner, Henry 167
Caribbean *see* West Indies
Carleton, Sir Guy 163, 168
Carmelite order 138
Carolina 83, 94, 103, 109, 155, 164
Cartagena 114
Castine 163, 168
Catherine of Braganza, Queen of England 121
Chakrabarty, Dipesh 4
Chamberlayne, John 94
Champion, Justin 60
Charles I, King of England 51, 88
Charles II, King of England 51, 79, 80, 83, 85–91, 103, 105, 106, 121, 125, 130, 133, 137
Charles II, King of Spain 39, 100
Charles III, King of Spain 19
Charles IV, King of Spain 163
Charles VI, Archduke of Austria and Holy Roman Emperor 40, 47
Child, Sir Josiah 34n14, 36n46, 43, 44, 104, 108
Chile 23, 25, 27, 46
Church of England, 9, 61, 70–1, Chapter 4 *passim*, Chapter 5 *passim*
Churchill, John, 1st Duke of Marlborough 18, 19, 147
Clerk, Sir John 81

Clifford, Thomas, 1st Baron Clifford, Lord Treasurer 92
Cohn, Bernard 194n41
Coke, Daniel Parker 149
Coke, Roger 43, 100, 103, 109, 110, 111
Colbert, Jean-Baptiste 43
Collet, Joseph 95
Colley, Linda 117n8
Columbus, Christopher 24
compensation 12, Chapter 8 *passim*, 163, 195n52
Cook, James 169
Cooke, Humphrey 125, 126, 131, 134, 138
Cooper, Anthony Ashley, 1st Earl of Shaftesbury 92, 111, 113, 118n25, 120nn71, 77
Cooper, Grey 151, 152
Corn Laws 171
corruption Chapter 10 *passim*
Council of the Indies (Spain) 47
Council of Trade (England) 3, 82, 83, 86, 111
Cranfield, Edward 88
Cromwell, Oliver 3, 7, 40, 50, 64, 66, 68, 69, 78

Darien 146, 157n28
Darwin, John 31
Davenant, Charles 34n14, 43, 47, 53, 90
De Krey, Gary 44, 45
Declaration of Breda (1660) 86
Defoe, Daniel 24, 36n39, 40, 45, 85
Denmark 130
Devine, Tom 31, 32
Dickinson, H. T. 35n24
Dingley, Charles 142
Dirks, Nicholas 180, 191
Diu 128, 136
Dominion of New England 3, 51, 89
Dover, Treaty of (1669) 92
Dow, Alexander 72
Du Rivage, Justin 9
Dunkirk 18
Dunn, R. S. 146
Dutch West India Company 55n37, 105

East Florida 163, 165, 166, 175
East India Company 3, 11, 24, 25, 63, 70, 71, 84, 85, 95, 104, 106,

[199]

INDEX

118n24, Chapter 7 *passim*, 153, 178, 179, 180, 195n47
Eburne, Richard 77, 78, 80
Eliot, John 83
Elizabeth I, Queen of England 43, 58, 78, 92
Elkins, Stanley 171
Elliott, Sir John 8, 17, 34n5
Elsinore 130
English Civil War 60, 78, 80, 86, 87, 90, 142
English Enlightenment 60, 61, 70
English (or British) law 179, 184, 186, 187, 190, 191, 194n41
European state system 11, 48, 49, 53, 92
Evelyn, John 83
Examiner, The 22, 34
Exclusion Crisis (1679–81) 88, 90, 108

Federalists 167
Ferdinand VII, King of Spain 175
Ferguson, Niall 32
Ferguson, Robert 93
Ferguson, Sir Adam 149
Fernandès, João, de Almeida 137
Fiennes, William, 1st Viscount Saye and Sele 87
Financial Revolution 22, 26, 42
Finch, Daniel, 2nd Earl of Nottingham 22
Fitzpatrick, John 163
Flavel, John 80
Florida 151, 167, 173, 174, 175
Fort Confederación (or Fort Tombecbe), Alabama 166
Fort Nogales, Treaty of (1793) 166
Fort San Fernando de las Barrancas, Memphis 166
Fort St George, India 85
Fox, Charles James 185
France 5, 18, 19, 21, 28, 34, 40, 46, 47, 49, 51, 52, 56, 70, 79, 87, 92, 93, 94, 105, 117n13, 118n43, 138, 143, 144, 147, 148, 153, 154, 161, 162, 170, 171, 172, 173, 174
Franklin, Benjamin 20
Fryar, John 70, 71, 124, 126

Gallagher, John 3, 4, 171
Galloway, Joseph 150, 152, 154, 158n44
Galvéz, Bernardo de 163
Games, Alison 10, 29–30, 50
Gary, Henry 126
Gassiot, Juan 166
Gayoso, Manuel 174
George III, King of England 162, 172, 175, 176
Georgia 172
Germain, George, Lord 167
Germany 94
Ghaylān, al-Khadir 69
Gibraltar 17, 28, 33, 45, 95
Glasgow 153
Glickman, Gabriel 9
Glorious Revolution (1688–9) 3, 7, 38, 51, 79, 92, 120n78
Goa 121, 122, 123, 124, 127, 130, 131, 133, 134, 136, 137
Godolphin, Sidney, 1st Earl of Godolphin, Lord Treasurer 144, 145
Godwyn, Morgan 80, 81, 84, 88, 90
Goffe, William 88
Goldie, Mark 60
Gondomar, Count of *see* Sarmiento de Acuña, Diego
Gookin, Daniel 83, 87
Gookin, Vincent 87
Gordon Riots (1780) 142, 153
Gordon, Patrick 81
Gore, John 23
Gould, Eliga 12
Green Mountain Boys 172
Greene, Jack 51, 156
Grillo, Domingo 105
Grotius, Hugo 149, 152, 197n83
Guinea 25
Guiscard, Antoine de, Marquis de Guiscard 23
Gujarat 131

Hakluyt, Richard 80, 81
Halhed, Nathaniel Brassey 182, 187
Hall, Catherine 37n73
Hall, Joseph, Bishop of Norwich 81
Hariot, Thomas 59

[200]

INDEX

Harley, Robert, 1st Earl of Oxford 21, 22, 23, 24, 25, 26, 27, 29, 34, 36n39, 44, 46, 49
Harrington, James 60
Hastings, Warren 10, 13, 72, Chapter 10 *passim*
Havana 114
Hedges, Sir Christopher 143
Henchman, Humphrey, Bishop of London 85
Henry VII, King of England 24, 29
Henry VIII, King of England 24, 65
Hill, Aaron 71, 72
Hill, B. W. 34n4
Hinduism 63, 71, 72
Hispaniola 107
Hoare, Sir Richard 23
Hobbes, Thomas 154
Hobson, John 2
Holmes, Geoffrey 18
Holroyd, John Baker, 1st Earl of Sheffield 160, 164, 165, 168, 170, 171
Holwell, J. Z. 72
Honduras Bay 169
Hopkins, Antony 3, 5
Hoppit, Julian 12, 17
Howard, Martin 152
Howe, Anthony 31
Hudson Bay 28, 33
Hume, David 154
Hyde, Thomas 84

Illinois 173
India 11, 13, 17, 29, 36n46, 57, 61, 62, 71, 95, Chapter 7 *passim*, Chapter 10 *passim*
  laws 13, 179, 182, 183, 184, 185, 186, 187, 188, 190, 191, 194n40
Indian Stream Republic 174–5
Inez de Miranda, Donna, Lady 123
informal and formal empire 3, 20
Innes, Harry 174
Ireland 30, 51, 84
Islam 10, 61, 62, 63–71, 72, 81, 84
Islamic law 179, 183, 194n37, 195n59, 196n64
Isle of Man 151, 152, 153

Jackson, Andrew 167
Jacobites 142, 149
Jamaica 44, 86, 87, 94, 105, 107, 108, 112, 113, 114, 115, 118n43
James I, King of England 58
James II, King of England (formerly Duke of York) 36n46, 43, 51, 83, 89, 90, 93, 103, 105, 106, 108, 115, 118n25
James III (James Francis Edward Stuart, the Old Pretender) 40
Jasanoff, Maya 162
Jay Treaty (1795) 168, 176
Jefferson, Thomas 174
Jeffreys, George, 1st Baron Jeffreys, Lord Chief Justice 84, 106
Jesuits 68, 89, 92, 122, 130, 131, 132, 133, 134, 136, 137, 138
Jones, Sir William 73, 183
Jones, Thomas, Chief Justice, New York 162

Karanja 124, 125, 127, 128, 130, 134, 137
Keene, Edward 193n19
Kennedy, Dane 1, 4
Kennett, White, Bishop of Peterborough 93
Kentucky 166, 174
King Philip's War (1675–78) 85, 90
Knox, William 167
Koot, Christian 6
Kramnick, Isaac 35n24
Kupperman, Karen 78

Lake Champlain 172
Lake Pontchartrain 163
Lambert, Sir John 23
Lancashire 21
Law of Nations 125, 128, 129, 130, 152, 179, 181, 187, 188, 189, 190, 191, 193n20, 196n77
Law, Edward 182, 194n30
Leeds, Duke of *see* Osborne, Peregrine
Leeward Islands 86, 87, 89, 143, 157n14, 168, 171
legal pluralism 12, 13, 53, 121, 122, 126, 135, Chapter 10 *passim*

[201]

INDEX

Leonard, Daniel 167
Levant Company 63, 84, 118n24
Lexington, Lord *see* Sutton, Robert
Ley, James, 3rd Earl of Marlborough 122
Lille, Battle of (1708) 18
Lisbon 121, 123, 128, 133
Littleton, Edward 20
Locke, John 19, 20, 41, 43, 46, 82, 111, 113, 118n25, 120nn71, 77, 142, 151
Long Island 176n8
Long, Samuel 113
Louis XIV, King of France 18, 29, 39, 40, 70, 91, 92, 93, 100
Louis XVI, King of France 170
Louisiana 47, 166, 167, 174, 175
Lucas, Gervase 126, 131
Lynch, Thomas 113, 114
Lyttleton, Sir Charles 118n25

Macarthy, Harry 175
McGillivray, Alexander 166
McGillivray, Lachlan 166
McKitrick, Eric 171
MacMillan, Ken 7, 10, 11, 12, 50, 51
Madras 95, 135
Madrid 29
Mahim 124, 127, 128, 131, 133, 137, 138
Maine 168, 173
Malplaquet, Battle of (1709) 17, 21
Manchac 163
Manchester, Earl of *see* Montagu, Edward
Mansfield, Lord *see* Murray, William
Manuel de Zéspedes, Vincente 166
Maratha Empire (India) 121, 130, 132
Marīn family 68
Marlborough, Duke of *see* Churchill, John
Marlborough, Earl of *see* Ley, James
Marshall, Peter 4, 5, 194n31
Martha's Vineyard 83
Maryland 77, 90, 93
Massachusetts 47, 51, 82, 83, 86, 87, 88, 89, 153, 167, 168
Master, Harcourt 23
Mather, Cotton 83, 88, 94
Mayhew, Thomas 83

Mazagon 124, 132, 135
Mecca 68
Medina 68
Mediterranean 28, 63, 84
Mello de Castro, Antonio de 122, 131
mercantilism 31–2, 42, 52–3, 55n34, 101, 102, 108–9
Mexico 20, 40, 41, 42
Michigan 173
Milan 70
Milton, John 92
Minorca 17, 33, 45, 95
Miranda, Dona Inez de 131
Mississippi River 166, 172
Mississippi 175
Mobile 166
Modyford, Sir Thomas 107, 118n35
Mokyr, Joel 31
Molesworth, Hender 114
Monck, George, 1st Duke of Albermarle 107, 118n35
Monroe Doctrine (1823) 176
Montagu, Edward, 2nd Earl of Manchester 87
Montesquieu *see* Secondat, Charles-Louis de
Montreal 165, 173
Moore, Arthur 23
Morgan, Edmund 117n14
Morgan, Kenneth 31, 32
Morgan, Sir Henry 107, 108, 118nn35, 39
Morocco 63, 65, 66, 67, 68, 69, 71, 90
Morris, Lewis 94
Mosquito Coast 169
Mughal Empire (India) 57, 71, 121, 130, 132, 135, 136
Muhammad (Prophet) 63, 64, 65, 66, 69, 72, 193n28
Muhammad ibn Aḥmad 68
Mukherjee, Mithi 192n4
Murray, John, 3rd Duke of Atholl 151
Murray, William, 1st Earl of Mansfield, Lord Chief Justice 183, 184, 196n74
Muskogee 175

Naples 70
Nasr, King of Fes 68

INDEX

Nassau 165
Natchez 174
Natick 83, 87
National Land Bank (England) 23, 24
Native Americans 59, 82, 83, 84–5, 87, 93, 94, 161, 162–3, 165–6, 168, 175
Nelson, Horatio 168, 171
Nevis 143, 144, 145, 146, 148, 149, 151, 156n10, 157n16
New Brunswick 164, 167, 172, 173, 174
New England Company (England) 83, 87, 88, 89
New England 3, 21, 82, 83, 85, 88, 90, 147, 164, 174
New Hampshire 86, 88, 172
New Imperial History 4, 5, 6, 7, 13, 33, 53
New Institutional Economics 7, 12
New Ireland 163, 167, 168
New Jersey 79, 89, 94, 103
New Orleans 163, 174
New York 82, 92, 103, 163, 172
Newfoundland 77
Nootka Sound 169
Norris, William 71
North American colonies 30, 34, 43, 44, 47, 51, 52, 78, 82, 83, 85, 86, 87, 88, 89, 90, 93, 94, 109, 111, Chapter 8 *passim*, Chapter 9 *passim*
North, Douglass 7, 154
North, Frederick, Lord North 142, 153, 195n47
Northwest Territory 165, 168
Nottingham, Earl of *see* Finch, Daniel
Nova Scotia 17, 33, 45, 164

O'Fallon, John 174
October Club 23
Ohio Valley 173
Ohio 171
Old Woman's Island 135
Oldmixon, John 19, 20, 24, 35n14, 42, 45, 147
Oliver, Thomas 167
Olson, Alison 7, 53
Ongley, Sir Samuel 24
Orgill, Andrew 110
Oriental despotism, 13, 179, 182, 183, 185

orientalism 4, 10, Chapter 4 *passim*, 194n32
Ormerod, Oliver 74n11
Orrery, Earl of *see* Boyle, Roger
Osborne, Francis 63, 64, 65, 66, 67, 69, 70
Osborne, Peregrine, 2nd Duke of Leeds 25
Ottoman Empire 62, 63, 65, 66, 67–9, 70, 71, 79
Oudenarde, Battle of (1708) 18
Ovington, John 71
Oxford, Earl of *see* Harley, Robert
Oxford 86
Oxinden, George 126, 131

Paget, William, 6th Baron Paget 71
Palmer, R. R. 160
Panama 114
Panton, Leslie (company) 165, 166
Panton, William 166
Pardo, Convention of (1739) 155
Paris, Treaty of (1783) 148, 150, 162, 163, 167, 168, 169, 170, 175
Parliament (English, or British) 52, 86, 90, 92, 106, 112, 113, 145, 150, 152, 154, 162, 164, 165, 167, 168, 183, 191, 195n50
    Act of Uniformity (1662) 88
    House of Commons 23, 28, 39, 40, 49, 92, 144, 145, 148, 151, 152, 153, 163, 178, 182, 189
    House of Lords 167, 178, 191
    India Bill (1783) 185
    Intolerable Acts (1774) 30
    lobbying and colonial agents 6–7, 51, 146
    Navigation Acts 7, 43, 111, 168, 170, 171, 172
    Stamp Act (1765) 30, 152, 153
    Sugar Act (1764) 30
    Tea Act (1773) 30
    Toleration Act (1689) 88, 93
    Townshend Acts (1767) 30
Parry, Francis 130
party politics (England) 7, 8, Chapter 2 *passim*, Chapter 3 *passim*, 60, 89, 91, 92, Chapter 6 *passim*
Passamaquoddy Bay 163, 173

INDEX

Penhallow, Charles 114
Penn, William 82
Pennsylvania 6, 83, 89
Pepys, Samuel 123
Perez, Alvaro, de Tavora 133, 134
Peru 20, 39, 40, 41, 42
Pestana, Carla 78
Peter, Hugh 88
Pett, Peter 89
Pettigrew, Will 9
Petty, Sir William 80, 89, 109
Petty, William, 2nd Earl of Shelburne, Prime Minister 149, 162, 163, 170
Philadelphia 164
Philip V, King of Spain (formerly Duke of Anjou) 39, 40, 51
Phips, William 107
Physiocrats 171
Pike, Zebulon 167
Pincus, Steve 7, 8, Chapter 3 *passim*, 60, 78, 101
Pindar, Thomas 25
Pitt, Thomas 163
Pitt, William, the younger 150, 151, 154
Pitts, Jennifer 13, 37n63
Pittsburgh 166
Pocock, J. G. A. 44
political economy 7, Chapter 2 *passim*, Chapter 3 *passim*, 78, Chapter 6 *passim*, 170–1
  'land-based' 19–27, 29, 33, 45, 46, 101, 103–8
  'labour-based' 19–21, 25, 34, 42, 43–4, 45, 46, 101, 102, 108–15
political parties (England) 8, Chapter 2 *passim*, Chapter 3 *passim*, 90–1, Chapter 6 *passim*, 171
Popish Plot (1678) 88
Port Royal 86, 107
Porter, Sir James 72
Portugal 11, 25, 26, 70, 100, 103, Chapter 7 *passim*
Potosi 46
Povey, Thomas 118n25
Pownall, Thomas 20
preaching and conversion 82–5, 87, 88, 90, 91, 93, 94
Prideaux, Humphrey, Dean of Norwich 85

priestcraft 60, 62, 65, 69–70, 71, 72
Prior, Matthew 29
Privy Council (England) 153
Protestant foreign policy 2–3, 9, Chapter 5 *passim*
Providence 87
Providence Island 107
Providence Island Company 118n24
public opinion 8, 18, 48
Pufendorf, Samuel 149, 152
Purchas, Samuel 59

Quakers 89
Quebec 164, 172

Raby, Lord *see* Wentworth, Thomas
Raleigh, Sir Walter 40
Ramillies, Battle of (1706) 17, 18
refugees 94, 173
Reilly, Hugh 85
Restoration (1660) 20, Chapter 4 *passim*, Chapter 5 *passim*, Chapter 6 *passim*, 146
Reynell, Carew 104
Rhode Island 83, 87, 152
River Plate (Rio de la Plata) 24, 25, 27, 28, 46
Robinson, Ronald 3, 4, 171
Rodger, Nicholas 46
Rome 52
Roxbury 83
Royal African Company 3, 6, 23, 24, 25, Chapter 6 *passim*, 146, 155
Royal Society 80, 84
Rudyard, Sir Benjamin 40
Rupert, Prince, of the Rhine 118n25
Rycaut, Sir Paul 57, 63, 64, 65, 66, 67, 70
Rye House Plot (1683) 88

Sa'dī dynasty (Morocco) 68, 69
Saba 107
Sacheverell, Henry 21
Safavid Empire (Persia) 71
Said, Edward 62
Saint-Domingue 170
Sale, George 71
Salsette 124, 127, 134, 136, 137, 138

[204]

INDEX

Sarmiento de Acuña, Diego, 1st Count of Gondomar 41
Saye and Sele, Viscount *see* Fiennes, William
Scot, George 79
Scotland 30, 90, 94, 142, 146, 165
Secondat, Charles-Louis de, Baron de Montesquieu 57, 58, 185, 186, 187, 195n48, 196n64
Seeley, Sir John 2
Serron, Simon 126
Seven Years War (1756–63) 30, 172
Sewell, Samuel 82, 94
Shaftesbury, Earl of *see* Cooper, Anthony
Shaldon 147
Sheffield, Earl of *see* Holroyd, John Baker
Shelburne, Earl of *see* Petty, William
Sheppard, Samuel 138
Sheres, Sir Henry 20, 79
Sheridan, R. B. 148
Shipman, Abraham 122
Sicily 70
Sidney, Sir Philip 92
Sierra Leone 149, 165, 173
Simms, Brendan 8, 48
Singh, Chait, Raja of Benares 189, 193n18
Sion 135
Slack, Paul 53
slavery and the slave trade 17, 25, 27, 28, 29, 48, 49, 83, 90, 93, 95, 102–3, 104–5, 106, 107, 108, 111–12, 114, 115, 119n70, 120n88, 161, 168, 173–4, 175, 177n84
  see also Asiento
Smith, Adam 20, 53, 170
Smith, Nathaniel 194n32
Society for the Promotion of Christian Knowledge (SPCK) 94
Society for the Propagation of the Gospel (SPG) 93, 94
Somerset 77
Sonora 166
South Carolina 166
South Sea Company 18, 23, 24, 27, 25, 26, 27, 28, 29, 33, 35n33, 36n38, 44, 45, 46, 49, 116

sovereignty, 10, 11, 12, 13, 51, Chapter 7 *passim*, 181, 184, 188, 192n4, 193n19, 193n28, 194n43
Spain, 5, 17, 18, 19, 20, 24, 25, 26, 28, 29, 32, 39, 40, 41, 42, 43, 47, 48, 51, 52, 56, 79, 81, 85, 86, 91, 92, 93, 100, 101, 102, 103, 104, 106, 107, 108, 110, 112, 113, 114, 115, 151, 161, 162, 163, 164, 165, 166, 167, 168–9, 171, 172, 173, 174, 175
Spanish America, 18, 20–9, 32, 33, 34, 40, 46, 49, 100–8, 112–15, 169, 171
  gold and silver mines, 24, 25, 40, 41–2, 46, 55n37, 92, 103
Spencer, Charles, 3rd Earl of Sunderland 19
Spencer, Robert, 2nd Earl of Sunderland, Secretary of State 157n14
Sprat, Thomas 80
St Andrews (New Brunswick) 163
St Christopher/St Kitts 17, 27, 28, 33, 45, 143, 145, 146, 148, 149, 150, 151, 153, 157nn12, 16
St Croix River 173
St Eustasia 107
St John, Henry, 1st Viscount Bolingbroke 21, 22, 23, 28, 34, 47, 57n44
St Lawrence River 172
St Lucia 107
Stanhope, James 19
state power 7, 10–11, 29–30, 49–51
Stern, Philip 11, 12, 13
Stiggins, George 165
Stillingfleet, Edward 92
Strafford, Earl of *see* Wentworth
Straits of Magellan 25
Stratford, Francis 23
Stringer, Dr Moses 23
Stubbs, Philip 80
Sunderland, Earl of *see* Spencer, Charles; Spencer, Robert
Surat 125
Surinam 86
Sutton, Robert, 2nd Baron Lexington 28
Sweden 130

[205]

INDEX

Swingen, Abigail 9
Switzerland 87, 94

Talbot, John 94
Tangier 10, 63, 79, 89, 90, 103, 121
Tavora, Bernardino de 131
Teignmouth 147
Temple, Sir William 91
Tennessee 166
Terry, Edward 63
Texas 175, 176
Thana 125, 127, 128, 130, 134, 137
Theibert, Leslie 8
Tierra del Fuego 25, 28
toleration 86, 88, 89, 93
Tombigbee River 166
Tordesillas, Treaty of (1494) 105
Townshend, Charles, 2nd Viscount Townshend 19
Travers, Robert 10, 57, 180, 191, 194nn34, 43
Trombay 124, 127, 137
Twining, William 179, 180

United Provinces 18, 21, 28, 32, 34, 40, 41, 42, 44, 46, 47, 48, 56, 60, 86, 87, 91, 102, 103, 104, 105, 106, 107, 117n13, 122, 133, 197n83
United States of America Chapter 9 *passim*
  Congress, 164, 165, 166, 170, 172, 176
  Constitutional Convention 164
  Declaration of Independence (1776) 176
universal monarchy 21, 40, 42, 60
Utrecht, Treaty of (1713) 17, 18, 28, 33, 34, 38, 39, 45, 48, 49, 161

Valdivia 25, 28, 46, 55n37
Vane, Sir Henry, junior 88
Vattel, Emer de 149, 152, 181, 189, 193n22
Vaughan, John, Lord Vaughan (later 3rd Earl of Carbery) 105, 107
Venezuela 175
Venner, Thomas 88
Vermont 172
Vicksburg 166

Villiers, George, 2nd Duke of Buckingham 91
Virginia Company 2, 118n24
Virginia 59, 85, 86, 90, 117n13
virtual representation 191
Voltaire (Francois-Marie Arouet) 59

Wafer, Lionel 25
War of 1812 176
War of Jenkins' Ear (1739–48) 36n59
War of the Spanish Succession (1701–14) 17, 18, 19, 22, 29, 34, 39, 42, 49, 51, 153
Washington, George 164
Weber, David 165
Wedderburn, Alexander (later 1st Earl of Rosslyn, Attorney General) 168
Weingast, Barry 154
Welland, Heather 33
Wentworth, Thomas, 3rd Baron Raby and 1st Earl of Strafford 21, 28
West Florida 151, 163, 165, 166, 172, 175
West Indies 19, 20, 27–8, 34, 40, 44, 85, 86, 87, 89, 90, 91, 100, 102–3, 105–16, 121, 143–8, 153, 168, 170, 171, 172
Western Design 40, 78, 91
Westminster 7
Westphalia, Treaty of (1648) 11
Whalley, Edward 88
Whitefoord, Caleb 170
Whitley, Roger 81
Wilkes, John 153
Wilkinson, James 166
William III, Prince of Orange and King of England 39, 51, 78
Wilmot, John 149, 150
Wilson, Kathleen, 7, 37n74
Winthrop, John 82
Wisconsin 173
Wither, George 92
Worsley, Benjamin 82

Yorktown 162

Zahedieh, Nuala 31, 119n45

[206]

EU authorised representative for GPSR:
Easy Access System Europe, Mustamäe tee 50,
10621 Tallinn, Estonia
gpsr.requests@easproject.com

www.ingramcontent.com/pod-product-compliance
Lightning Source LLC
Chambersburg PA
CBHW070354240426
43671CB00013BA/2499